345.02523

Items should be returned on or before the last date
shown below. Items not already requested by other
borrowers may be renewed in person, in writing or by

MADNESS AND MURDER

MADNESS AND MURDER

Gender, Crime and Mental Disorder
in Nineteenth-Century Ireland

PAULINE M. PRIOR
Queen's University, Belfast

Foreword by
ANGELA BOURKE

IRISH ACADEMIC PRESS
DUBLIN • PORTLAND, OR

First published in 2008 by Irish Academic Press

44, Northumberland Road,   920 NE 58th Avenue, Suite 300
Ballsbridge,   Portland, Oregon,
Dublin 4, Ireland   97213–3786

www.iap.ie

British Library Cataloguing in Publication Data
An entry can be found on request

ISBN 978 0 7165 2937 8 (cloth)
ISBN 978 0 7165 2938 5 (paper)

Library of Congress Cataloging-in-Publication Data
An entry can be found on request

Typeset by Carrigboy Typesetting Services
Printed by Biddles Ltd., King's Lynn, Norfolk

Dedicated to Bobbie Hanvey

Contents

List of Tables

List of Abbreviations

Asylums Report	The annual report on the district, criminal and private lunatic asylums in Ireland, with appendices
CSO	Chief Secretary's Office (Ireland)
CSORP	Chief Secretary's Office Registered Papers
CRF	Convict Record File
DMP	Dublin Metropolitan Police
Dundrum	Central Mental Hospital (formerly, Central Criminal Asylum), Ireland
GPB	General Prisons Board
HC	House of Commons
HL	House of Lords
IC	Irish Constabulary
ICR	Irish Crime Records
Irl	Ireland
LL	Lord Lieutenant
MPA	Medico-Psychological Association
NAI	National Archives of Ireland
NUI	National University of Ireland
PEN	Penal servitude file
RIC	Royal Irish Constabulary
RMS	Resident Medical Superintendent
UK	United Kingdom
US	United States of America

Preface and Acknowledgements

IN 1893, WHEN Catherine Wynn, a 35-year-old Catholic married woman from Sligo, drowned her three children in a bath of boiling water, there was no doubt in the public mind that she was not responsible for her actions. She was perceived as 'mad' or 'insane' and was sent to the Central Criminal Asylum for Ireland, at Dundrum, County Dublin, as a 'criminal lunatic'. The same was true for Allan Spiller, a 26-year-old Presbyterian salesman from Belfast, who cut the throats of his wife and two children in 1892. In both cases, it was generally acknowledged that the crimes were such that they could not be committed by a person in their 'right mind'.

However, there were other serious crimes where the outcome was the same but where there was disagreement as to the level of responsibility of the perpetrator of the crime. In 1902, John Logue, a policeman from Woodford, County Galway shot his ex-girlfriend and her mother. The girl recovered, but her mother died. In spite of medical reports by an inspector of lunacy and a prison doctor to the effect that Logue was 'feigning insanity' as he awaited trial, the court found him to be insane at the time of the crime and sent him to Dundrum as a 'criminal lunatic'. Similarly, in 1891, Margaret Rainey, a 19-year-old single Episcopalian servant from Belfast, was found 'not of sound mind' when she threw her newborn baby out of an upstairs window into the yard below. Margaret was one of many women who found themselves before the court for the killing of an infant during this period. Some of these women were found guilty of murder and sentenced to execution, while others, like Margaret, were sent to Dundrum.

These stories illustrate the complex relationship between crime and mental disorder (referred to as 'insanity' or 'lunacy' in nineteenth-century discourse) – a relationship that has been the subject of extensive debate and research for the past two centuries. The focus of the debate is the extent to which the experience of having a mental disorder relieves the individual of responsibility for a crime. The difficulties arise from the fact that not only is the definition of mental disorder highly contentious, but so also is the nature of its impact on the actions of the individual who commits a crime.

The original purpose of this book was to explore the cases of some of the people for whom the theoretical debates on the interaction between crime and mental disorder was a reality in their lives. These were people who found their way into the Central Criminal Asylum for Ireland, now the Central Mental Hospital (Dundrum). As the book took shape, it became evident that to understand what happened to them, we needed to know about the general patterns of crime and punishment in the nineteenth century. This led to the inclusion of much more material on the general context of these crimes.

The book is organized into two parts. The first part presents the debates on crime and punishment, on gender and crime, and on mental disorder and crime, in the context of nineteenth-century Ireland. The second presents the stories of men and women who became involved in murder. These include young women who killed an unwanted illegitimate baby, older women who lashed out at abusive husbands, men who killed their wives during a bout of drinking, and families that turned in on themselves and killed 'one of their own', sometimes influenced by superstition and sometimes by greed for land.

Writing a book like this raises a number of ethical issues, as all of the people whose lives are discussed were real people. Because they had committed a crime, they officially lost the right to privacy and their records became public property. For example, because their names and the details of their crimes were in the public domain at the time of their arrest and conviction, these details can be published now also. However, for the author, this was something of a double-edged sword. Information that might be regarded as confidential (in medical records in Dundrum) was often duplicated in convict records held at the National Archives of Ireland. These records contain reports from medical staff at Dundrum, including diagnostic information on individual patients. Some of these patients are also easily identifiable in the published reports of the inspectorate of lunacy and in journal articles in the medical press of the time. However, notwithstanding the fact that these records are in the public domain, I am aware that some of the people, who are discussed in the following chapters, may have relatives still alive in Ireland or in another country. The book was not written with the intention of offending any of these relatives, but I apologize in advance for any hurt that may be caused.

Like any other book, this has taken a number of years to complete and I have become indebted to many people who have helped me both professionally and personally with this project. I would like to express my appreciation to each of them. On a professional level, these include: The Wellcome Trust, which funded part of the research on which the book is based; Lisa Hyde, the editor at Irish Academic Press, for her good humour and encouragement; the anonymous referees, whose comments led to the revision of many chapters; colleagues at Queen's University Belfast, whose input and advice were invaluable – Professor Leslie Clarke, Dr Margaret Crawford, Dr Jim Campbell, Dr Leon Litvack, Professor Sean Connolly, Professor Bernadette Hayes; colleagues at other Universities – Professor Elizabeth Malcolm, University of Melbourne, Professor Angela Bourke, University College, Dublin, Professor Maria Luddy, University of Warwick, Professor Maryanne Valiulis and Dr Bill Vaughan, Trinity College, Dublin; archivists and librarians who helped me access records and nineteenth-century publications – Norma Menabney and other staff of Queen's University libraries, Gregory O'Connor, National Archives of Ireland, Dr Art O'Connor, Central Mental Hospital, Dundrum, and staff of the Wellcome Trust library, London.

On a more personal note, I would like to thank my family and friends who are always positive about my literary endeavours – especially my mother, Rita Prior, who is still going strong at 93, and my other half, Bobbie, to whom this book is dedicated.

I have made every effort to comply with copyright regulations, but if any copyright holders have been inadvertently overlooked, we will be pleased to make the necessary arrangements at the first opportunity.

PAULINE M. PRIOR
January 2008

Foreword

THE HIGH STONE WALLS of the Central Mental Hospital in the south Dublin suburb of Dundrum tower over the double-decker buses, the cars, bicycles and pedestrians that pass constantly beneath them. Opened in 1850 as the Central Criminal Asylum, the hospital housed women and men who had committed serous crimes but, following police investigation and medical assessment, had been judged 'mad' rather than 'bad'. Murderers deemed sane were routinely sentenced to death in the nineteenth century, though this was increasingly commuted to penal servitude, while those found guilty of manslaughter were incarcerated in Mountjoy and other convict prisons. Killers thought to have been temporarily insane at the time of their violent actions – typically new mothers (especially unmarried), and men who had been drinking heavily – might spend only a short time in Dundrum before being set free, but others remained there for life. Between the lines of the official statistics, medical reports and prison records that Pauline Prior has researched so extensively for this book, lie stories of unhappiness, exclusion, exploitation and abandonment, along with vivid illustrations of class and gender stereotype in action. Her expert and compassionate exploration of the legal issues and social contexts of murder and madness in nineteenth-century Ireland is richly illustrated with the first-hand accounts of observers and the verbatim testimony of offenders. Some seem to have been clever manipulators, but most of them come across as bewildered and distraught.

It is a mark of changing preoccupations that 'Dundrum' in the twenty-first century calls to mind a sprawling shopping centre, with marble floors, luxury brands and a complicated outdoor fountain, rather than the high-security institution, whose buildings or inmates few who pass its walls have ever seen. Crime and mental disorder were powerful modern concepts when Ireland's asylums, prisons and workhouses were built: converging lines along which society could be divided and organized. By the middle of the nineteenth century, famine, disease and emigration had left the country in a state of shock. The Irish language had given way to English over much of the country, literacy was advancing, and ideas of nationhood and national identity were taking root, but large numbers of people still lived in an oral, localized culture that was exotic and incomprehensible to administrators whose ideas and expectations came from London. As science seemed set to solve all the problems of the world, the state penetrated deeeper into the lives of families and individuals, as if order and uniformity among the lower classes might bring peace and prosperity to all. Those who did not fit in could be locked up, and, all going well, would emerge from their incarceration in prison or asylum as quiet, industrious and well-conducted subjects of the Crown. Or they might obligingly emigrate and disappear from view.

Crime and mental disorder remain uneasily connected, but they stand now at a different angle to each other, and to gender, the other key theme of this book, than they did in nineteenth-century Ireland. Murder sold newspapers in the nineteenth century the way sex does today, and never more effectively than when women and children were involved. A woman's mind was believed to be innately passive and suggestible, its delicate balance easily knocked out of kilter by the workings of her reproductive system: hysteria, then, was the unpredictable, uncontrollable action of the womb. Chapters on women who killed children, or killed men, and on men who killed women, show Victorian society in Ireland both at its most unbending and at its most charitable.

Gender, crime and mental disorder offer administrators and interpreters ways to classify people and their problems, but the ways the three phenomena are understood and interpreted have changed radically and repeatedly in the last two hundred years, as the the ground of cultural and political meaning has shifted beneath them. By focussing on the links between them in nineteenth-century Ireland, articulating the dynamic connections between ideas, this book makes visible patterns that have been hiding in the social and cultural landscape.

Pauline Prior's mother Rita and my mother Rosaleen are sisters, born three years apart on a farm in County Cavan in the second decade of the twentieth century, a few years before partition drew the Border a couple of miles away from their home. The energy, intelligence and resourceful imagination our mothers shared with their five sisters and three brothers, the Magees (or McGees) of Staghall, have made educational opportunity available to us, and paved the way for both our academic careers; they are certainly at the heart of our shared interest in the intimate history of Irish society and in what it meant for women.

ANGELA BOURKE
Dublin, 2 December 2007

PART I

The Context

CHAPTER ONE

Crime and Punishment

Lawless, predatory specimens of the human race were they; men, women and children, whose civilisation had never even been attempted. More dangerous neighbours were they by far than the warlike Zulus, inasmuch as the 'strong back' on which they leant, was that body of human beings professing Christianity, and arrogating to themselves the right to remit sins.[1]

T HESE ARE THE WORDS of a visitor to Ireland in the late nineteenth century. She was Matilda Charlotte Houstoun, who gave this rather colourful account of the tenant farmers of County Mayo. She clearly thought the local people were 'predatory' and uncivilized, and that their adherence to the Catholic religion added to their dangerousness. Another, equally scathing account of the Irish peasantry comes from a Tipperary magistrate, who described some of the agrarian murders that took place in the early 1840s as 'so heinous in their nature – so marked by cruelty, atrocity and barbarity – as to equal, if not exceed in their details, those of the most savage nations of the earth, excepting only the absence of cannibalism'.[2] These views were not unusual at the time. Rather they formed the basis for the popular view of the Irish as violent and untamed.

Historians of Irish crime have tended to focus on 'acts of defiance against a colonial state' – riots, uprisings and violence against authority figures.[3] However, newer approaches to the study of crime and punishment in Ireland have opened up areas formerly hidden, such as the impact of policing on crime, the importance of studying 'ordinary' crime including domestic violence, the role of the judiciary and, finally, changes in patterns of sentencing and in ideologies of punishment.[4] These studies provide the basis for new insights into the plight of the people who are the main focus of this book – convicted offenders who were directed out of the prison system into the mental health care system. Known as criminal lunatics in the nineteenth century, they are now generally referred to as mentally disordered offenders. Though diverted from prison, the sentencing and management of these individuals fell squarely within the criminal justice system. To understand what happened to them, we need some knowledge of common patterns of crime and of the judicial response to it.

In the early nineteenth century, the administration at Dublin Castle was greatly concerned with the maintenance of law and order.[5] This concern was based on the British perception of the Irish as a violent nation. Whether or not this perception was valid is the subject of great debate. Neal Garnham, in his study of violence in eighteenth-century Ireland, argues that it was only true if the comparison was with England. If, for example, Ireland had been compared with a similar peasant society, such as France, the level of violence would not have seemed unusual.[6]

However, it cannot be denied that, as the century progressed, there was widespread agrarian unrest in rural Ireland – 'a combination of sedition, agrarian discontent, faction fighting and general lawlessness'.[7] There were various reasons for the unrest and related criminal activity. Some crimes arose from disputes between tenants and landlords over rents and evictions. Others were caused by rivalries between and within classes and disputes between and within families.[8] Family disputes over land often led to violence and sometimes to murder, as happened in the Stackpoole family from County Clare in 1853 and the Shiel family from King's County (Offaly) in 1870. These cases, which are discussed in a later chapter, led to the murder of two men and the execution of two men and three women.[9] Both cases were unusual because of the direct involvement of women in the act of murder. However, it was not unusual for disputes over land (between families or neighbours) to escalate into violence and murder. Some of these disputes found their way into works of fiction, such as *The Field* by John B. Keane, while others were known only to the perpetrators. Agrarian unrest continued throughout the century, reaching a peak in terms of reported crime during the Famine. The annual reports of the inspectors of prisons show an increase from an annual average of 19,000 indictments for all crimes between 1842 and 1846 to an annual average of 31,000 between 1847 and 1850. This upward trend was reflected in transportation statistics, with a large increase in the number of transportation sentences in the years 1847–49.[10]

Contrary to what might be expected from a 'violent' race, the most common form of crime before and during the Famine was an 'offence against property without violence'. This covered a multitude of offences, including house-breaking, robbery and the stealing of horses, cows and sheep.[11] These non-violent crimes increased from 33 per cent of indictments before the Famine to 54 per cent during its peak. It was inevitable that this would happen, as people competed for scarce sources of food and sustenance. The object of the exercise was to acquire the desired goods without hurting anyone. However, it would be untrue to say that violence disappeared at this time. 'Offences against property with violence' remained stable (at around 7 per cent of indictments). In contrast, 'offences against the person' almost halved – from 26 per cent before the Famine to 14 per cent during it.[12] It is worth remembering that as the total number of indictments was much higher during the height of the Famine, the actual numbers of attacks on people did not diminish.

The second half of the nineteenth century was characterized by a decline in the overall crime rate and a decrease in violent crime. As W.E. Vaughan points out, the number of outrages (crimes) reported to the constabulary office (the police) fell from 10,639 in 1850 to 4,351 in 1870.[13] When compared with England and Wales in 1870, Ireland had a lower rate of serious crime. However, the Irish had higher rates of assaults against people, including police officers, and of malicious offences against property. According to the report on judicial statistics for 1863:

> The increase of 'malicious offences against property' took place under the head of setting fire to dwelling houses, persons being therein; and attacking and injuring dwelling houses and lands. The former increased from seven in 1862, to twenty four in 1863; twelve of the offenders were chiefly disorderly inmates, committed for setting fire to workhouses. The attacking of dwelling houses increased from thirteen to twenty six. Other cases of burning decreased.[14]

Vaughan suggests that there was little difference in serious crime against human life between Ireland and England by 1880, making it 'one of the safest places in Europe' when compared with France, Germany or Rumania.[15] This view is contested by S.J. Connolly, who argues that 'the murder rate in Ireland was about twice that recorded in England and Wales from the 1860s to the 1890s.[16] However, it is the view put forward in official reports on criminal and judicial statistics, which compared crime in Ireland with that in England and Wales. For example, in the report for 1868, the writer claimed that the greater number of murders recorded from Ireland in that year was due to statistical errors in police reports.

> The apparent excess of murders in Ireland appears to arise from some defect in the police statistics for murders in both countries. Thus, whilst the coroners return 404 verdicts of wilful murder in England and Wales, the police report only 135; and in Ireland, whilst coroners return fifty eight verdicts of wilful murder, the police report forty five.[17]

According to the same report, less serious crimes 'against the person' were less prevalent in Ireland than in England.

> As regards the offences of attempts to murder, shooting at, wounding, stabbing etc, to do bodily harm, the Irish statistics are more favourable than the English, and also the statistics on unnatural offences, rape and immoral offences, perjury, and attempts to commit suicide.[18]

While it may be true that offences such as rape or perjury were less common in Ireland than in England, it is more difficult to come to any conclusion on suicide statistics. These are always likely to be under-reported in a population dominated by the Catholic religion, which was the case in Ireland.

Crime rates continued to fall as the nineteenth century drew to a close. According to Brewer, Lockhart and Rodgers, this was associated with a rise in urbanization in the latter decades of the century.

> Judicial statistics for the year 1915 show a total of only 7,873 indictable offences and 4,833 persons apprehended for the whole of Ireland. Of these 31 per cent (2,451 crimes) occurred in the DMP (Dublin Metropolitan Police) District and twenty-one per cent (1,622 crimes) in the Belfast city area. This meant that just over half of all the crime recorded in Ireland occurred in these two urban areas.[19]

In other words, crime was becoming increasingly an urban phenomenon. The only exception to this was the crime of murder which, in 1915, 'was still predominantly a rural or small town offence, most likely with victim and perpetrator known to each other'.[20] This was not an unusual pattern, as has been shown in studies on homicides and attempted homicides in late nineteenth-century England. For example, Clive Emsley found that: 'a closer look at Victorian homicide reveals that, while the fear may have centred around being murdered by a burglar or a similarly ferocious member of the "dangerous classes", in most homicides assailant and victim were known to each other, and often they were related'.[21]

HOMICIDE

In spite of the fact that patterns of crime, particularly of violent crime, changed over the nineteenth century – increasing in the first half and decreasing in the second – the administration at Dublin Castle remained steadfast in its perception of the Irish as an unruly and violent nation.[22] However, this violence was not always lethal. Ian O'Donnell's analysis of trends in lethal violence from 1841 to 2003 shows that, following a peak in the homicide rate during the Famine, there was a long-term decline in all forms of homicide (murder, manslaughter and infanticide) in the second half of the nineteenth century, a trend that continued until the middle of the twentieth century.

> The highest level of homicide – 54.5 killings per million population – was recorded in 1847, when the Famine was heading for its catastrophic peak. Thirty years later, it had fallen by half (the rate in 1877 was 27.3) and there was a similar proportionate decline by 1907, when the rate stood at 14.6.[23]

This decline was significant in real terms.

> To appreciate the magnitude of this change, consider that there were 2,786 homicides recorded on the island of Ireland between 1841 and 1850, compared with 260 between 1941 and 1950 . . . Even taking account of the substantial decline in the island's population (from 8.2 million in 1841 to 4.3 million in 1941), this is a remarkable transformation.[24]

This trend reflected a reduction in overall violence in Irish society, brought about by a combination of factors including population decline, economic development and increasing state control. To understand more fully what was happening to homicide rates, O'Donnell disaggregated baby-killing (victim under one year) from overall homicide statistics and found two quite different patterns within an overall trend of declining homicide rates. The killing of babies (aged under one year) decreased dramatically in the ten year period following the Famine. This was followed by a long period during which the rates of baby-killing continued to decline, so that by the middle of the twentieth century, it had become an extremely rare crime.[25] In contrast, the killing of individuals over the age of one year (mostly adults) decreased after the Famine but increased again to a relatively high but stable rate towards the end of the nineteenth century.[26]

The overall decline in homicide in Ireland in the second half of the nineteenth century has to be placed within the context of major changes in social behaviour. As O'Donnell suggests, the reasons for the decrease in the killing of babies were highly complex. They were linked, on the one hand, to the growing importance of celibacy and, on the other, to changing social attitudes towards children.[27] In post-Famine Ireland, economic conditions aligned with religious beliefs to ensure that those who married did so later in life and those who did not remained celibate.[28] In spite of the postponement and rejection of marriage by many, the number of children born 'out of wedlock' remained low and abortion was rare. The percentage of illegitimate births in Ireland in the 1890s was much lower than in other countries – at 2.6 per cent in Ireland, 4.1 per cent in England and Wales, and 12.1 per cent in Portugal.[29] Those that did occur were the subject of fear and stigma, a situation that led, in some cases, to infanticide.

GENDER AND CRIME

Infanticide is of interest not only to scholars of Irish history, but also to those interested in the wider academic debate on gender and crime.[30] This debate focuses on gender differences in criminal behaviour and in legal outcomes. Throughout the world, men feature more visibly in crime statistics than do women, but certain crimes, such as baby-killing, have been historically the domain of women. The term 'infanticide', which is sometimes used in a generic way to describe the killing of a child under the age of one year, in its strictest meaning, refers to the killing a baby by its mother in the early months of its life. It derives from the legal definition of a crime which came onto the statute books of many countries to provide a legal way out of a 'murder' conviction for women who had killed a baby, but who were not seen as responsible for their actions, due to a disruption in their mental state brought on by the birth. The mental condition attributed to these mothers was known then as 'puerperal mania' – a condition that will be discussed in a later chapter.

In nineteenth-century Ireland, it was still possible for a murder conviction to be handed down to a woman who had killed a child but, as the verdict led directly to the death sentence, courts were reluctant to do this. What is interesting about this crime, in terms of the gender debate, is the fact that the main perpetrators are women. Men sometimes kill children, but it is not now, nor was it then, a common crime. This is a very unusual situation, as shown in numerous studies by leading feminist criminologists such as Frances Heidensohn and Clarice Feinman.[31] They argue that while it is statistically 'normal' for men to commit crime, it is statistically 'abnormal' for women to do so. This argument is based on the fact that in almost every jurisdiction and in every time-period, women have a consistently lower level of officially recorded crime than men. This, they say, is related to their roles and position in society. Women are not only subject to more oppressive social control mechanisms, but they are also the custodians of those very mechanisms, leading to a high level of compliance with the law.

Others theorists argue that the low representation of women in official crime statistics is a function of the fact that they engage in criminal activities that are not recorded – part of the 'dark figure' of crime. However, this is not borne out by current or historical statistics, as it is clear that women engage in all sorts of criminal activity, but they have very low levels of participation in some. Criminal activity is also highly related to socio-economic opportunity and low crime rates among women often reflect their relative lack of opportunity in comparison with men. Crimes committed by women mirror their lives. As their opportunities increase, so does their field of crime. Current studies show that while women are unlikely to engage in acts of violence against adults, they are highly likely to become involved in violence against children. They are also likely to engage in offences against property, but when compared with men, their rates of participation in such crimes as robbery and shoplifting are lower.[32]

In nineteenth-century Ireland, criminal activity for women was often opportunistic and always highly related to their socio-economic opportunities. Three studies by Inez Bailey, Sinead Jackson and Rena Lohan, confirm the fact that women were accused and convicted of criminal activities covering the full range of crimes – from drunkenness and disorderly conduct to murder.[33] However, the rates of participation by men and women in crime and the ways in which the law dealt with them varied over time. In 1850, the number of people arrested in Ireland reached a peak of around 65,000 (approximately 40,000 men and 25,000 women).[34] The majority of these arrests were for anti-social behaviour such as drunkenness, prostitution and disorderly conduct.[35] The popularity of drunkenness as an offence was reflected in Jackson's study of crime in Mayo and Galway in the late century. 'Drunkenness figures far exceeded those for any other crime, with large numbers of women and men being convicted every year'.[36] Officials were very concerned about alcohol consumption, as over-indulgence was often linked to other crimes. However, this was not a problem specific to Ireland, as drunkenness featured in the circumstances of arrest for many women in prison in England at the time.[37]

But, of course, many of the arrests for drunkenness, disorderly behaviour and other minor offences in Ireland did not lead to a conviction. Of the 65,000 people arrested in 1850, only 750 were convicted – 492 men and 258 women.[38] A substantial number of the crimes that led to conviction were in the category 'offences against property'. An analysis of crimes in the decade after the Famine, 1850–60, shows that women predominated in arrests for these crimes, a trend that reversed after that, although it continued to be their most likely crime.[39] The involvement of women in this area of crime is confirmed in Lohan's study. She found that the majority of women convicts in Dublin prisons (Grangegorman and Mountjoy) in the second half of the century had been convicted of offences against property.[40] Their crimes were very like those committed by female convicts transported to Australia from Ireland in the first half of the century. They included the stealing of clothing, money, food, animals, jewellery, and household items.[41] The main gender difference in relation to these 'offences against property' was the very small number of women involved in offences involving violence. Women throughout the century did steal goods and animals, but they rarely used violence.

The gender pattern was quite different for 'offences against the person'. With the exception of infanticide, it was very unusual for women to become involved in assaults or murder. However, when women did participate in serious assaults leading, in some instances, to murder, they were arrested and tried. Some of these women were found guilty and sentenced to death, but as will be discussed in a later chapter, most of these sentences were commuted to penal servitude, and very few women were actually executed.

POLICING AND PUNISHMENT

Crimes then, as now, became a public affair only when reported to the authorities. Today, the local policeman or woman is a rarity, but not so in nineteenth-century Ireland. Robert Peel, who became Chief Secretary for Ireland in 1812, began the process of setting up an Irish police force. At the time, agrarian unrest was regarded as a contributing factor to the general state of lawlessness in many areas of rural Ireland.[42] It had to be quelled and soon Ireland was 'the most heavily policed part of the United Kingdom'.[43] By the middle of the century even the remote parts of Ireland were subjected to a high level of police activity.

There were two major police forces in the country by the second half of the century. The Royal Irish Constabulary (RIC), was established in 1822 as a country constabulary, restructured in 1836 as the Irish Constabulary (IC) and, finally, renamed the RIC in 1867. The second was the Dublin Metropolitan Police (DMP) force, which was established in 1836 under the command of two commissioners (usually former army officers), who were directly responsible to the office of the Chief Secretary for Ireland.[44] The RIC was by far the larger force, with small barracks scattered throughout Ireland. Sir Frances B. Head, a Canadian who visited Ireland in 1852, counted 1,594 barracks, manned by constables who knew their localities and their inhabitants pretty well.[45] A third police force – the Peace Preservation Force – existed from 1814 to 1836. When it was disbanded, most of the members joined one of the two newly established forces.

As a result of this high level of policing, a great deal of information not only on crime, but on behaviour that might result in a crime, found its way to the administration at Dublin Castle. Because of their close proximity to the communities they were policing, it would have been difficult for a crime such as murder or manslaughter to be hidden. However, as will be clear in later chapters, in the murky world of domestic violence, the police often found it difficult if not impossible to uncover the truth.

The nineteenth century saw the emergence not only of a highly organized police force in Ireland, but also of a highly regulated system of punishment for crime. Scholars have explored different aspects of this system, showing that the century divides neatly into two distinct approaches to the criminal.[46] The first half of the century was dominated by transportation policies and the second by a convict system based on institution-centred punishment and rehabilitation.

Throughout the century, the death penalty remained as a possibility for a list of crimes, some of which are still viewed as serious (such as murder) and some that now appear quite trivial (such as the theft of an item of clothing). In the eighteenth century, there were other forms of non-prison punishment that continued into the early nineteenth century. For example, an offender could be publicly whipped or transported to 'his majesty's plantations in America' for seven years for stealing 'lamps, iron posts or furniture' which were public property.[47] The object of the exercise was to deter the offender and others from committing a similar offence. The major deterrent from crime was, of course, the death sentence, which was at the heart of the penal system throughout the nineteenth century. It remained on the statute books in Ireland until 1949, but its use was increasingly questioned after the Famine. The debate was kindled by the ending of public executions in 1866 and was re-ignited later by the reluctance of the judiciary to carry out death sentences on women who had killed a baby.[48] This debate, which will be discussed in a later chapter, focused on the need to exclude certain crimes from the death sentence, by redesignating them as essentially different to those requiring capital punishment. The best example of this was the re-designation of the killing of a baby (under certain circumstances) from murder to infanticide, and the exclusion of infanticide from the death penalty.

In the early decades of the nineteenth century, the possibility of a death sentence was very real for those who broke the law. In 1821 'all crimes, from murder to larceny of five shillings privately in a shop, were punishable with death'.[49] In 1828, new legislation allowed for the death sentence for the stealing of an animal such as a horse, a cow or a sheep. This law was repealed in 1832, when transportation for life replaced the death penalty for these offences. It is interesting that, although the death sentence continued to be a possibility for many crimes until the mid-century, the number of convictions was lower than might be expected, as was the number of executions. For example, in 1851, seventeen people were sentenced to death, but only two were executed. Of the others, fourteen were transported to the colonies for life and one was sent to prison.[50] In the following year, twenty-two people were sentenced to death, but only six were executed. All of the others were transported – thirteen for life and three for fourteen years.[51]

Between 1827 and 1847, the number of capital convictions plummeted – from 346 in 1827 to twenty-five in 1847. It increased during the Famine to a peak of sixty in 1848, decreasing again immediately, so that in the years after 1854 the number fell to single figures. Executions followed a similar pattern. They decreased between 1827 and 1847 from thirty-seven to eight. The number was high in 1848 (twenty-eight people executed) and in 1849 (fifteen people executed), corresponding to the peak years for rural unrest and crime. From then on, the number fell to single figures, reflecting the lower level of capital convictions.[52] There was only one exception to this pattern. In 1883, twelve men were executed – this was the year following the murders of the Joyce family at Maamtrasna and of Lord Frederick Cavendish, the Chief Secretary for Ireland, in the Phoenix Park, Dublin.[53] An extract from the judicial statistics for Ireland for 1863, gives a picture of the kind of people executed in that period.

> Antrim: Daniel Ward, aged twenty three, a labourer; murder of his companion by a blow of a stone in a handkerchief, and then throwing the body in a river – for a watch.
> Limerick County: Charles MacCormack, aged twenty four; murder of a young man in the presence of his father, for giving evidence at a trial.
> Wexford: Joseph Kelly; murder arising from a dispute about the disposal of the purchase money of land.[54]

The use of the death sentence in Ireland has been the subject of important studies by S.J. Connolly and Desmond Greer. Connolly compared the use of the death sentence and the actual carrying out of executions in Ireland with those in the other areas of the United Kingdom. He argues that the use of the death sentence was at its highest in the early part of the nineteenth century – at 32.7 per million of the population in the period 1823–30 – but, even then, it was much lower than in England and Wales, which had a rate of 87.6 per million for the same period.[55] This rate fell dramatically in both countries after 1840, so that by the 1880s, the rates were 1.4 per million for Ireland and one per million for England and Wales. This was mainly due to the fact that by the 1850s, the death penalty was restricted to crimes of murder and treason. Only a minority of those sentenced to death were executed, although a higher proportion met this fate before the Famine than after it. Greer suggests that this may have been due to the absence of a formal appeal system in the early decades of the century.[56] After its introduction, the Lord Lieutenant exercised a great deal of discretion in relation to appeals for clemency. For example, great compassion was extended to women who had been sentenced to death – with only three women being executed in the second half of the nineteenth century (in comparison to 106 men).[57]

Table 1.1 *Sentences passed on criminal offenders in Ireland 1845–51*

Sentence	1845	1846	1847	1848	1849	1850	1851
Death	13	14	25	60	38	17	17
Transported for life	39	49	87	79	61	35	27
for 15 or 14 years	14	29	71	71	32	50	67
for 7 years	428	504	1,587	2,075	1,896	837	1,165
for other periods	134	121	440	473	1,061	927	719
Imprisoned above 3 yrs	—	—	—	—	—	—	—
3 years & above 2	—	3	11	5	4	5	6
2 years & above 1	115	193	342	263	344	365	250
1 yr & above 6 m	534	758	1,428	1,410	1,721	1,547	1,498
6 mths and under	4,347	4,897	9,440	11,289	13,369	10,935	9,209
Fined or discharged	1,349	1,852	1,621	2,235	2,336	2,124	1,231
Sentence respited	128	219	181	245	335	465	143

Source: Criminal statistics for Ireland 1851. *Ireland: Tables showing the number of criminal offenders committed for trial or bailed for appearance at the assizes and sessions in each county, in the year 1851.* HC 1852–53, (1556) lxxxi. 71, p. 75.

Table 1.1 shows sentencing patterns for the middle of the century, while transportation was still an option. It is extracted from a report on the progress of criminal offenders through the court system for the period 1845–1851.[58] In this table, we see a number of patterns already discussed. Just as the level of crime increased during the Famine, so too did the levels of capital punishment, transportation and imprisonment. In 1848, the worst year in terms of serious crime in Ireland, sixty people were sentenced to death, 2,698 to transportation, and 12,967 to imprisonment.

TRANSPORTATION

Transportation to the British colonies formed a major part of penal policy in Ireland for almost two hundred years. It was introduced in 1717 as a replacement for the death sentence.[59] The assumptions underlying convict transportation schemes were similar to those in 'assisted emigration' schemes, with the additional aim of improving the home country (England, Ireland, Scotland or Wales) by getting rid of unruly elements, especially those who had been convicted of a crime.

Transportation was viewed very positively by the Dublin authorities. Not only was it an alternative to capital punishment, but it also gave the convict a second chance at a new life. Although transportation was intended initially as a replacement for the death sentence, it was more widely interpreted than this when it came into effect.[60] Thousands of people left Ireland under these schemes. The transportation of convicts from Ireland to North America began as early as 1703, until it was interrupted by the American War of Independence. Brian Henry estimates that excluding the suspension period between 1775 and 1784, the total number transported from Ireland to the Americas from 1718–89 was 14,400 people.[61]

Transportation to the Americas continued after the War of Independence even though the US authorities had made it known to the British government that it did not want to receive any more convicts.[62] However, it had to be discontinued after two ships (the *George* and the *Mercury*) which sailed in 1783 and 1784, had difficulties landing in the US. The *George*, renamed the *Swift*, managed to land at Baltimore, Maryland, where the convicts were sold. The *Mercury* was refused entry by all American ports and finally managed to land on the British Honduras, much to the disgust of the residents. The protests brought the transportation of convicts to the US from the British Isles to an end.[63] Instead, from 1786, England began to transport convicts to New South Wales in Australia. However, Irish convicts did not go to Australia until 1791 when the first ship sailed directly from Cork to Botany Bay.[64]

Although operating under similar laws and policies to those in England, the Dublin administration continued to transport people to the Americas until 1789, when the *Duke of Leinster* sailed twice from Ireland, bringing 115 convicts to Newfoundland and eighty-nine to the Leeward Isles.[65] Officials at Whitehall had informed Dublin Castle of the decision by the British government to change the destination for transported convicts to Australia. However, because of the pressure on gaols caused by the lack of transportation as an option, Dublin officials went ahead with the final journeys, with disastrous consequences for the convicts, many of whom died of disease and hunger.

As shown by Brian Henry, the negative attitude of the people of Newfoundland towards Irish convicts was first demonstrated in 1788, when two Irish convicts were expelled from the port of St Johns and a messenger sent to Dublin Castle to claim a refund for their return fares. In the following year, a special ship was commissioned by the authorities in Newfoundland to return the seventy-nine convicts who had been sent out from Dublin on the *Duke of Leinster*. Though officials in Dublin claimed they were acting legally (under the Police Act 1786), they were told to stop this practice as it was 'highly improper'.[66]

The Lord Lieutenant of Ireland took over responsibility for transportation in 1790, and in the following year, the first convict ship, the *Queen*, sailed from Cobh to Port Jackson, Australia.[67] Transportation had originally been introduced as an alternative to capital punishment. When, during the period 1820–34, a number of offences were exempted from capital punishment, the result was a decrease in those requiring transportation. However, as Carroll-Burke points out, 'even after the repeal of the majority of capital offences, the government continued to depend on that alternative, transporting a record of 1,298 persons from Ireland in 1835'.[68] Transportation from Ireland to Australia continued throughout the first half of the nineteenth century until it was abolished in 1853, when it was replaced by a system of penal servitude. During that period, over 40,000 convicts were transported to Australia directly from Ireland in the period 1791–1867, with an additional 8,000 of Irish birth transported from Britain.[69] According to Rena Lohan, approximately one third of the transportees from Ireland were women, though the proportion changed over time. For example, during the Famine, more than half of the convicts transported from Ireland were female.[70]

In Table 1.2 we see the names of some of the women who were convicted of the serious crime of murder and were sentenced to death, but who had their sentences commuted to transportations for life.[71] These women were among the last to be punished in this way. It would be misleading to suggest that all of the convicts transported during this era were guilty of serious crimes, such as murder or manslaughter. On the contrary, just like their male counterparts, many had been involved in the much less serious crime of stealing – which included shoplifting, pick-pocketing, receiving stolen goods and burglary. As shown by Deborah Oxley, in her analysis of crimes committed by Irish convict women transported to Australia, the majority had been convicted of stealing (clothing, money, food, etc.) with only a minority convicted of other crimes including vagrancy and violence.[72]

Table 1.2 *Women convicted of murder and transported for life*

Name	Year	County	Victim
Catherine Grennan	1838	Cavan	Child
Ann Myles	1839	Meath	Child
Una Berhagra	1846	Tipperary	Husband
Peggy Crumeen	1847	Donegal	Father in law
Bridget Mann	1850	Roscommon	Child
Charlotte Gribbin	1853	Antrim	Child
Anne Moloney	1853	Cork	Child
Mary Boland	1853	Cork	Child
May Murphy	1853	Cork	Child

Source: Convict records (National Archives of Ireland)

Oxley paints a pen picture of a typical female transported from Ireland.

> Brown hair, hazel eyes, with skin pitted with pock marks, Bridget Kennedy looked typically Irish. Raised a Catholic in a Meath countryside, she remained in the rural sector employed as a housemaid, and also did some washing. Literacy was not her strong point, as she could neither read or write. She had not married. At the age of 24, Bridget was tried in nearby Wicklow for her second offence, stealing butter.[73]

For this crime, she was sentenced to seven years transportation. After two years in prison in Ireland, she was sent to New South Wales to serve the remaining five years of her sentence.

IMPRISONMENT AND DISCHARGE

Throughout the nineteenth century, imprisonment in Ireland was accepted as a major strand of the criminal justice system. This approach was strengthened by the replacement in 1853 of transportation by a system of penal servitude as a method of dealing with convicted offenders. The legislation decreed specific substitutions for former sentences to transportation. For example, transportation for life became penal servitude for life, transportation of seven years or less became four years of penal servitude, and 10–15 years of transportation became 6–8 years of penal servitude.[74]

In order to support a prison system that could cope with the extra numbers that would inevitably result from the abolition of convict transportation, a new approach was necessary. In 1853, after the passing of the penal servitude legislation, the Chief Secretary for Ireland, John Young, set up a commission of inquiry to look into the conditions and discipline in the Irish prison system. The commission made a number of recommendations, including the addition of cellular accommodation at Mountjoy Gaol, the building of a separate prison for women at Mountjoy, with capacity for 600, the employment of convicts in the building of new prisons and the teaching of trades in all prisons.[75] As a result of the work of the commission, an overhaul of the prison system took place, leading to new legislation – the Irish Convict System Act in 1854.[76] This legislation laid the foundation for the centralization of the prison system and the introduction of a highly regulated system of management.

These regulations covered a 'licence'/'ticket of leave' system that was later used to allow convicts to 'emigrate' to the US and elsewhere. The prison service recognized that some of the problems that had led to the rejection of convicts by the American and the Australian authorities were related to the fact that they were very far from being ready for 'industry and self reliance'.[77] In fact, they were likely to engage in burglary and physical violence almost as soon as they arrived in their new land of opportunity. Now that the options of both capital punishment and of transportation were diminishing, the problem of what to do with the increasing numbers of convicts was a major headache for the Dublin administration. In January 1855, for example, there were 3,427 convicts in prison, 330 of whom were women.[78] By the late century, the numbers of convicts had decreased substantially but the problem of what to do with them on discharge remained problematic. In 1884, for example, the Royal Commission on Prisons in Ireland was told that the number of convicts in custody was 837 (749 males and 88 females) and by 1893, the numbers had dropped farther to 486 (447 males and 39 females).[79] The question remained – how best might these people be integrated back into society, a society that was often quite hostile to them?

The 'ticket of leave' system was introduced as part of a programme to prepare convicts for discharge, within an overall approach of 'disciplinary and reformatory treatment within the newly reformed prison system'.[80] The law enabling a 'ticket of leave' system was passed in 1853 (for England and Ireland) and came into force in Ireland in 1856. This meant that any convict could be released early (before the sentence expired) on licence or ticket 'to be at large'. The ticket had printed on it the conditions of release and it could be revoked at any time by the government.[81] The licences (as they were normally called) were, according to the directors of prisons,

> a sort of guarantee to the community that in consequence of a prisoner having been subjected to a proper course of prison discipline and reformatory treatment, he is considered a fit subject to be received and employed outside the prison.[82]

The 'ticket of leave' system was not universally popular. Many of those released in this way in England re-offended within a short time and were re-convicted. Some of the commentators at the time were more positive about convicts released in this way in Ireland, attributing it to the higher level of surveillance. However, there may have been another reason for the lack of opposition to the system in Ireland. Many of them left the jurisdiction.

The 'ticket of leave' was legally valid only within the UK, as illustrated in an extract from the licence issued to Mary Lavelle on her release in 1892. Mary, who had been a victim of domestic violence, had killed her husband. She, together with her son and daughter, was found guilty of manslaughter and sentenced to penal servitude for life. After spending eleven years in prison, she was released on licence. The licence or 'ticket if leave' was similar to those issued to other prisoners who were discharged before the end of their sentences.

> Her Majesty is graciously pleased to grant Mary Lavelle, who was convicted of manslaughter at the Assizes for the Connaught Winter Assize on the 12th day of December 1881 and was then and there sentenced to be kept in penal servitude for life and is now confined in the Grange Gorman Convict Prison, her Royal Licence to be at large from the day of her liberation under this Order during the remaining portion of her said term of penal servitude, unless the said Mary Lavelle shall before the expiration of the said term be convicted on indictment of some offence within the United Kingdom, in which case such Licence will be immediately forfeited by law, or unless it shall please Her Majesty sooner to revoke or alter such Licence.

And

> This licence will be forfeited if the Holder does not fulfil the following conditions. The Holder shall preserve her Licence and produce it when called upon to do so by a magistrate or police officer. She shall abstain from any violation of the law. She shall not lead an idle and dissolute life, without visible means of obtaining honest livelihood. If her Licence is forfeited or revoked in consequence of a conviction for any offence, she will be liable to undergo a term of Penal Servitude for the remaining portion of her natural life.[83]

Mary was delivered to the Liverpool Boat, leaving for Jersey City just two days after her release (which was the date stamped on the licence). Like convicts who had been transported to the US in the first half of the nineteenth century, these 'ticket of leave' people – who were ex-convicts – were not welcome. Towards the end of the nineteenth century, the US was making great efforts to keep out undesirables. Ellis Island, the first port of call for newly arrived immigrants to New York, is a monument to the bureaucratic practices introduced to weed out anyone who might be troublesome or a burden on the state. However, this was the route used by many convicts released from prison in Ireland on a 'ticket of leave'.

However, it would be untrue to suggest that all convicts were released early and went on to happier lives elsewhere. Many served out their time within the prison system in Ireland, a system that was hailed as exemplary in the 1860s. During that period, imprisonment was viewed as rehabilitation and everything was geared towards that end. The separation of females from males was part of this endeavour, with the new female prison at Mountjoy replacing the 'depot for female convicts' at Grangegorman in 1858.[84] This helped relieve some of the overcrowding at Mountjoy, which had been caused by the ending of transportation. It also provided a unique opportunity for the training and rehabilitation of women within an all-female environment. Though women were subjected to the same regime as men, working through each stage of the convict system, earning marks and gratuities, there were some concessions. For example, after complaints from the chaplains that solitary confinement often led to mental disturbance, its use was limited.[85] Other differences in approach to men and women were more controversial. In the final stage of serving out a sentence within the convict system, men were transferred to intermediate prisons from which they could be released into the community on a 'ticket of leave'. This did not happen for women.

They were transferred to a refuge, such as that at Goldenbridge, Dublin (opened in 1856), where they were supervised while on 'ticket of leave'. Goldenbridge was run by the Sisters of Mercy, and was fully integrated into the criminal justice system. While some commentators at the time were critical of the system, others viewed this as a positive feature of the rehabilitation process.[86]

As the century progressed, conditions deteriorated within the prison system, leading to two major enquiries in 1878 and 1884.[87] As a result of these enquiries, the male public works prison at Spike Island, Cork, was closed and the Mountjoy female prison taken over for male convicts. The women were transferred back to Grangegorman Prison in 1883. By then, the female convict population had dropped to ninety-nine from a peak of 674 in 1858.[88] Ten years later, in 1893, the number of women in convict prisons declined even further – to thirty-nine. In the same year, the number of males in convict prisons was 447. It had also declined – from 833 in 1872.[89] However, this was not a reflection of the overall trend in the prison population. In fact, the trend there was in the opposite direction. The total number of males in prisons (of all kinds) in 1893 was 5,962, and the equivalent number for females as 5,067. In addition, a further 8,434 (5,058 males and 3,376 females) had been transferred to asylums, but were still officially listed as criminals. The equivalent numbers for 1872 are 4,824 for males and 3,657 for females in the prison system, and an additional 3,693 (2,246 males and 1,447 females) in the asylum system.[90]

What these statistics tell us, for the purposes of the discussion here, is that thousands of men and women served their time within a range of prisons in Ireland. Some were released unconditionally after serving their sentences or after a successful appeal to the Lord Lieutenant of Ireland. Others gained freedom early through the 'ticket of leave' system, allowing them to return to their friends and relatives in Ireland or the US. Finally, there were those who showed signs of insanity while in prison. They were transferred to what was perceived as a less punitive and more appropriate regime within an asylum. Most of these 'insane' prisoners went to district asylums, but some were sent to the Central Criminal Asylum at Dundrum – a special facility opened in 1850 for criminal lunatics.

NOTES

1 Matilda Charlotte Houstoun, *Twenty years in the Wild West: or Life in Connaught* (London: 1879), p. 228, quoted in Brian Griffin, *Sources for the Study of Crime in Ireland, 1801–1921* (Dublin: Four Courts Press, 2005), p. 72.

2 Anonymous magistrate, *The present state of Tipperary, as regards agrarian outrages, their nature, origin, and increase, considered, with suggestions for remedial measures* (Dublin: 1842), quoted in Griffin, *Sources*, p. 70.

3 John D. Brewer, Bill Lockhart & Paula Rodgers, *Crime in Ireland 1945–95* (Oxford: Clarendon Press, 1997), p. 1.

4 See, for example, Patrick Carroll-Burke, *Colonial Discipline: The Making of the Irish Convict System* (Dublin: Four Courts Press, 2000); Desmond Greer, 'Crime, Justice and Legal Literature in Nineteenth-century Ireland', *Irish Jurist (n.s.)*, 37 (2002): 241–68; Brian Griffin, *The Bulkies* (Dublin: Irish Academic Press, 1998); Elizabeth Malcolm, *The Irish Policeman, 1822–1922: A Life* (Dublin: Four Courts Press, 2005); Ian O'Donnell and Finbarr McAuley (eds), *Criminal Justice History* (Dublin: Four Courts Press, 2003).

5 For sources, see Griffin, *Sources*, p. 11.

6 Neal Garnham, 'How violent was eighteenth-century Ireland?, in O'Donnell and McAuley, *Criminal Justice History*, [pp. 19–34] p. 34.

7 R.B. McDowell, 'Administration and the public services, 1800–1870', in W.E. Vaughan (ed), *A New History of Ireland, V: Ireland under the Union, 1. 1801–1870* (Oxford: Clarendon Press, 1989), [pp. 538–561,] p. 544.

8 For discussion, see Griffin, *Sources*, pp. 11–13.

9 NAI, CRF, 1853/S. 6 (Stackpoole); NAI, CRF, 1870/S. 7 (Shiel).

10 Nicholas Woodward, 'Transportation convictions during the Great Irish Famine', *Journal of Interdisciplinary History*, xxxvii, 1 (Summer, 2006), pp. 59–87.

11 Ibid., p. 68.

12 Ibid., Table 2, p. 67.

13 W.E. Vaughan 'Ireland c. 1870', pp. 726–98 in Vaughan (ed.) *A New History*, p. 764.

14 *Judicial statistics for Ireland 1863*, HC 1864 (3418) lvii. 653, p. 672.

15 Vaughan, 'Ireland c. 1870', p. 765.

16 S.J. Connolly, 'Unnatural death in four nations', in S.J. Connolly (ed.), *Kingdoms United? Great Britain and Ireland since 1500: Integration and Diversity* (Dublin: Four Courts Press, 1999), p. 205; C. Conley, Homicide in late-Victorian Ireland and Scotland, *New Hibernia Review*, 5, (Autumn 2001), pp. 66–86.

17 *Criminal and judicial statistics for Ireland 1868*, HC 1868–69 (4203) lviii.737 p. 751.

18 Ibid.

19 Brewer *et al. Crime in Ireland*, p. 15.

20 Ibid.

21 Clive Emsley, *Crime and society in England 1750–1900*, 2nd edition (London and New York 1996), p. 44.

22 See Mark Finnane, 'A decline in violence in Ireland? Crime, policing and social relations, 1860–1914', *Crime, History and Societies*, 1, 1 (1997), pp. 51–70; William Wilbanks, 'Homicide in Ireland', *International Journal of Comparative and Applied Criminal Justice*, 20, 1 (Spring 1996), pp. 59–75.

23 Ian O'Donnell, 'Lethal Violence in Ireland, 1841–2003', *British Journal of Criminology*, 45 (2005), pp 671–95, p. 676.

24 Ibid.

25 Ibid., Figure 3, p. 678.

26 Ibid., Figure 2, p. 678.

27 Ibid., p. 686.

28 See Joseph Lee, *The Modernization of Irish Society 1848–1918* (Dublin: Gill and Macmillan, 1973).

29 K.H. Connell, *Irish Peasant Society: Four Historical Essays* (Oxford: Clarendon Press, 1968), pp. 82–3.

30 Clarice Feinman, *Women in the Criminal Justice System* (Westport, CT: Praeger, 1994); Lorraine Gelsthorpe and Allison Morris (eds), *Feminist Perspectives in Criminology* (Milton Keynes: Open University Press, 1990); Frances Heidensohn, *Women and Crime*, 2nd Edition (Basingstoke: Macmillan Press, 1996); Alido V. Merlo and Jocelyn

M. Pollock, *Women Law and Social Control* (Boston, MA: Allyn and Bacon, 1995); Sandra Walklate, *Gender and Crime: An Introduction* (London: Prentice Hall, 1995).

31 Heidensohn, *Women and Crime*; Feinman, *Women in the Criminal Justice System.*

32 Heidensohn, *Women and Crime*, p. 7.

33 Inez Bailey, *Women and Crime in Nineteenth-Century Ireland: Mayo and Galway examined* (Unpublished MA thesis, NUI, Maynooth, 1992); Sinead Jackson, *Gender, Crime and Punishment in late Nineteenth-Century Ireland: Mayo and Galway examined*, (Unpublished MA thesis, NUI, Galway, 1999); Rena Lohan, *The Treatment of Women Sentenced to Transportation and Penal Servitude 1790–1898* (Unpublished M. Litt. thesis, Trinity College, Dublin, 1989).

34 Bailey, *Women and Crime*, p. 7.

35 Ibid.

36 Jackson, *Gender, Crime and Punishment*, p. 182.

37 Heidensohn, *Women and Crime*, p. 65.

38 Bailey, *Women and Crime*, p. 8.

39 Ibid., p. 9.

40 Lohan, *The Treatment of Women*, Appendix 14, p. 345.

41 Deborah Oxley, *Convict Maids: the Forced Migration of Women to Australia* (Cambridge: Cambridge University Press, 1996), Tables A9, A10, pp. 260–1.

42 Mc Dowell, 'Administration 1800–1870', p. 544.

43 Griffin, *Sources*, p. 21.

44 Ibid., pp. 21–2; McDowell, 'Administration 1800–1870', pp. 551–3.

45 F.B. Head, *Fortnight in Ireland* (London, 1852), p. 42, cited in Griffin, *Sources*, p. 21.

46 These include Carroll-Burke, *Colonial Discipline*; Brian Henry, *Dublin Hanged*, (Dublin: Irish Academic Press, 1994); Lohan, *The Treatment of Women*; Gerard Moran, *Sending out Ireland's Poor* (Dublin: Four Courts Press, 2004); Bob Reece, *The Origins of Irish Convict Transportation to New South Wales* (Basingstoke: Palgrave, 2001)

47 Carroll-Burke, *Colonial Discipline*, p. 26.

48 Lohan, *The Treatment of Women*, p. 365, Note 10; Correspondence in relation to the death sentence in the 1880s (NAI, CRF, Misc 1888/no. 1862).

49 Carroll-Burke, *Colonial Discipline*, p. 28.

50 *Ireland: Tables showing the number of criminal offenders committed for trial or bailed for appearance at the assizes and sessions in each county, in the year 1851*, HC 1852–53, (1556) lxxxi. 71, p. 75.

51 *Criminal Tables for* HC 1852–53 [338] lxxxi. 347, p. 436.

52 Carroll-Burke, *Colonial Discipline*, pp. 30–1.

53 Data on executions, *Death Book (Male and Female) 1852–1932* (NAI, GPB, CN5).

54 *Judicial statistics for Ireland 1863*, HC 1864 (3418) lvii. 653, p. 674.

55 Connolly, 'Unnatural death', p. 213.

56 Greer, 'Crime, justice', p. 252.

57 Executions for the period 1852–99, in the *Judicial statistics for Ireland, 1863*.

58 *Ireland: Tables showing the number of criminal offenders committed for trial … in the year 1851*, p. 75.

59 Transportation Act 1717 (6 Geo 1 c. 12).

60 Lohan, *The Treatment of Women*, p. xv.

61 Henry, *Dublin Hanged*, p. 156.

62 Ibid., p. 154; Reece, *The Origins of Irish Convict Transportation*, p. 17.

63 Henry, *Dublin Hanged*, p. 154.

64 Bob Reece (ed.), *Exiles from Erin Covict Lives in Ireland and Australia*, (Dublin: Gill and Macmillian, 1991), p. 111.

65 Henry, *Dublin Hanged*, p. 155.

66 Ibid., pp. 160–4.

67 Ibid., p. 167.

68 Carroll-Burke *Colonial Discipline*, p. 31.

69 Reece (ed.) *Exiles from Erin*, p. 1.

70 Lohan, *The Treatment of Women*, p. 1 and Appendix 1, p. 30.
71 Each entry found in two sources: Transportation Database (NAI); Death Book (Female) 1852–1930; Individual convict files – NAI, CRF, 1846/ B51 (Behagra); NAI, CRF, 1847/C16 (Crumeen); NAI, CRF, 1838/G58 (Grennan); NAI, CRF, 1850/M17 (Mann); NAI, CRF, 1839/M99 (Myles).
72 Oxley, *Convict Maids*, Tables A9, A10, pp. 260–1.
73 Ibid., p. 134.
74 Carroll-Burke, *Colonial Discipline*, p. 95; 16 & 17 Vic c. 99 (1853) UK (untitled)
75 *Copies of correspondence relative to the management and discipline of convict prisons, and the extension of prison accommodation, with reports of commissioners*, HC 1854 (344) lviii. 6; Carroll-Burke, *Colonial Discipline*, pp. 95–9.
76 Irish Convict System Act 1854 (17 & 18 Vict. c.76).
77 Carroll-Burke, *Colonial Discipline*, p. 100.
78 Ibid., p. 104.
79 *Second Report of the Royal Commission on Prisons in Ireland*. HC 1884 (c. 4145) xlii. 671, p. 698; Jackson, *Gender, Crime and Punishment*, Tables 9, 10, p. 219 derived from *Judicial and Criminal Statistics for Ireland 1892*, HC 1893 (c. 7534) xcv. 105.
80 *First report of the directors of convict prisons in Ireland for 1854*. HC 1854–55 (1958) xxvi, 609, p. 3; Carroll-Burke, *Colonial Discipline*, pp. 95–100.
81 *First report on convict prisons for 1854*, p. 3.
82 Ibid., p. 4.
83 Copy of licence in the convict file NAI, PEN, 1892/118 (Mary Lavelle).
84 Lohan, *The Treatment of Women*, pp. 39, 44; Grangegorman opened in 1836.
85 Ibid., p. 183.
86 Ibid., p. 132.
87 *Report of the commissioners appointed to inquire into the working of the penal servitude acts, Vol. iii, Minutes of evidence, continued with appendix and index 1878*, HC 1878–79 (c. 2368), xxxviii. i; *Preliminary report of the royal commission appointed to inquire into the administration, discipline, and condition of prisons in Ireland 1884*, HC 1883 (3496), xxxii. 803; *First report with evidence and appendices 1884*, HC 1884–85 (4233), xxxviii. 1; *Second Report 1884*, HC 1884 (4145), xlii. 671.
88 Lohan, *The Treatment of Women*, pp. 278–9.
89 Jackson, *Gender, Crime and Punishment*, Tables 9, 10, p. 219, based on *Judicial and Criminal Statistics of Ireland*, HC 1872 (c. 851) lxx. 247; and HC 1893 (c. 7534) xcv. 105.
90 Ibid.

CHAPTER TWO

Criminal lunacy

IRELAND, IN THE NINETEENTH CENTURY, was subjected to waves of legislation not only in relation to crime and punishment, but also to vagrancy and lunacy.[1] While some of this legislation was aimed at controlling unruly elements in society, some had the more positive aim of providing services for people with a mental disorder. Arthur Williamson's work on the events that led up to the establishment of a publicly funded asylum system in Ireland, highlights the influence of the debates on lunacy reform taking place in Britain at the time.[2] These debates aroused political and public attention due to the third 'attack of madness' suffered by King George the third in 1801.[3] Members of Parliament focused on how best to deal with people suffering from mental disorder in ways that protected them from harm and the public from danger.[4] Sir John Newport, Member of Parliament for Waterford was one of these parliamentarians. He was also the chairman of the board of governors at the Waterford house of industry and, as such, was well aware of the difficulties encountered by people suffering from mental disorder as they competed for space and care within the workhouse system. He became a champion of lunacy reform in Ireland, supported by another prominent Whig politician, Thomas Spring Rice, who was also a life governor of the Limerick house of industry.

Following the report of the Select Committee on the Aged and Infirm Poor of Ireland in 1804, which found that little was being done for 'idiots or insane persons', an attempt by Newport to introduce legislation for the building of four asylums failed.[5] However, houses of industry were allowed to develop lunatic wards to help the situation. At the Dublin house of industry, a separate institution was deemed necessary and the Richmond Asylum was opened in 1815.[6] As plans were going ahead for the Richmond Asylum, Robert Peel came to Ireland as Chief Secretary in 1812.[7] He initiated an investigation in 1814 into all institutions that had lunatics as inmates.[8] This investigation, by Foster Archer, the inspector of prisons, showed that only nine of the thirty-two counties in Ireland had any provision for lunatics. Dublin was best served, with a private asylum, Saint Patrick's, and plans for a public asylum the Richmond.[9] There was also a public asylum in Cork, but elsewhere, the only public provision was within workhouses and prisons. There were also a few small private 'madhouses' in Ireland at the time, including the Bloomfield Retreat, at Donnybrook in Dublin, run by the Society of Friends on the same principles of moral management as the York Retreat. These principles included the rejection of physical treatments (such as bleeding and the use of drugs) in favour of a psychological approach, incorporating creative work, 'a sound diet, gentle amusements, and religious instruction'. The York Retreat had been founded in 1796 by William Tuke, a Quaker laymen, for the treatment of 'insane English Quakers', as an alternative to medical treatment in large public institutions.[10]

Archer's investigation showed that conditions in both workhouses and prisons were grossly inadequate and unsuitable for individuals suffering from a mental disorder. The abject state of some of these people was brought to the attention of the public during the deliberations of the Select Committee on the Lunatic Poor in Ireland, which reported in 1817.[11] All the evidence presented to the Select Committee strengthened the arguments, already advanced by Newport and Spring Rice, that the current situation could not continue. The select committee recommended the establishment of a network of district lunatic asylums throughout Ireland. It also recommended that the emphasis in these asylums should be on moral treatment as practiced at the Quaker Retreat at York, England.[12]

In 1817, the first of many laws to establish district asylums was passed, followed by a number of amending acts to strengthen the smooth running of the system.[13] Based on this legislation, the first district asylum in Ireland opened at Armagh in 1825. Seven more opened within the following ten years, and by the middle of the century there were ten district asylums dotted throughout the country, providing over 3,000 beds in total.[14] The second wave of asylum building, more vigorous than the first, took place between 1852 and 1869, when twelve more district asylums opened. These asylums were bigger than those built in the first half of the century, due to the ever increasing demand for places from the public. By 1900, there were twenty-two asylums in Ireland, providing over 16,000 beds.[15]

The emphasis in the early years was on care and treatment. The annual reports of the inspectorate of prisons in Ireland (also responsible for asylums until the middle of the century) were full of optimism and a promise of recovery. In 1824, the Inspector General of Prisons praised the Cork asylum, which had as its medical superintendent one of the early Irish converts to moral treatment, Dr William Saunders Hallaran.

> Dr Hallaran has within a few years been enabled to introduce a system of classification, the good effects of which he speaks in terms of great encouragement ... With respect to the employment of the insane, Dr Hallaran observes that the accomplishment of this object has been but partial, but that so far as the trial has been in Cork, the success has greatly exceeded his expectations; he finds that with the pauper insane, horticulture has proved to be the most welcome employment of any other.[16]

Dr Hallaran led the way among asylum managers in following the philosophy of moral treatment that had emerged from the Quaker approach to mental disorder. With a view to bringing out the best in patients, they were divided into groups based on their behaviour. Patients who were amenable to direction were encouraged to engage in semi-skilled and manual labour – one of which was gardening, as promoted by Dr Hallaran. As well as being popular, it was deemed therapeutic for certain forms of mental disturbances. As Elaine Showalter shows in her seminal work on women in English asylums, particular forms of activity were pursued as a means of curing certain diseases and as promoting tranquility and a return to health.[17]

By the 1840s, the inspectors were still confident about the methods of containment used in the asylums, methods that excluded physical restraint. In 1844, the annual report of the inspectorate painted a picture of contentment at Armagh Asylum:

> In going through the asylum, it is very gratifying to witness the cheerfulness and apparent contentment of these poor creatures ... The absence of all kind of severe or unnecessary restraint forms a prominent feature in the treatment of the patients in this as, indeed, in all the district asylums in Ireland.[18]

The inspectors presented a rosy picture of the benevolent moral management regime that prevailed not only in Cork and Armagh, but throughout Ireland. In 1851, they reported:

> We have reason to express satisfaction at the general arrangements and domestic economy of these Institutions. Constant to our visitations of them, we invariably observe the utmost kindness of manner and considerate attention on the part of the physicians and superior officers to the various inmates, while the attachment of the lunatics themselves

to their immediate attendants, affords a satisfactory proof that the latter fulfill their duties with humanity, good temper, and forbearance – moral powers, for which mechanical coercion will be ever found from experience both a harsh and inefficient substitute.[19]

Every now and again in the annual reports of the lunacy inspectorate, we get a glimpse of treatment regimes that were less than therapeutic and which incurred their wrath. Wexford Asylum was held up as one such example in 1845. Dr Frances White, the inspector, was extremely angry at what he found there.

I proceeded next into the yard outside this apartment, and was ushered to an out-house, where a patient was locked up; on asking to see him, the keeper said that I could see him through the window, appearing unwilling, at the same time, to open the door. On looking in, I saw the unfortunate man standing at his cell door, nearly in a state of nakedness, chained by the wrists and ankle, and padlocked; he wore an old torn jacket and a short petticoat; a trencher of potatoes lay on the floor, as also a porringer of milk. I had the door unlocked and caused him to be let out, his chains to be struck off, and allowed to walk about the place. He was represented as a very dangerous idiot; however, I could perceive that he had intellect enough to convince me that he felt grateful so far for having been allowed his liberty. This man's name was Thomas Edwards.[20]

White personally appointed and sent an attendant to Wexford, who took over as warden and initiated a number of improvements. Within a year, Thomas was helping with general cleaning within the asylum and enjoying the company of his fellow inmates. What this case illustrates is that underneath the apparently benevolent management style being promoted within the asylums, there were undercurrents of control and even cruelty towards some patients. These were the 'difficult to handle' individuals who were increasingly being labelled as 'dangerous lunatics'. Their plight was made worse by the increasing demand for places within asylums, which led to over-crowding and inadequate care.

DANGEROUS LUNATICS

To solve the immediate problem of asylum overcrowding, a new Act was passed in 1838, which meant that lunatics who were deemed to be dangerous and for whom a place could not be found within an asylum, could be admitted directly to prison.[21] These people could then be transferred to a district asylum, without any further recourse to local magistrates, whenever a place became available. Though some people continued to be admitted to district asylums as 'ordinary' lunatics (of unsound mind), the proportion of 'dangerous' lunatic admissions to asylums increased as the century progressed. This was due primarily to the fact that the asylums could not refuse admissions from the prison system. However, the district asylum system was constantly overcrowded and the numbers in prison awaiting transfer to an asylum accumulated as the years went by. In the annual report of the inspectors of lunacy for 1866, the numbers were used to show the need for additional asylums. In 1864, there were 441 dangerous lunatics in prison, in 1865 there were 505, and in 1866 the number was 495 – all waiting for places in the district asylum system.[22]

One of the many problems with the 1838 Act was that after confinement to prison, these people could only be discharged as sane from the asylum to which they were later transferred. Even if they never showed any signs of insanity while in prison, they could not be discharged directly from there. The practice of imprisoning lunatics caused great concern within both the prison system and the lunacy system. Prison governors complained that the presence of lunatics made discipline difficult. Asylum managers complained about the stigma arising from the procedure itself and about the practical difficulties – they had no control over the numbers of lunatics being transferred from prison. All of these concerns were made known to the Select Committee (House of Lords) on the State of the Lunatic Poor in Ireland in 1843.[23] In its report, it commented on the misuse of the legislation.

> The Act of the 1 & 2 Vic c. 27, objectionable as it is, has been rendered still more so by the practice it has produced. Cases are stated where unfortunate lunatics are encouraged to commit trivial acts of mischief and violence, in order to afford a colourable [sic] pretence for their commitment to prison, thus saving their family or friends the expense of providing for them otherwise.[24]

However, these comments did not lead to any immediate change, as became clear in the evidence given to the Commission of Inquiry into Lunatic Asylums in Ireland in 1858.[25]

Evidence of Dr John Thomas Banks, Physician at the Richmond Asylum, Dublin

Question: Are you satisfied that those who are committed as dangerous lunatics, and come to you as such, have been fairly committed as dangerous lunatics?

Answer: Indeed in many cases, I think no. I cannot say but they may have done something that might be construed to be dangerous. The legal proceeding is to swear before a magistrate a person is dangerous and owing to the crowded state of the house, they constantly remain weeks and sometimes months in the gaol.

Evidence of James Corry Connellan Esq., Inspector General of Prisons

Question: Supposing the law to be altered, by which dangerous lunatics may not be committed by the magistrates direct to gaols, what amendment would you suggest?
Answer: I see no reason why they should not be sent direct to asylums. The whole question with regard to the confinement of lunatics in gaols resolves itself into this – first that the greatest injury is done to the discipline of a prison; and secondly, with regard to the lunatics themselves, they are either curable or incurable; if they are curable, it is surely a gross injustice to them to detain them in a place so deficient in the proper means of treatment for their disease as our ordinary gaols; if they are incurable you are perverting the gaol from the object for which it was established.[26]

The report of the Commission of Inquiry led to a change in the law in 1867, which made the admission of 'dangerous lunatics' to prison illegal and authorized their direct admission to asylums.[27] However, in spite of this change, the upward trend in the number of dangerous lunacy admissions continued. The only difference was that the burden had been transferred from the prison system to the asylum system to which dangerous lunatics were now admitted directly. By the last quarter of the century, only a very small percentage of admissions to district asylums were 'ordinary' admissions (of unsound mind). Most of the admissions were legally classified as 'dangerous'. For example, in 1888, out of a total of 1,821 admissions to all asylums in Ireland, only 10 per cent (181 people) were ordinary admissions. The rest were admitted either as dangerous lunatics or as urgent cases.[28]

However, many were not really dangerous.[29] Rather the designation of dangerousness was the simplest way of ensuring admission for the person with a mental illness. There were two obvious practical advantages to families who used 'dangerous lunacy' admission procedures rather than 'ordinary' admission procedures. Firstly, the police transported the patient from home to the asylum regardless of the distance and, secondly, the asylum could not refuse admission to someone legally deemed dangerous. These people, though labelled as dangerous, often turned out to be docile and easy to manage after admission to a prison or an asylum.

CRIMINAL LUNATIC ASYLUM

There was however, another group of people with mental illnesses who proved to be more difficult to place and treat. These were individuals who had engaged in criminal activity and who were deemed to have a mental disorder. In Britain, this group of people had been categorized as criminal lunatics in 1800.[30] This law highlighted the need for a distinct method of sentencing and of confinement in Ireland. The Lunacy (Ireland) Act 1821 began the process by providing the basis for an acquittal on the grounds of insanity – 'any person charged with an offence should be acquitted, if found to have been insane at the time the crime was committed'.[31] He or she could then be confined to an asylum or prison at the pleasure of the Lord Lieutenant.

Because of the lack of specific accommodation for criminal lunatics and the scarcity of places in district asylums, these individuals were detained in prison pending transfer to an asylum. The category of criminal lunatic was broadened in 1838 to include prisoners whose original crime had not been linked in any way to insanity, but who developed a mental disorder while in prison. Two doctors were required to certify the prisoner as insane.[32] Within the context of the gradual expansion of the district asylum system, the authorities hoped that criminal lunatics would gradually move out of the prison system into an asylum. However, things did not work out as planned and by the 1840s, it was clear that the system was not working.

The whole issue of criminal lunacy was brought to public attention in Britain and Ireland in January 1843, when a crime occurred that was to form the basis for future trials in which the insanity defence was used. This was the murder by Daniel McNaughton of Edward Drummond, secretary to Robert Peel, who was the Brtish Prime Minister at the time. McNaughton was later found not guilty on the grounds of insanity, his case forming the basis for the M'Naghten Rules.[33] The meaning and influence of these rules will be discussed in the next chapter. For the moment, suffice it to say that the debate that took place in both houses of Parliament in London, as a result of this crime, had a profound effect on policies and laws in relation to criminal lunatics in Britain and Ireland.

In 1843, the year that Daniel McNaughton killed Edward Drummond, a decision was taken to open a central criminal lunatic asylum for Ireland. This decision was based on the recommendation of the Select Committee (House of Lords) on the State of the Lunatic Poor in Ireland which reported in 1843.[34] The committee heard substantial evidence on the problems created by the presence of criminal lunatics in the prison system. They numbered 110 in January 1841, rising to 214 in January 1843.[35] The Committee also heard evidence on possible solutions to the problem from Dr Francis White, the inspector of prisons with responsibility for overseeing lunatic asylums in Ireland.[36] White favoured the opening of a new central asylum specifically for criminal lunatics, rather than the addition of smaller units to existing prisons or asylums. In his evidence to the Select Committee, White quoted a letter from the Lord Chancellor, Edward B. Sugden, to make his point – a central asylum would save money and increase security.

> Solid objections exist to criminal lunatics being received into district asylums which never were intended for prisons. As there is a want of room for pauper lunatics, it would save expense to remove all the criminal lunatics to one spot ... The advantages of bringing together all the criminal lunatics under the immediate eye of the Governor is obvious; their security could readily be provided for, and strangers could be prohibited from visiting that department from motives of curiosity. It might be attended with great advantage if a power were given to send Irish criminal lunatics to England, or English ones to Ireland, for security.[37]

As a result of the efforts of Dr White and the support of the Lord Chancellor, the Select Committee recommended that a central asylum 'for insane persons charged with offences in Ireland' be opened.

> The committee is of the opinion that all persons of this class should be maintained and treated throughout the whole United Kingdom on the same principle; and there are many obvious reasons why their removal to one central establishment, near the seat of the executive government in Ireland, is expedient.[38]

The recommendation was accepted by the government and the Central Criminal Lunatic Asylum (Ireland) Act was passed in 1845.[39] This Act also made provision for the setting up of a separate inspectorate of lunacy and the appointment of two qualified persons to act as inspectors. All of the responsibilities for oversight and inspection of lunatic asylums were transferred from the inspectorate of prisons to this new body.

Five years later, a special building, with a separate infirmary, was opened at Dundrum village on the outskirts of Dublin. It had room for 120 people – eighty places for men and forty for women.[40] When Dr Frances White was asked to estimate the number of people most in

need of this facility (from the 214 in the system in 1843), he reported
that there were eighty-five criminal lunatics ready for immediate transfer
in 1844 – seventy-five in asylums and ten in prisons.[41] By the time
Dundrum opened, there were many more ready for transfer. The
selection process was carried out by the inspectors and is discussed later.

As already noted, the debate on criminal lunacy in Ireland was
preceded by similar discussions in England. These discussions formed
the context within which politicians and civil servants in Ireland
developed their ideas. Since the opening of two criminal wings at
Bethlem Hospital in 1816, different views were being publicly aired as
to the value of having a separate institution for criminal lunatics.[42]
Although Fisherton House, an asylum in Salisbury, had added a criminal
ward in 1848, it had not solved the problem of a growing population of
criminally insane people. However, as Nigel Walker points out, the idea
of a central asylum for offenders was not acceptable to all.[43] There were
two main objections to having one large asylum for criminal lunatics
– that it would not be desirable to mix different social classes in the
same building and that there might be a problem with security. Dr
W.C. Hood of Bethlem Asylum voiced the concerns of many people at
this time. Dr Hood, who went on to be knighted after his appointment
by the Lord Chancellor as the Visitor of Chancery Lunatics in England,
was an extremely influential figure.[44]

> Would it be fair or humane to shut up a lady or a gentleman who
> may ... have committed a very trivial misdemeanour, in the same ward
> or even in the same establishment with women or men belonging to the
> lowest classes of society, who may have committed revolting and
> nameless offences?

and

> There is a feeling, I am aware, abroad, that lunatic asylums should be
> built in the style of palaces, and surrounded with beautiful and attrac-
> tive scenery ... It is however obvious that where security and safe
> custody of a dangerous criminal lunatic is an object, pleasant and
> umbrageous avenues would afford opportunities for concealment.[45]

However, despite objections, such as those from Dr Hood, Broadmoor
opened in 1863 and, like Dundrum, continues to be a special hospital
for mentally disordered offenders.[46]

By the time Dundrum opened, it was already clear that running a
criminal lunatic asylum would cost more than an ordinary asylum,
but this seemed a price worth paying if it relieved the prisons of the

problems associated with housing convict lunatics. This was the argument put forward in the reports from the inspectorate of lunacy for Ireland. When it became a separate entity in 1846, Dr Francis White, who had been responsible for the oversight of asylums within the inspectorate of prisons, became the first inspector of lunacy. He was joined by Dr John Nugent a year later, and the two men oversaw the first years of the new asylum.[47] In their 1854 annual report on Dundrum, they wrote:

> The general expense of supporting the Dundrum Asylum will be found greater than that in ordinary institutions for the insane, principally in consequence of the staff being more numerous for the safe custody of the peculiar classes confined in it, and from the somewhat higher rate of wages paid to the attendants there than elsewhere, from the more responsible nature of their duties.[48]

The extra cost of staff seemed to pay off in the early years, as the quality of care reported by Dr White and Dr Nugent seemed quite good. However, by the end of the century, the staffing levels at Dundrum had fallen far behind those at Broadmoor, contributing to disciplinary problems among patients and staff. As the century progressed, the management of patients reflected the approach of the medical superintendent in post at the time. The first, Dr G.M. Corbett, was very much in line with that of the lunacy inspectorate – a regime informed by theories of 'moral management'. The second, Dr Isaac Ashe (appointed in 1872) was more controversial and idiosyncratic.[49] He became embroiled in a number of disputes with the visiting physician, Dr C.J. Nixon, which escalated into a lengthy dispute with the lunacy inspectorate on matters of discipline and of expenditure.[50] Ashe's replacement, Dr George Revington (appointed in 1892) was expected to reform Dundrum, which he did under the direction of the lunacy inspectors of the time, Dr G. Plunkett O'Farrell and Dr E. Maziere Courtenay. This led to increased staffing levels, increased security measures (such as a higher periphery wall), and a tighter administrative regime. The impact of these changes in regime on the patient population will be discussed in the next chapter.

DUNDRUM PATIENTS

When Dundrum opened in 1850, with accommodation for 120 patients, the inspectors of lunacy had to make a selection from those being put forward for admission, as the demand far exceeded the supply. Many prison governors saw the opening of this new asylum as an opportunity to get rid of their most troublesome, or most dangerous, inmates. The selection process was described by the lunacy inspectors, Dr John Nugent and Dr George William Hatchell, in the annual report in 1864.[51]

> The principle adopted was in the first instance to remove to it (Dundrum) all who had committed homicide, or attempted capital crimes, or perpetrated deeds of violence against the person; such parties having been acquitted at trial on the plea of irresponsibility, or having become insane consequent to conviction. The character of the offences, however, was not the only criterion for transference to the Asylum. Lunatics, though indicted of simple misdemeanors, if in disposition violent, dangerous or ungovernable, were regarded as fit subjects for admission. The total received in the first year was 89 – 59 males and 30 females.[52]

From then on to the end of the century, the number of occupants was higher than anticipated. There were usually around 140 patients in the asylum at any one time, with more pressure on male than on female accommodation.[53] Patients were admitted for different types of criminal behaviour and there was constant turnover, as some were transferred back to prison and others discharged home or to a local asylum.[54] From the scant medical records that still exist at Dundrum, it is possible to learn some facts about the patient population – information on age, gender, place of origin and offence committed.[55] The medical records are more complete for some periods than for others and, when considered together with lunacy inspectorate reports and convict records, held at the National Archives, they give us a picture of the people confined as criminal lunatics in the second half of the nineteenth century.

In looking at the age and gender of people admitted to Dundrum between 1850 and 1900, a number of interesting patterns emerge (see Table 2.1). The first is a gender pattern, which shows that of the 823 admissions, only 21 per cent were women.[56] This is not an unexpected finding, as historical and current research confirms the under-representation of women in crime statistics.[57] The numbers did not quite match the plan drawn up before Dundrum was built – to accommodate eighty men and forty women – allowing one third of places for women – but it confirmed the gender pattern that was to continue throughout the next two centuries – a predominance of males.[58]

Table 2.1 *Gender and age on admission of Dundrum patients 1850–1900*

Age	Females		Males		Total	
	Number	%	Number	%	Number	%
14–19	8	4	20	3	28	3
20–29	51	29	204	32	255	31
30–39	66	37	212	33	278	34
40–49	28	16	128	20	156	19
50–59	10	5	47	7	57	7
60–69	5	3	26	4	31	4
70–79	5	3	2	0	7	1
80–89	1	1	0	0	1	0
Unknown	3	2	7	1	10	1
Total	**177**	**100**	**646**	**100**	**823**	**100**

Source: Central Criminal Asylum Ireland, Dundrum, Registers of admissions. (Some statistical error due to rounding.)

The age profile was similar for both men and women, with 66 per cent of women and 65 per cent of men aged between 20 and 39 years of age. There were some very young people locked up in Dundrum – the youngest male admitted between 1850 and 1900 was only 14 and the youngest female 17 years of age.[59] The predominance of men and the concentration of admissions in the age range of young adulthood are patterns in prison populations even today, but they were also mirrored in the district asylum population in Ireland of the time. One of the reasons for this over-representation of young men in the asylum population was no doubt due to the impact of the Land Acts that had left many young men dispossessed of their land.[60] The social context of post-Famine Ireland, forcing the general population to delay or postpone marriage, also provided an explanation for another pattern to emerge from the medical records – an over-representation of single people.[61] In the annual report on Dundrum for 1872, the inspectors of lunacy commented on the protection from insanity offered by marriage.

> We have long noticed a characteristic difference between the general insane in this country and in England, without venturing or indeed being able to assign a reason; the same holds at the Central Criminal Asylum, viz. – the marked disparity between the mentally affected in respect to celibacy and marriage. We have much less of lunacy among the married, an illustration of which we may adduce the fact that out of

172 patients at Dundrum, the single amount to 128, of whom 89 are males and 39 females.[62]

As demonstrated by Finnane, marriage protected both men and women from admission to district asylums in post-Famine Ireland, a pattern that was reflected in the Dundrum statistics. This pattern continued to hold until the end of the twentieth century, as shown by Gibbons and colleagues who analyzed the data on admissions for the period 1850–1995. During that time, single people outnumbered married people by around two to one.[63]

Religion
Most of the patients in Dundrum were Roman Catholics (80 per cent). Another 12 per cent were Protestant (probably Church of Ireland) and 6 per cent Presbyterian. Only a tiny minority – 2 per cent – did not give a religious affiliation (see Table 2.2).[64] As Roy Foster has shown, this pattern reflected the religious composition of the population in Ireland during the same period.[65]

Table 2.2 *Religion on admission of Dundrum patients 1850–1900*

Religion	Females		Males		Total	
	Number	**%**	**Number**	**%**	**Number**	**%**
Roman Catholic	136	77	522	81	658	80
Protestant	25	14	70	11	95	12
Presbyterian	6	3	46	7	52	6
Unknown	10	6	8	1	18	2
Total	**177**	**100**	**646**	**100**	**823**	**100**

Source: Central Criminal Asylum Ireland, Dundrum, Registers of admissions. (Some statistical error due to rounding.)

The impact of religious preaching and worship on people with a mental disorder was hotly debated in some parts of Ireland during the mid-nineteenth century.[66] The debate extended from the medical press to the newspapers, when the Belfast District Asylum took legal action against the Lord Lieutenant of Ireland in order to avoid employing chaplains. On the one hand, there were those who argued that religious services could be a comfort to people deprived of other comforts in life. Others emphasized the potential divisiveness of religious disputes. This latter view was expressed in its most extreme form in the editorial of the *Northern Whig* in December 1851, at the height of the Belfast controversy.

> There seems to be something eminently absurd – and we will add mischievous – in the notion of appointing a chaplain to a number of insane persons, whose mental condition renders them utterly incapable of appreciating the teachings and practices of religion. Everybody knows that lunatics, when strongly seized with the religious idea, become often dangerously and hopelessly mad. Religious discourse (can) excite the most alarming displays in the insane, and in such cases, fearful results, murder or suicide frequently follow.[67]

This opinion was based on evidence from the province of Ulster particularly, where the preaching methods of the American revivalist campaign were being used to increase the fervour of the Presbyterian faithful. In County Antrim and County Tyrone during the 1850s, religious frenzies, precipitated by preachers who prophesied hell and damnation to those who would not mend their evil ways, was said to have led to an increase in admissions to asylums. According to Joseph Robins:

> A Belfast clergyman claimed that it had given rise to at least fifty cases in his own immediate area. The medical superintendent of Omagh Asylum reported the admission of twenty six cases for which the movement was the 'exciting cause'.[68]

Religious fervour, the argument went, when taken to extremes, could precipitate an attack of insanity. Because this fervour could occur in any religious group, there was an onus on public institutions, such as asylums, to provide facilities for all faiths.

The counter argument, which was the official line, emphasized the positive impact of religion on recovery from mental illness. The first inspectors of lunacy, Dr White and Dr Nugent, were both convinced of the positive influence chaplains would have on the patients and they oversaw the employment of chaplains in all asylums. They had no difficulty with Dundrum on this score and the work of the chaplains was highly commended in annual reports during the 1850s.

> The regular performance of Divine worship should on no account be neglected; as nothing could tend more to the discontent of the sane and convalescent, or further depress the mentally afflicted, than the negation of religious observances. Were we to adduce an instance from the institution itself to corroborate this opinion we should refer to the

case of a patient, tranquil, but still unrecovered, who, many years ago, in an excess of maniacal fury, killed seven of his fellow-creatures, and whose only solace and employment are now, in his own words to be derived from 'sacred reading and the practice of religion'.[69]

The man referred to in this report was Captain Stewart who, after sailing from Bermuda, had murdered his entire crew just before they docked at Cork harbour. This had happened in 1828. Stewart had killed the seven men by beating them with an iron bar, after they had allowed themselves to be tied down on the deck.[70] At the time of his transfer to Dundrum from Cork Asylum, where he had been confined since 1828, he was described as being a 'religious monomaniac' and was still convinced that he had prevented a mutiny on his ship.[71] Luckily for the staff, his religious mania did not make him more difficult to deal with. In fact, as with many other patients in Dundrum, religion had a tranquillizing effect on Captain Stewart.

> With respect to the attendance of clergymen at the Asylum, we regard it practically of great utility, as being conducive to the tranquillity, satisfaction, and good conduct of the patients … The utmost cordiality exists between all the inmates on matters of religion, and we are unacquainted with a single instance of a disposition to indulge in party or sectarian feelings.[72]

Almost twenty years later, in 1880, religion was seen by the inspectors of lunacy as having a dual role. They argued that it created a peaceful atmosphere in the asylum and kept the patients connected to the wider society.

> As a means of quietude and consolation to some of the inmates [religious observances] are found to be highly desirable and serve particularly to the reasonable and convalescent, forgotten by their families as a sort of tie between them and the outer world.[73]

From its opening, chaplains in Dundrum were appointed on substantial salaries, which placed them among the senior staff of the asylum. In 1852, for example, the Catholic chaplain was paid £60 and the Protestant chaplain £30 per year (for two to three visits per week), while male attendants were paid £18 and females £12 for their much more labour-intensive occupations.[74] The chaplains' salaries were higher than those paid in the district asylums, where the top salary for a chaplain was £50 per year.[75] However, a comparison with the salary of the medical superintendent (or governor) shows the exalted social position of the latter. Dr G.M. Corbett, who was the medical super-intendent at the time, was receiving a salary of £240 per year in addition to his housing and other services.[76]

Poverty
The high social status of the medical superintendent was in sharp contrast to that of the patients over whom he had power. As in the wider asylum system, most of the patients came from extremely poor backgrounds. In fact, at the time, it was generally agreed that there was little difference between pauper and criminal lunatics. In this respect, Ireland was not different to England. In the words of the report of the Departmental Commission on Criminal Lunacy for England and Wales in 1882:

> All the witnesses who were examined in connexion [*sic*] with this subject, unanimously admitted that pauper lunatics are largely drawn from the lowest and worst classes of the community, that is from the same classes which yield largely the inmates of prisons, thieves, pros-titutes, drunkards, the idle and dissipated, persons leading turbulent lives and given to violence, persons unrestrained either by intelligence or morality.[77]

The people most likely to find themselves in an asylum, workhouse or prison were those from the lower socio-economic layers of society. Guillais, in his analysis of crimes of passion in nineteenth-century France, came to the conclusion that 'violence, while not the prerogative of the working class, was certainly more visible among its members'.[78]

The literacy levels in Dundrum reflected the general trends in literacy in Ireland, although they were probably lower than the general population. As shown by both Mary Daly and Joseph Lee, literacy levels rose steeply during the second half of the nineteenth century, after the establishment of a national school system in 1831.[79] Over half of the population was illiterate in 1841, but by 1900, this had dropped to 16 per cent. In Dundrum, the 1874 annual report tells us that that out of 160 patients in Dundrum at that time, sixty-six (41 per cent) were completely illiterate, twenty-six (16 per cent) could read and write well, and the remainder could read or write 'indifferently'.[80] The occupations of the patients for the same year show a similar picture. There were 133 (83 per cent) patients with backgrounds in agriculture (labouring) or with no occupation. The remaining twenty-seven (17 per cent) were from skilled jobs such as shoemaking, weaving and carpentry.[81] A decade later, the literacy level seems to have improved somewhat. The inspectors commented in the annual report of 1886 that only one third of the 178 patients were illiterate, with the others able to read and write. This corresponded to a lower number of patients from an agricultural background – just under 50 per cent – and a higher number from skilled occupations and from the security forces (army and police).[82]

In an analysis of Dundrum statistics for the longer period of 1850–1995, Pat Gibbons and colleagues found a similar pattern – an over-representation of unskilled labourers and an under-representation of professionals or business owners. Among those found 'unfit to plead', 50 per cent were unskilled labourers; 45 per cent were tradesmen or farmers; and 4 per cent were professional or business people.[83] Among those found 'guilty but insane' the pattern was even more pronounced – 64 per cent were unskilled labourers; 27 per cent were tradesmen or farmers; and 8 per cent were professional or business people.[84]

However, although poverty featured in many of the stories of people in Dundrum, it would be wrong to conclude that all were socially deprived. In the annual report for 1852, the inspectors wrote:

> We have individuals in [Dundrum] far removed from the lower or pauper classes, but in whose regard, beyond a permission to indulge in occupations congenial to their own taste, no practical distinctions are allowed.[85]

They cite the case of Allan Spiller, the 26-year-old salesman from Belfast, who was admitted in 1892 for cutting the throats of his wife and two children. He went on trial for murder and was found 'insane on arraignment'.

> The anxiety of trying to support his family, he had been out of work for seven months, family troubles between his wife's people and himself, want of sleep and sufficient nourishment, all these worries in a delicate constitution … caused an attack of homicidal melancholia.[86]

Spiller was lucky. Though poverty had precipitated his crime, he was not a pauper. Seven years later, he was described by the medical staff as a 'pleasant, fairly well educated man, possessed with a certain amount of ability and far superior to the penal class of asylum patients'. As he showed no signs of insanity, he was discharged to friends in 1899. He had been confined for only seven years for the killing of three people – his wife and two children. Among Spiller's talents were his ability to socialize with the staff and to play cricket – he was described as 'a fair wicket keeper'.[87] Another man who came from a privileged background was Dr Terence Brodie, a dispensary doctor from Spiddal, County Galway, who shot his wife in 1886. He was found to be insane at the time of the murder, due to delusions brought on by his alcoholic state. Brodie was well liked by the staff in Dundrum and not regarded as one of the 'criminal classes'. His family, which included three brothers who were doctors, began to appeal for his discharge almost immediately after his conviction.[88] Supported by the medical staff at Dundrum, Brodie's personal plea to the Lord Lieutenant was successful and he was released in 1892, having spent just six years in confinement. However, Brodie, whose case will be discussed in more detail later, was not typical of the general population in Dundrum or in any district asylum in Ireland. This population was drawn mainly from people whose lives were dominated by poverty and hardship.

Crimes

The term 'criminal lunatic' conjures up a picture of an extremely dangerous person – of someone who has broken the law and who is out of control. However, it is clear from the records of those unfortunate enough to acquire this label, that the reality could be very far removed from this description. As early as 1849, it was accepted by the inspectors of lunacy that there was great variation in both the seriousness of the crime committed and the level of the mental disorder experienced by people destined for Dundrum.

> Under the denomination of criminal lunatics are enumerated offenders varying from the most trivial transgression to the taking of human life itself. In the Waterford Asylum, for example, one of the two criminal lunatics confined in it is 'for trial, charged with stealing vegetables, value 3d.', another was committed to Wexford Gaol 'for having in her possession a workhouse cap': the great proportion, however, are assault cases ... of parties swearing against their relatives as being insane, with a 'disposition and purpose to commit some act', when they are simply returned 'dangerous', or as frequently happens after some scuffle has ensued, in an attempt to control the individual by force, when they are committed as 'criminal lunatics'.[89]

The inspectors did their utmost to keep a limit on the numbers admitted to Dundrum and, as discussed already, the first criterion for admission was the seriousness of the crime. Priority was given to people who had 'committed homicide, or attempted capital crimes, or perpetrated deeds of violence against the person'.[90] The second criterion for admission was the level of dangerousness to others. 'Lunatics, though indicted of simple misdemeanors, if in disposition violent, dangerous, or ungovernable, were regarded as fit subjects for admission'.[91] However, Dundrum had also to accept people who had committed minor offences but who could not be controlled within the prison system because of their mental disturbance. In the 1861 annual report, the inspectors describe some of these minor offences.

> It is no unfrequent occurrence for a lunatic to be arrested in the act of committing some very trivial offence – such as tearing his neighbour's coat, breaking a window, or inflicting a blow – for any of which transgressions he might be afterwards acquitted on the plea of insanity or, on arraignment, found incompetent to plead.[92]

Table 2.3 shows clearly that in the first fifty years of its operation, over half of the patients (57 per cent) in Dundrum had indeed been involved in serious crimes 'against the person', while the others (43 per cent) had not. Crimes 'against the person' included murder, manslaughter, assault and rape. Crimes 'against property' included the whole range of those that came before the Irish courts – fraud, burglary, animal stealing and arson (see Table 2.3).[93]

Table 2.3 *Offences of patients in Dundrum 1850–1900*

Offences	Females		Males		Total	
	Number	%	Number	%	Number	%
Murder, manslaughter	55	31	206	32	261	32
Assault	27	15	162	25	189	23
Rape, indecent assault	0	0	17	3	17	2
Theft, larceny, burglary	66	37	141	22	207	25
Attempted suicide	8	5	13	2	21	3
Arson	5	3	30	5	35	4
Miscellaneous	16	9	77	11	93	11
Total	**177**	**100**	**646**	**100**	**823**	**100**

Source: Central Criminal Asylum Ireland, Dundrum, Registers of admissions. (Some statistical error due to rounding.)

The statistics given here are based on the depleted collection of the Dundrum medical records from the nineteenth century.[94] It is extremely difficult to verify some of the facts given in these records, but a summary of statistics in the 1886 lunacy inspectorate report confirms the general pattern of crime emerging from the Dundrum records. Between 1850 and 1886, according to this report, 58 per cent of all admissions had been for murder or assault, with the remaining 42 per cent for other less serious offences, including burglary and arson.[95]

One of the patterns to emerge from a detailed examination of the medical and judicial records that are available from this time, is the gendered nature of murder and manslaughter when linked to mental disorder. The most common pattern for men was the killing of their wives or other female relatives. The most common pattern for women was the killing of their children. Both of these patterns will be discussed in later chapters. Here, we look briefly at some of the less serious crimes committed by the patients in Dundrum. In the early years (the 1850s), the lunacy inspectors tried to avoid admitting people who had committed trivial offences. For example, in the annual report of the inspectorate in 1855, we read:

> There are many insane persons both in district asylums and in prisons, charged with minor offences and assaults, which, on investigation, for the most part, turn out to be of a trivial character ... They cannot reasonably be deemed fit subjects for state confinement, probably too, if incurable, for the whole term of their existence.[96]

As the years went by, however, a number of people convicted for less serious offences were admitted to Dundrum, some for short periods of time and others for much longer stretches. In the annual report of 1886, Dr Isaac Ashe, the medical superintendent at Dundrum, wrote about the sixteen men and four women who had been admitted as criminal lunatics in the previous year.[97] Some had committed a murder, but others had been involved in assaults, larceny and burglary. For example, a 47-year-old grocer, referred to as P. M., was found 'incapable of pleading' for 'feloniously wounding' an unnamed person. He had spent some time in Mullingar Gaol, but was transferred to Dundrum because of 'his religious mania with delusions'. Two Galway brothers, aged 30 and 25, who were described as labourers, were convicted of a violent assault on another brother. Having been sentenced to five years penal servitude, they spent time in Mountjoy Prison before being transferred to Dundrum 'suffering under delusional mania'. Both had previously been treated in Ballinasloe asylum. A 64-year-old tailor from County Fermanagh, referred to as J. Mc C., was quite a different character. He had been sentenced to seven years penal servitude for larceny. He had a history of criminal behaviour, which included stealing and masquerading under different aliases. He also spent time in Mountjoy, where he suffered from delusions that the staff were trying to poison him. Another man, convicted of larceny and suffering from delusions, was Kilkenny born J.K., aged 30. He was also sent initially to Mountjoy, where his delusions were on 'monetary and religious subjects'. According to the records, this man had been employed as a butler and was from a good family. His crime had been to steal from his employers and 'one of the articles stolen ... was nothing less than the watch worn by the Duke of Wellington at the battle of Waterloo'.[98]

Among the four women admitted that year, one had murdered her child, but the other three had been involved in the less serious crime of larceny. It is interesting that all three of these women were single. They obviously had to fend for themselves economically and had resorted to stealing. One of these women, referred to as W. K., was a 40-year-old single woman from Sligo, who had stolen a cow. Having been sentenced to seven years penal servitude, she went initially to Grangegorman Prison, from which she was transferred to Dundrum as insane. She was described as a 'case of chronic mania', who was generally 'a quiet and well-conducted patient, though noisy in her conversation'.[99]

Another female (M.R.), a 22-year-old single woman from Dublin, was also convicted of larceny and sentenced to five years penal servitude. She was sent to Grangegorman Prison to serve her time, but was certified as insane within a month and transferred to Dundrum. She was obviously difficult to manage and was described as a 'troublesome case of mania, noisy, passionate, and of an incurable grumbling habit: always imagining herself the subject of ill-usage and conspiracy'.[100] Another troublesome Dublin woman convicted of larceny in the same year and sentenced to five years penal servitude, was 38-year-old A.C., who was also single. She had been sent to Grangegorman Prison but was certified as insane and transferred to Dundrum within a few weeks of conviction. She was described as 'a patient labouring under dementia, of noisy behaviour, foul language and filthy habits'.[101] One of the interesting features of these female cases was the speed at which they were transferred to Dundrum. It is likely that, as the demand for female places was not as high as that for males, women who had committed less serious offences were more likely than their male counterparts to be admitted to Dundrum soon after showing signs of mental disorder.

Lohan, in her study of female convicts in Mountjoy Prison, found a record of sixty women transferred to Dundrum between 1857 and

1879, with some descriptions of the behaviour that had led to the decision to have them certified as insane.

> In addition to persistent breaches of prison rules and destruction of prison property, other descriptions include 'paroxysmal insanity', 'refusal to attend chapter' and 'speaking disrespectfully to the priest', 'considering herself an object of persecution', 'unfit for prison discipline', 'an unfortunate', 'persisting in refusing to have her photograph taken', and 'suicidal'.[102]

In other words, these women were very difficult to deal with within a prison system, where the only option was to punish bad behaviour with solitary confinement and a diet of bread and water. The medical officers at Mountjoy, Dr Banon and Dr Young, were very reluctant to use these punishments on women whom they regarded as vulnerable. In their view, the punishments had no effect except to injure the health of these women.[103]

As the century came to a close, the crime patterns of the Dundrum population continued to reflect the efforts of the lunacy inspectorate to prioritize those who had been involved in serious crimes. However, some people who had originally committed minor offences continued to be transferred from prisons unable to cope with their behaviour. In 1895, the medical superintendent, Dr George Revington (appointed 1892), wrote about the admissions for the previous year – they included the following six men and four women convicted of offences against property.

> T. P., male, admitted from Mountjoy Prison, charged with burglary. A case of dementia ...
> P. C., male, admitted from Waterford Prison, charged with arson. A case of congenital imbecility ...
> G. R., male, admitted from Mountjoy Prison, charged with highway robbery. A case of chronic mania ...
> P. O'L. or P. T., admitted from Tullamore Prison, charged with attempt to upset trains. A case of general paralysis of the insane ...
> R. M., male, admitted from Mountjoy Prison, charged with house-breaking, second admission. Family history of drinking, personal history bad. A dangerous character ...[104]

In contrast to the male admissions, only six (out of twenty-nine) of whom were admitted for less serious offences, all of the four women admitted in that year fell into this category.

L. R. or C., female, admitted from Grangegorman Prison, charged with malicious injury. Seventy four previous convictions, and previous attack of insanity ...

K. B. or L. D., female, admitted from Wexford Gaol, charged with obtaining goods by false pretences. A case of delusional insanity, with a mania for intrigue ...

K. B. or M. E. D., female, admitted from Grangegorman Prison, charged with suicide: found on admission to be pregnant and, for this reason, the clemency of His Excellency was exercised and she was discharged to a district asylum. Three previous attacks of insanity ...

M. McB., female, admitted from Grangegorman Prison, charged with larceny ... Personal history of drink, several convictions for drunkenness.[105]

The common thread was not the type of crime but the mental state of these convicts. They were described as suffering from a range of conditions, including delusions, mania, melancholia, maniacal dementia, chronic delusional insanity and of being 'a moral imbecile'.[106]

It is clear from this and other reports that give information on the type of crime and the mode of admission, that then, as now, people who committed serious crimes (such as homicide or violent assault), usually came directly from the court, having been found either 'unfit to plead' or 'guilty but insane'. People who had been convicted of less serious crimes, on the other hand, usually came from the prison system, where they had shown signs of mental disorder after their sentences had begun. In order to be eligible for a transfer to Dundrum, they had to be certified as insane by two doctors and then subjected to a selection process by the inspectors of lunacy.[107] Though many patients were discharged from Dundrum to asylums, to prisons, or to freedom, the demand for places was always greater than the capacity within Dundrum. In the next chapter, we will look at the approaches to confinement and treatment at Dundrum – the management of criminal lunacy.

NOTES

1 See Appendix 3: List of notes selected statutes on mental disorder and crime.
2 Arthur Williamson, 'The beginnings of state care for the mentally ill in Ireland', *Economic and Social Review*, 10, 1 (January 1970), pp. 281–90, p. 282.
3 T.P.C. Kirkpatrick, *History of the Care of the Insane in Ireland to the end of the nineteenth century*, (Dublin: University Press, 1931), p. 22; Kathleen Jones, *Lunacy, Law and Conscience*, (London: Routledge, 1951).
4 Kathleen Jones, *A History of the Mental Health Services*, (London: Routledge, 1972).
5 *Report of the Select Committee on the Aged and Infirm Poor of Ireland, 1804*, HC 1803–04 (109) iv. 771; Williamson, 'The beginnings', p. 282; Kirkpatrick, *History of the Care*, p. 23.

6 Kirkpatrick, *History of the Care*, p. 23.
7 Virginia Crossman, *Politics, Law and Order in Nineteenth-century Ireland*, (Dublin: Gill and Macmillan, 1996), p. 194.
8 Williamson, 'The beginnings', p. 283.
9 For a history of St Patrick's, see Elizabeth Malcolm, *Swift's Hospital* (Dublin: Gill and Macmillan, 1989).
10 Kirkpatrick, *History of the Care*, p.24; Williamson, 'The beginnings', p. 285. S.E.D. Shortt, *Victorian Lunacy: Richard M. Bucke and the Practice of Nineteenth-century Psychiatry* (Cambridge and New York: Cambridge University Press, 1986), p. 128 G.E. Berrios and H. Freeman (eds), *150 Years of British Psychiatry 1841–1991*, (London: Gaskell, 1991), p. 34. Andrew Scull, *Museums of Madness: The Social Organization of Insanity in Nineteenth-century England* (London: Allen Lane, 1979), p. 246.
11 *Report of the Select Committee on the Lunatic Poor in Ireland 1817*, HC 1817 (430) vii.1.
12 Williamson, 'The beginnings', p. 287. For discussion of moral management, see Jones, *Lunacy, Law and Conscience*.
13 Lunatic Asylums (Ireland) Act 1817 (57 Geo. 3 c. 106); Lunacy (Ireland) Act 1821 (1 & 2 Geo. 4 c. 33) (see Appendix 3.) For a list of further legislation, see Williamson, 'The beginnings', p. 281, Note 3.
14 Mark Finnane, *Insanity and the Insane in Post-Famine Ireland* (London: Croom Helm, 1981), Table A, p. 227; Williamson, 'The beginnings', p. 288.
15 Finnane, *Insanity and the Insane*, Table A, p. 227.
16 *Report of the inspectors general on the general state of prisons in Ireland*, HC 1824 (294) xxii, 269, p. 279. For discussion on Dr Hallaran, see Joseph Robins, *Fools and Mad: A History of the Insane in Ireland* (Dublin: Institute of Public Administration, 1986), p. 57.
17 Elaine Showalter, *The Female Malady: Women, Madness and English Culture, 1830–1980* (London: Virago Press, 1987).
18 *Report of the inspectors general on the district, local and private lunatic asylums in Ireland 1843*, HC 1844 (567) xxx, 69, p. 90.
19 *Asylums Report* HC 1851 (1387) xxiv, 231, p. 238.
20 *Asylums Report*, HC 1845 (645) xxvi. 269, p. 46.
21 Criminal Lunatics (Ireland) Act 1838 (1 & 2 Vic. c. 27); For discussion, see P.M. Prior, 'Dangerous Lunacy: The Misuse of Mental Health Law in Nineteenth-Century Ireland', *Journal of Forensic Psychiatry and Psychology*, 14,3 (2003), pp. 525–53.
22 *Asylums Report*, HC 1866 (3721) xxxii.125, p. 145
23 *Report of the Select Committee (HL) on the State of the Lunatic Poor in Ireland 1843*, HC 1843 (625) x. 439, p. 25. (Hereafter, *Select Committee Report on Lunatic Poor 1843*).
24 *Select Committee Report on Lunatic Poor 1843*, p. xii.
25 *Report of the Commission of Inquiry into Lunatic Asylums in Ireland 1858*, HC 1857–58 (2436) xxvii.1 (Hereafter, *Commission of Inquiry 1858*).
26 *Commission of Inquiry 1858*, Evidence p. 185.
27 Lunacy (Ireland) Act 1867 (30 and 31 Vic. c. 118).
28 *Asylums Report*, HC 1889 (c. 5796) xxxvii. 641, p. 641.
29 For discussion, see Finnane, *Insanity and the Insane*, ch. 3; Prior, 'Dangerous Lunacy'.
30 Criminal Lunatics Act 1800 (39 & 40 Geo. 3 c. 94); Robins, *Fools and Mad*, p. 147.
31 Lunacy (Ireland) Act 1821.
32 Criminal Lunatics (Ireland) Act 1838; Robins, *Fools and Mad*, p. 148.
33 For a full discussion of the case and of the many versions of the man's name, see R. Moran, *Knowing Right from Wrong: The Insanity Defense of Daniel McNaughtan*, (New York: The Free Press, 1981). See also F. McAuley and J.P. McCutcheon, *Criminality: A Grammar*, (Dublin: Round Hall Sweet and Maxwell, 2000).
34 *Select Committee Report on Lunatic Poor 1843*, p. 25.
35 Ibid., p. ix.

36 This responsibility was strengthened in 1842 under the Private Lunatic Asylums (Ireland) Act 1842 (5 & 6 Vic. c. 123); Kirkpatrick, *History of the Care*, p. 32.
37 *Select Committee Report on Lunatic Poor 1843*, Evidence on 20 July, question 123, p. 13.
38 *Select Committee Report on Lunatic Poor 1843*, p. xii.
39 Central Criminal Lunatic Asylum (Ireland) Act 1845 (8 & 9 Vic. c. 107).
40 *Asylums Report*. HC 1861 (2901) xxvii. 245, p. 254; *Asylums Report*. HC 1864 (3369) xxiii, 317, p. 376.
41 *Report of the inspectors general on the district, local and private lunatic asylums in Ireland*, HC 1845 (645) xxvi, 269, p. 324.
42 D. Forshaw and H. Rollin, 'The history of forensic psychiatry in England', in R. Bluglass and P. Bowden (eds), *Principles and Practice of Forensic Psychiatry* (Edinburgh : Churchill Livingstone, 1990), pp.61–101, p. 94; Nigel Walker, *Crime and Insanity in England, Vol. 2* (Edinburgh: Edinburgh University Press, 1973), p. 8.
43 Walker, *Crime and Insanity*, Vol. 2, p. 9.
44 See Anonymous, 'Obituary: Sir William Charles Hood, M. D. Knight', *Journal of Mental Science*, xvi, 74 (July 1870), p. 152.
45 Cited in Walker, *Crime and Insanity*, Vol. 2, p. 9.
46 Forshaw and Rollin, 'The history', p. 95.
47 For a list of Inspectors of Lunacy in Ireland, see Appendix 4.
48 *Asylums Report*, HC 1854–5 (1981) xvi, 137, p. 157.
49 According to the Inspectors report on salaries for 1873, Dr F. MacCabe was also appointed as medical superintendent at Dundrum in 1872 and he was still in position in 1873. However, his name does not appear in any other record, *Asylums Report*, HC 1874 (c. 1004) xxvii, 363, Appendix F, Table 14, p. 257.
50 Dundrum Letter Book 1878–88.
51 For a list of Inspectors of Lunacy, with dates of appointment, see Appendix 4.
52 *Asylums Report*, HC 1864 (3369) xxiii. 317, p. 376.
53 *Asylums Report*, HC 1886 (c. 4811) xxxiii, 559, p. 571.
54 See Appendix 1: Legal basis for admissions to Dundrum 1850–1900.
55 Register of Inmates 1850–1900; Register of Admissions, Discharges and Deaths 1850–93 and 1893–1920s; Male and Female Casebooks 1893–1920s; Physician's Book 1872–1920; Letter Book 1878–88.
56 This number may be an underestimate as some of the annual reports from the inspectors of lunacy give higher numbers e.g. *Asylums Report*, HC 1886 (c. 4811) xxxiii, 559, p. 571.
57 K. Daly, *Gender, Crime and Punishment* (New Haven, CT: Yale University Press, 1994): A. Morris, *Women, Crime and Criminal Justice* (Oxford: Basil Blackwell, 1987).
58 *Asylums Report*, HC 1864 (3369) xxiii, 317, p. 376; P. Gibbons, N. Mulryan, A. McAleer and A. O'Connor, 'Criminal responsibility and mental illness in Ireland 1850–1995: Fitness to plead', *Irish Journal of Psychological Medicine*, 16, 2 (1999), pp. 51–6, p. 52; P. Gibbons, N. Mulryan and A. O'Connor, 'Guilty but insane: the insanity defense in Ireland 1850–1995', *British Journal of Psychiatry*, 170 (1997), pp. 467–72, p. 447.
59 Based on data drawn from the *Registers of Patient Admissions*, held at the Central Mental Hospital, Dundrum, Dublin.
60 For discussion, see Finnane, *Insanity and the Insane*.
61 Ibid., pp. 131–2.
62 *Asylums Report*, HC 1872 (c. 647), xxvii, 323, p. 351.
63 Gibbons *et al*, 'Criminal responsibility', p. 52; Gibbons *et al.*, 'Guilty but insane', p. 447.
64 Based on data drawn from the *Registers of Patient Admissions*, held at the Central Mental Hospital, Dundrum, Dublin.
65 R.F. Foster, *Modern Ireland 1600–1972*, (London: Penguin Books, 1988), Ch. 14.
66 P. M. Prior and D. V. Griffiths, 'The Chaplaincy Question: The Lord Lieutenant of Ireland versus the Belfast Lunatic Asylum', *Eire-Ireland*, 33, 2–3 (1997), pp. 137–53.

67 *Northern Whig*, 4 December 1851, 2, col. 6.
68 Robins, *Fools and Mad*, p. 120.
69 *Asylums Report*, HC 1852–53 (1653), xli, 353, p. 17.
70 *Asylums Report*, HC 1874 (c. 1004) xxvii. 363, p. 469; see also Robins, *Fools and Mad*, p. 59.
71 *Asylums Report*, HC 1851 (1387) xxiv, 231, p. 244.
72 *Asylums Report*, HC 1854–55 (1981) xvi, 137, p. 156.
73 *Asylums Report*, HC 1880 (c. 2621) xxix, 459, p. 19.
74 Inspectors of Lunatics Report Book 1852 (NAI, OLA 6/1, Item 472).
75 *Asylums Report*, HC 1874 (c. 1004) xxvii. 363, Table 22, p. 211.
76 Inspectors of Lunatics Report Book 1852 (NAI, OLA 6/1, Item 472).
77 *Report of the commission appointed by the Home Department to enquire into the subject of Criminal Lunacy* (England & Wales), HC 1882 (c. 3418) xxxii. 841, p. 11.
78 J. Guillais, *Crimes of Passion: Dramas of private life in Nineteenth-century France*, (Oxford: Polity Press, 1986), p. 19.
79 Mary Daly, *Social and Economic History of Ireland since 1800*,(Dublin: The Educational Co., 1981); Joseph Lee, *The Modernization of Irish Society 1848–1918*, (Dublin: Gill and Macmillan, 1973).
80 *Asylums Report*, HC 1874 (c. 1004) xxvii. 363, Appendix F, Table 7, p. 256.
81 Ibid., Appendix F, Table 10.
82 *Asylums Report*, HC 1886 (c. 4811) xxxiii. 559, p. 571.
83 Gibbons *et al.*, 'Criminal responsibility', p. 52.
84 Gibbons *et al.*, 'Guilty but insane', p. 447.
85 *Asylums Report*, HC 1852–53 (1653) xli, 353, p. 14.
86 Dundrum, Male Casebook 1, A. Spiller, 1892, Case M.851, p. 25.
87 Ibid.
88 NAI, CRF 1897/ Misc.1420 (Brodie).
89 *Asylums Report*, HC 1849 (1054) xxiii, 53, p. 61.
90 *Asylums Report*, HC 1864 (3369) xxiii, 317, p. 376.
91 Ibid.
92 *Asylums Report*, HC 1861 (2901) xxvii, 245, p. 254.
93 Based on data drawn from the *Registers of Patient Admissions*, held at the Central Mental Hospital, Dundrum, Dublin.
94 Register of Inmates 1850–1900; Register of Admissions, Discharges and Deaths 1850–93 and 1893–1920s; Male and Female Casebooks 1893–1920s; Physician's Book 1872–1920; Letter Book 1878–88.
95 *Asylums Report*, HC 1886 (c. 4811) xxxiii, 559, pp. 682–5.
96 *Asylums Report*, HC 1854–55 (1981) xvi, 137, p. 153.
97 *Asylums Report*, HC 1886 (c. 4811) xxxiii, 559, pp. 682–6.
98 Ibid., p. 684.
99 Ibid., pp. 682–5.
100 Ibid., p. 685.
101 Ibid.
102 Lohan, *The Treatment of Women*, pp. 185–6.
103 Ibid., p. 185.
104 *Asylums Report*, HC 1895 (c. 7804) liv. 435, p. 64.
105 Ibid., p. 66.
106 *Asylums Report*, pp. 440–1, HC 1893–94 (c. 7125) xlvi, 369.
107 Criminal Lunatics (Ireland) Act 1838 (1 & 2 Vic. c. 27); Central Criminal Lunatic Asylum (Ireland) Act 1846 (9 & 10 Vic. c. 115).

CHAPTER THREE

Managing crime and mental disorder

PSYCHIATRISTS (ALSO KNOWN AS ALIENISTS) in nineteenth-century Ireland were influenced by their British counterparts when they spoke for individual men and women who stood before the courts accused of serious crime. Many had received their specialist training in England or Scotland and most of them were members of the Medico Psychological Association of Great Britain and Ireland.[1] The AGM of this Association was held occasionally in Ireland, giving Irish doctors an opportunity to share ideas with colleagues from England, Wales and Scotland.[2] Dr Isaac Ashe, later medical superintendent at Dundrum, for example, presented a paper on 'General paralysis' to the AGM held in Dublin in 1875.[3] In addition, a few individuals, such as Dr E.M. Courtenay, Dr Oscar Woods and Dr Connolly Norman, were active members of the executive committee.

The debates in British and Irish medical and legal literature of the time show that there was a wide range of opinion on the meaning of insanity and on its impact on criminal behaviour. G.W. Abraham in his major treatise on *Law and Practice of Lunacy in Ireland*, written in 1886, summarized the legal view of the period.

> The jurist views the condition of mind called lunacy or insanity with an exclusive eye to its effect upon the doings of the lunatic, whether in relation to the safety, the rights, and the accountabilities of that person himself, or to the safety and to the rights of the other members of the commonwealth, under the protection and dominion of the laws. Considered in his capacity of citizen, the person alleged to be of unsound mind may, through apparent absence or disorder of intellect, create the belief among his friends and neighbours that he ought to be placed under tutelage, for safety of person and property; and it is to the judicial ascertainment of the truth on this particular that the common inquisition of office is directed.[4]

Judicial certification of 'lunacy', 'idiocy', 'insanity' or 'unsoundness of mind', was thus seen in terms of protection for the person from

exploitation, or the protection of society from troublesome or dangerous citizens. Certification was introduced not as a slur on the character
of the person, but as a protective measure. It was based on the
assumption that the State should protect its citizens from loss of
liberty or of property rights. As the 'lunatic' continued to be a citizen,
any decision to remove civil rights had to remain in the public domain
– this was the function of certification. Because of this, nineteenth-
century lunacy law offered no definitions of what mental disorder
was, but rather considered the impact it had on the reasoning and
behaviour of the individual.

The legal view on insanity ran parallel to the medical view, which
changed in line with medical advances during the century. In a paper
read to the York Law Students Society and published in the *Journal of
Mental Science* in 1886, Dr S.W. North, visiting Medical Officer to the
York Retreat, told his audience:

> There is no definition of insanity. No one has ever yet framed a defini-
> tion of mental disorder capable of embracing all cases of derangement
> of the intellectual facilities, and at the same time of excluding sanity.[5]

However, doctors did define mental disorder for the purpose of
treating patients in both the private madhouse system and in the
public asylum system. A brief glance at the summary of admissions to
any district asylum in Ireland shows the wide range of conditions that
could be classified as insanity. In the annual report of 1874, the
inspectors of lunacy refer to some of the most common diagnoses
accepted by the medical establishment of the time. These were –
'Mania, Melancholia, Dementia, Monomania, Imbecility, Idiocy and,
finally, Mental Affections complicated with Epilepsy'.[6] The first four of
these diagnoses: 'Mania, Melancholia, Dementia and Monomania'
referred to people who, today, would be recognized as having some
form of mental illness. The following two – 'Imbecility and Idiocy' –
referred to people who, today, would be seen as having intellectual
disabilities. The final diagnosis – 'Mental Affections complicated with
Epilepsy' (a form of psychosis) – is now a rare condition.

It would be wrong to suggest that there was total agreement among
medical men on all of these diagnoses, but they were generally
accepted as the framework for treatment at that time. Though the
phrase 'mental disorder' is a modern term, it is very like the term
'mental aberration' used by Dr Francis White and Dr John Nugent, the
first inspectors of lunacy in Ireland. These two men dominated the
medical debate on lunacy in Ireland in the middle of the nineteenth

century. They achieved this through the pages of their annual reports on asylums. In the 1851 report, they gave a description of 'mental aberration'.

> The individuals in Ireland, who labour under mental aberration, in its endless diversity of aspect and variety of symptoms, from simple imbecility to the lowest grade of congenital idiocy on the one hand, and from moral insanity with its comparative clearness of intellect, to raving madness on the other ... [add up to] a proximate total of 15,000 human beings affected to a greater or less degree with a disease the most serious to which mankind is liable; not alone from the melancholy nature of the malady itself, its hereditary character and facile transmission, but from the danger to which society is exposed, from its too frequent excitement to deeds of fatal violence.[7]

When it came to the definition of insanity for the purposes of deciding the level of responsibility for a crime, it was generally agreed by doctors that the legal concept of insanity was of a different nature than that described in medical text books. A recognised expert in the field of medico-legal definitions was Dr Joseph W. Williams, a member of both the Royal College of Surgeons of Ireland and of the King and Queen's College of Physicians. In an article published in 1854 in the *Dublin Quarterly Journal of Medical Science*, he explored the question of 'unsoundness of mind' in medico-legal discourse.

> Justice demands that the grounds on which insanity be received as a plea for exculpation from punishment, or as a pretext for exclusion from social rights, should be as uniform as possible.[8]

He went on to categorize the mental conditions that might lead to insane crimes.

1. Insane states manifested chiefly by delusion, or what has been termed 'monomaniacal insanity', in which the intellectual or reasoning powers seem to be those more particularly involved.
2. Insane states in which the exaggeration or perversion of the moral intelligence or affective faculty is that most evident, constituting the 'moral mania' of writers, when the intellectual powers are apparently unaffected.
3. Insane states in which neither the moral or intellectual faculty is of necessity inadequate to appreciate the relations of a particular act, whose commission is alone explicable on the admission of an irresistible impulse: a form of disease described as 'impulsive insanity'.[9]

Williams gave his readers some indication of how the legal arguments might be framed. In the first case, that of *monomaniacal insanity*, the person suffers from the recurrence of similar thoughts, to the point where these thoughts become intrusive and delusionary, leading to a criminal act. Obviously, there has to be a connection between the delusion and the criminal act before this defence can be used – for example, Dr Brodie, whose case will be discussed later, laboured under the delusion that everyone was plotting to kill him. Therefore, his act of shooting his wife was (in his mind) a mode of self-defence. The second condition – that of *moral insanity*, occurs when the person's sense of right and wrong is either underdeveloped, or distorted, and manifests itself through the 'perversion of the affective faculties'. As an example of this, Williams discusses the 'distortion' of emotion that occurs in some women due to childbirth, leading to the destruction of the child by the mother, an act that completely negates the normal maternal instinct and emotional response.

The third condition – that of *impulsive insanity*, is said to exist when the person commits a violent act without any indication beforehand of the intention to do so. In some cases, the victim is known to the perpetrator (parent/child-killing) while in others, the victim is a stranger. No explanation is offered by Williams as to why this occurs. He sees this as a different form of insanity than any outlined before. In other medical literature this is sometimes referred to as a 'transitory frenzy', which could be attributed to an epileptic attack or to an over-indulgence in alcohol. For example, Dr Yellowlees, of the Glasgow Royal Asylum, writing in the *Journal of Mental Science* in 1883 about a murder in Scotland, argued that 'Hallucinations or delusions leading to dangerous violence are, of course, frequent in the insanity of intemperance'.[10] This argument was used in Ireland in the case of Mary Rielly, accused of the murder of a man in her care.[11] These arguments will be explored in a later chapter.

The difficulty involved in distinguishing 'disease' from 'vice', as a cause of a particular crime, was reflected in an article by Dr S. North, visiting Medical Officer to the York Retreat, England. This article appeared in 1886 in the *Journal of Mental Science* (the forerunner of the *British Journal of Psychiatry*), the only specialized journal available to Irish doctors working with mental disorder.

> While groups of acts, in themselves criminal, may be, and often are, the direct outcome of insanity – acts of destruction, murder, arson, every form of violence, and the acts of lust and appetite – that which calls the passions into play being disease not vice. The same motives may influence an insane as a sane man. Investigation alone will prove their character, and in which category the act should be placed.[12]

In other words, the motives for committing a crime (jealousy, fear, lust, love) are not different in the insane man. What is different is the mental condition underlying the motivation. However, as North explained, the final judgement as to whether an offender was a criminal or a lunatic often depended on legal arguments rather than on medical opinion. Dr North reflected on some of the aspects of 'mental unsoundness' that caused most difficulty at the point of trial, due to differences in the approaches taken by law and medicine. These are almost identical to the conditions proposed by Dr Williams, in the *Dublin Quarterly Journal of Medical Science*, in 1854.

- Deficiency of mental power from whatever cause, including every form of imbecility and dementia, forms of mental unsoundness, either congenital or the direct result of positive disease.
- Delusions – embracing every form of illusion or hallucination – auditory, optical etc.
- Impulse – destructive fury without necessary delusion, or any marked weakness of intellect.[13]

In relation to the first of these conditions, North argued that the question of responsibility only becomes important when the crime is serious. In the case of homicide, for example, the offender is excused of responsibility on the grounds of not having reasonable control over his actions due to his or her weak intellect. However, as 'weakness of intellect' could vary greatly from one individual to another and from one situation to another, the judgement as to legal responsibility for a particular crime is not always clear. In cases characterized by delusions, similar problems exist. Many people with mental disorders have delusions, but this does not cause them to commit a violent act. However, they may not be perceived as responsible for their actions because 'their reason is disturbed'. The final condition is also fraught with difficulty – this refers to people who commit a crime as a result of an impulse or 'transitory frenzy' and who have no other signs of mental defect or of insanity. In some of these cases, the court accepts the plea and in others rejects it. The relevance of North's article to the discussion here is the fact that he highlighted the difference between the medical and legal approaches to the relationship between insanity and crime. Doctors sought to prove the presence or absence of a disease while lawyers aimed to establish if the disease (or symptom of the disease) provoked the individual into engaging in the crime or of preventing him or her from knowing that the act was wrong.[14]

The only Irish contribution to the debate on insanity and crime in the *Journal of Mental Science* was on the topic of *folie à deux*. Dr Oscar

Woods, medical superintendent at Killarney Asylum, wrote a number of articles on the subject in relation to the killing in 1889 of a 13-year-old boy, Patsy Doyle, by his mother and other members of the family.[15] In these articles, Dr Woods argues that all of the family members suffered from 'group insanity' at the time of the crime. Dr M. J. Nolan, Assistant Medical Officer at the Richmond Asylum, Dublin, joined in the debate on *folie à deux*, with an article on the case of two brothers, John C. and Richard C., admitted to the asylum after becoming violent and anti-social, destroying neighbouring property, during an attack of 'simultaneous insanity' in 1888.[16] In both cases, which will be discussed more fully in a later chapter, the individuals involved recovered their sanity. However, tragically for the Doyle family, a young boy had died. One of the questions of interest to Dr Woods was how to determine how responsible these individuals were for the crime they had committed, a topic on which he had also written.[17]

THE INSANITY DEFENCE

The question of culpability for crime is basic to all sentencing decisions. Countries have different approaches to the establishment of grounds for the removal of responsibility for crimes, and this is clearly shown in different legal systems. However, some general principles prevail. For example, in the western world, some notion of criminal insanity has been recognized since the thirteenth century. Legal systems in Ireland, the UK and the US, though different now, are based on a common intellectual tradition. While there were laws prior to the nineteenth century, one of the legal landmarks occurred in 1800, when ex-army officer, James Hadfield, attempted to kill King George the third in London by shooting at him as he sat in the royal box at Drury Lane Theatre.[18] Fortunately for the King, he did not succeed, but Hadfield was arrested for attempted murder. He had been discharged from the army on the grounds of insanity. His main delusion was that God was going to destroy the world. In an effort to have himself killed (by execution) without committing suicide (which he regarded as a mortal sin leading to damnation), Hadfield decided to kill the King. Due to the brilliant oratory of his defence lawyer, he was not executed. This case created a new set of rules for pleading 'not guilty on the grounds of insanity' and introduced the practice of presenting medical evidence to the court. As suggested by McAuley and McCutcheon, this was probably the first reported case of someone suffering from schizophrenia being acquitted on the grounds of insanity.[19] Within a month of Hadfield's trial, the Criminal Lunatics Act 1800 was passed.[20]

The next legal landmark was the case of Daniel McNaughton, who shot and killed Edward Drummond, private secretary to the British Prime Minister, Sir Robert Peel, in 1843. He had meant to kill Peel, as he suffered under the delusion that he was being persecuted by the Tories. He was found 'not guilty on the grounds of insanity' and sent to Newgate Prison until 'Her Majesty's pleasure' be known.[21] Many people were unhappy with the verdict, judging it to be too lenient. After a heated public debate in the press, the Law Lords developed a set of rules for future cases, rules that became known as the M'Naghten rules. These rules state:

> [To] establish a defense on the grounds of insanity, it must be clearly proven that at the time of the committing of the act, the party accused was labouring under such a defect of reason, from disease of the mind, as not to know the nature and quality of the act he was doing; or if he did know it, that he did not know that what he was doing was wrong.[22]

These rules dominated Anglo-American law on criminal responsibility for over a hundred years. In the US, they were used in the majority of states (with the exception of New Hampshire and Alabama) until the 1950s. After that time, they became the basis for further developments in case-law, culminating in the revised American Law Institute Test of 1962.[23]

> A person is not responsible for criminal conduct if at the time of such conduct, as the result of mental disease and defect, he lacks substantial capacity to appreciate the criminality of his conduct or to conform his conduct to the requirements of law.[24]

Though there were different interpretations of this test throughout the US, it was nonetheless accepted by the public as well as the judiciary as being just. This was changed by the attempted assassination of President Ronald Reagan in 1981 and the subsequent acquittal of Hinkley, his attacker, on the grounds of insanity. The public outcry gave a new impetus to the move for the reform of the insanity law initiated by President Nixon. The result was the complete abolition of the insanity defence in a number of states, and a revision of the insanity test at federal level, making it much more difficult for the offender to avoid responsibility for crime.[25]

The laws in Britain and other countries in Europe are now quite different from those in the US, mainly because of different procedures to ensure psychiatric treatment for the offender, regardless of the level of responsibility for crime. In England, where the M'Naghten Rules remain as the legal definition of criminal insanity, they are rarely used, as it is no longer necessary to prove insanity to access treatment.[26] They were the only test of criminal responsibility until 1957, when the Homicide Act became law, introducing the legal concept of 'diminished responsibility' already in use in Scotland. Since then, there have been a number of changes in the law, giving courts a variety of means to divert mentally ill offenders away from the judicial system.

Other aspects of British criminal law affecting offenders who might have a mental disorder have been changed radically by the Criminal Procedure Law of 1991, covering 'fitness to plead' and the insanity defence. Before 1991, lawyers rarely argued that their clients were 'unfit to plead' as this led to involuntary commitment to a psychiatric hospital for an indefinite period, with criminal charges pending. The 1991 law opened the number of options available to the court, allowing for time limits on commitment and community treatment (rather than hospital). The most important change was the introduction of a time limited sentence – in contrast to the traditional indefinite commitment for psychiatric treatment. This change was due mainly to the influence of the European Court of Human Rights, to which many offenders, who have convictions and sentences related to their mental disorder, have taken their cases. It is no longer acceptable to confine individuals indefi- nitely without review. After they have completed their 'tariff time' for the offence, the onus is on the authorities to provide evidence of potential dangerousness. Otherwise, confinement in prison or in mental hos- pital constitutes a breach of the basic human right to liberty.[27]

In Ireland, the first two laws governing the outcome of trials in which the offender was deemed to have a mental disorder were the Criminal Lunatics Act 1800 and the Lunacy (Ireland) Act 1821.[28] Until 1800, the verdict was 'not guilty' and the accused was allowed to walk free, having been acquitted completely. In the 1800 Act, the verdict became 'not guilty on the ground of insanity' and the offender was sent for a period of indefinite detention subject to the 'pleasure of the Lord Lieutenant'. This verdict remained in force until 1883, when there was a major change as a result of the Trial of Lunatics (Ireland) Act. With this legislation, the verdict became 'guilty but insane' with no change in sentencing. In the words of the Act:

> ... the jury shall return a special verdict to the effect that the accused was guilty of the act or omission charged against him, but was insane as aforesaid at the time when he did the act or made the omission.[29]

As argued by McAuley and McCutcheon, the shortened version of this verdict – 'guilty but insane' – could be confusing. In the late 1970s, the Henchy Committee recommended a change to wording similar to that in the English Criminal Procedures (Insanity) Act 1964 – to 'not guilty by reason of insanity (or mental disorder)'.[30] This change did not happen until forty years later, when the Criminal Law (Insanity) Act 2006 was passed in Ireland.[31]

In a retrospective analysis of the patients admitted to Dundrum 1850–1995, Gibbons, Mulryan and O'Connor found that before 1910, the insanity defence was used successfully by an average of five patients per year. Of the 437 cases explored (for the complete period), 81 per cent were male and 19 per cent were female. The average age for males was 37 years and for females 34. Crimes against the person predominated as the 'index offence', with a significant gender difference in relation to homicide. While both men and women had been almost equally involved in murder (53 per cent of men and 59 per cent of women) almost half of these women had killed children. After 1910, the number of people admitted to Dundrum, using this defence decreased to one per year, with the greatest reduction among women. This was most probably due to a change in social and legal attitudes to infanticide, making it easier for the court to be more lenient and to find an alternative solution for these cases.[32]

Two of the cases referred to by Gibbons, Mulryan and O'Connor as illustrations of the use of the 'guilty but insane' verdict will be discussed in more detail later, but are of some interest here. These were two family murders. One was the case of the Doyle family from County Kerry, in which the 13-year-old son, described as 'an imbecile idiot', was beaten to death by his mother, Johanna Doyle, his father, his two sisters and a brother. Johanna was found 'guilty but insane' and admitted to Dundrum in 1888, where she was diagnosed as suffering from 'chronic mania'.[33] Other members of the family spent a short period in the Killarney asylum. This case was famous in both the media and the medical press – in the former because of the stories of 'fairies' and 'changelings' and in the latter because of its resemblance to *folie à deux* as described in French psychiatric literature of the time.[34] The second case was that of the Cunningham family from County Roscommon, in which James Cunningham (aged 35) was beaten to death by his three brothers during a fight which also involved his father and sister.[35] The three brothers, who had earlier shown signs of 'paranoid delusions, auditory, visual and olifactory hallucination', were found 'guilty but insane' and admitted to Dundrum in 1896.[36] Like the Doyle family, they had all been caught up in a frenzy based on superstition and fear, a frenzy that disappeared soon after their admission.

In both of these cases, which will be discussed later, there was no doubt in the eyes of the law that a murder had taken place, but there was also no doubt that the mental state of those involved had been seriously disturbed to such an extent that they could not be held responsible for their actions. However, most cases that came before the courts then, as now, were not as straightforward as this. Rather, the impact of a mental disorder on criminal behaviour was the subject of intense debate in each individual case.

PUNISHMENT OR TREATMENT?

Before 1850, views on how to manage criminal lunacy were rarely expressed in government documents in Ireland except in the context of arguments for reform in the law. These arguments stemmed from the misuse of the 'dangerous lunacy' legislation – the Criminal Lunatics (Ireland) Act 1838 – a law that led to the admission of large numbers of individuals with no criminal history into prisons throughout the country.[37] As in England: 'Criminal lunatics had an uneasy existence between prison and asylum, between discourses of guilt and disease.'[38] During this period in Ireland, officials from the prison service argued that lunatics were not criminals and should not be treated in the same way or on the same premises. In other words, lunatics and criminals were different kinds of people and warranted different institutional approaches. The debate expanded and changed during the second half of the century, based mainly on the experiences gained from the 'captive' population in Dundrum. From the 1850s onwards, the annual reports from the inspectors of lunacy became a vehicle for the discussion of criminal lunacy and its management.[39] Before Dundrum was built, potential inmates were viewed as lunatics rather than as criminals and in planning for a central asylum, Dr Francis White, argued for a facility that would be more like an asylum than a prison.

> It is not designed that the building should partake of the character of a 'prison'; more especially as experience has proved that in the district asylums (where criminal lunatics are now confined) such are not more inclined to attempt to escape than other patients.[40]

And, though there was some hope of cure, White realized that some people would be confined for long periods of their lives.

> The greater proportion of the inmates of this intended institution being
> destined to remain in it for life; it is proposed to have the structural
> arrangement as cheerful as circumstances will admit, so as to afford
> every possible facility for the recreation and occupation of the patients.[41]

Nice surroundings were viewed as an essential part of a treatment
plan, aimed at restoring the criminal lunatic to full health. The theory
underlying this approach was elaborated in the 1864 annual report on
Dundrum, written by Dr G.M. Corbet, the first medical superintendent. The underlying premise in the following extract from the
report is that the mind in its original state is 'healthy' and not prone to
violence.

> The deed of an individual manifestly labouring under aberration of
> mind may frequently and fairly be regarded, no matter how unfor-
> tunate in result, as simply symptomatic of the disorder, lasting be it
> from the irritation to which he is too often subjected, or from sudden
> impulse, or a fixed delusion, he commits the offence without weighing
> its consequences to himself or others. Now, if exciting causes be removed,
> and that the mind be restored to its primitive healthy condition, with its
> reasoning powers unimpaired; in other words if the patient sees, feels,
> and recognizes during a certain and continuous period the true
> character of his offence, for which, being a lunatic, he was held
> irresponsible, he surely ought not to be dealt with more unfavourably
> than the sane man, whose punishment for a similar act from
> extenuating circumstances would be little more than nominal. Insanity,
> as a bodily disease, is curable; consequently when there is recovery
> from it, and a justification to expect its continuance, it would be unfair
> to deny the benefit of mental health to the recovered lunatic.[42]

The views expressed here were not unique. Robert Menzies argues, in
his discussion of the treatment of criminal lunacy in British Columbia,
Canada: 'At the core of asylum ideology and practice was the widely
shared vision of a well-regulated citizen who was at once morally
reputable, disciplined (and) industrious.'[43] The object of treatment
based on this ideology was to return the mind to its original healthy
state. The argument, as presented by Dr G.M. Corbet in the 1864
report, often formed the preamble to appeals for discharge. It also
provided the basis for the introduction of all the best practices known
in the management of insanity at the time – most of which came from
the Quaker approach to 'moral treatment'. This included involving
patients in useful activities and providing some form of amusement
for them. The argument had been used before the opening of
Dundrum to show that there was little difference in the management

and care of criminal lunatics from that of ordinary lunatics. In 1849, the inspectors of lunacy had written:

> We believe that no ingenuity could distinguish the criminal lunatic by his actions or habits from his more unoffending neighbour. Much is due on this head to the considerate attention of the physicians and managers who treat these poor creatures with confidence, and employ them promiscuously with the other inmates of their respective asylums ... As no extra keepers are employed to watch over the criminally insane, and in one instance only was an escape effected, the cost of their support is not greater than that for the maintenance of the ordinary classes.[44]

This view changed later in the century, when the medical super-intendent and the inspectors realized they needed higher staffing levels and higher wages than other asylums if they were to attract the right kind of staff to manage this difficult population. However, the benevolent attitude toward the inmates and the optimism about the methods being used to manage them characterized all official reports in the early years of Dundrum's existence. In 1853, we are told:

> The attendants are directed, consistent with the efficient discharge of their duties, to afford every latitude to the patients, and to consult their wishes. Hence, a system of kindliness on their part with a considerate solicitude on that of the officers, administers not alone to the quietude of the insane but to the contentment of those who may be looked on as restored to reason.[45]

However, the quality of care could not have been all that good. As Joseph Robins reminds us, professional nursing training did not exist in Ireland before the 1860s. Neither was there a strong commitment to the employment of 'caring' professionals in asylums. Initially, men were employed as 'keepers' with the primary function of maintaining order. Women were employed as servants and were sometimes referred to as 'nurses'. Their primary purpose was to look after the female patients and to clean the male wards.[46] The relatively low status of the role meant that it was almost impossible to recruit educated women into this emerging profession. This difficulty had been brought to the attention of the Select Committee in 1843, by the medical superintendent of the Clonmel asylum: 'I may here mention that the difficulty in procuring educated females as assistants and nurses is also a sad calamity.'[47] As the work in Dundrum was even more dangerous than in an ordinary district asylum, it is highly likely that recruitment was not easy.

However, in spite of staffing difficulties, the inspectors, Dr White and Dr Nugent, and the medical superintendent, Dr G.M. Corbet, were very proud of the institution, which they thought was superior to others elsewhere.

> As a body, the patients are orderly and industrious – in the female no less than in the male departments; in fact, to a well devised system of employment, at trades or in field-labour, suiting their various inclinations and capabilities, we would mainly attribute the satisfactory condition of the whole establishment, so strongly contrasting with receptacles for criminal lunatics elsewhere, in which, without sufficient means for occupation, the sane, insane, and convalescent are confined together.[48]

In fact, the reader could be forgiven for mistaking the institution for a well-run private asylum, rather than a criminal lunatic asylum, housing seriously disordered convicts and people who had committed the most serious crimes in Ireland. The picture painted in 1853 was one of happily occupied individuals, who had ample opportunities for work and leisure.

> The portions [of land] immediately around the building are laid out in exercise and pleasure grounds, the garden affords an ample supply of vegetables of domestic use, and at present about ten acres are under oats and potatoes, the manual work being altogether performed by the patients. Besides the out-door labourers, there are some good tradesmen and mechanics usefully engaged; and perhaps, the best and most ingenious of them are the wildest in their delusions, occasionally, too, highly dangerous and uncontrollable. In the female department, both the insane and convalescent, with few exceptions, are all industriously occupied under the superintendence of the matron, and perform the common household duties – washing, spinning, knitting, mending clothes, &c.[49]

Dundrum was visited in the late 1850s by some of the commissioners of inquiry into the state of lunatic asylums in Ireland. In their report in 1858, they confirmed the opinion of the lunacy inspectorate, that it was 'well conducted' though there were complaints about heating and ventilation. However, they also observed that life was monotonous for the inmates.

> The observation we have made as to the general absence of any means of amusement of the patients, or of any prints or pictures to relieve the monotony of the whitened walls, in the day rooms and galleries, apply equally to this asylum.[50]

The recommendations of the commission were duly acted on and the inspectorate reports of the 1860s highlighted various amusements added to the daily routine of useful activity.

> We are disposed to attribute much of the success which last year, as hitherto, marked the working of the Criminal Asylum at Dundrum, to the varied employments, combined with a reasonable share of amusements, and of facilities for indulging in different pastimes, ball playing, dancing, evening parties and the like; whilst to those who desire them books, illustrated newspapers and light periodicals are supplied.[51]

Of course, the problem with supplying books was that many of the inmates could not read, a fact acknowledged by the inspectorate. However, undaunted by the fact that the amusements were based on middle and upper-class notions of drawing-room culture – a culture alien to all but the senior medical staff – music was added to the repertoire during the 1860s. In 1868, the annual report tells us:

> As regards amusements, the bulk of the inmates belonging to the little instructed classes, are not very sensible to the refinements of life, and take little interest in reading; but selected newspapers and books are supplied for the amusement of those few who are disposed to read them. A band of music has been instituted, the members consisting of attendants and patients and which affords great pleasure in its establishment.[52]

The practice of supplying games, books and other amusements continued throughout the century, and was recorded in each annual report from the inspectorate. For example, in 1873, the report tells us that 70 per cent of patients (112 out of 160) took part in reading or games. The games included 'hand-ball, drafts, cards, backgammon, cribbage, bagatelle, and parlour games'. Their reading material included *Illustrated London News, Graphic Fun, All the Year Round, Chambers Journal, Biography* and *Natural History* (and) some novels'.[53] In the same report, we learn that 41 per cent of patients could not read or write, so a significant number were excluded from taking part in any leisure activity that required any level of literacy.[54] However, there was always handball and, by the end of the century, cricket had been added to the list of activities.

CONTROL AND COERCION

In an asylum which was specially designed to take criminal lunatics, some of whom had committed very serious crimes and others who had been very troublesome within the prison system, one might expect to find some means of exerting physical control. However, this was not the case. In 1855, for example, the inspectors claimed that there was no use of force or coercion.

> The lunatics, as a body, seem equally industrious and well-conducted, owing to a system of kindness which is uniformly carried out in their regard, under the direction of the Resident Physician, Dr Corbet, and of the matron; and though the institution is, both from its nature and its name, a place of detention and safe custody, no coercion or restraint is employed to render it different in appearance from ordinary establish-ments for the insane.[55]

The argument here is twofold, that no force was being used to coerce patients and that Dundrum was like an ordinary asylum. This is an interesting argument, as it was legal within the 'ordinary' district asylum system to use restraint and seclusion, as long as it was carried out in accordance with strict rules. The 1858 commission of inquiry into the state of lunatic asylums in Ireland was very concerned with the way in which these rules were being ignored in some district asylums.

> We feel it is our duty also to notice the culpable disregard with which the 23rd Rule of the Privy Council has in many instances been treated. This rule requires that 'The Manager is to take charge of the instruments of restraint, and is not, under any pretence to allow the unauthorized use of them to any person within the establishment; all cases placed under restraint, seclusion, or other deviation from the ordinary treat-ment, are to be carefully recorded by him in the daily report, with the particular nature of the restraint or deviation resorted to; but in no case shall the shower-bath be used without the authority of the physician'.[56]

Under these regulations, the names of all patients under restraint or seclusion should have been written in the Morning Statement Book, so that the Visiting Physician could visit them 'to examine them, so as to ascertain that they are not cramped or injured'.[57] The commissioners found serious breaches of these rules in two asylums – Carlow and Armagh.

> On our visiting (Armagh), we found several of the inmates under restraint. A patient on the female side, was strapped down in bed, with body-straps of hard leather, three inches wide, and twisted under the body, with wrist-locks, strapped and locked, and with wrists frayed from want of lining to straps; this patient was seriously ill. There was no

> record of her being under restraint in the Morning Statement Book ...
> Another female was in the day room, without shoes, or stockings, with
> strait waistcoat and wrist-locks; she had been two years in the house
> and almost continually kept in that state day and night. Wrist-locks and
> body-straps were hung up in the day room, for application at the
> pleasure of the attendants.[58]

The commissioners were shocked not only by the state of the patients
they found in these appalling conditions, but also at the fact that the
incidents were not being recorded. They were also horrified that in
most of these cases, the use of restraints had not been authorized by
the senior medical staff (visiting physician or medical superintendent),
and that these cases had never come to the attention of the inspectorate of lunacy.

It was against this background that Dundrum was held up as an
example of good practice. In order to avoid the use of any coercion or
mechanical restraints, the management realized as early as 1853 that it
would cost more to run a criminal lunatic asylum than an ordinary
district asylum, because of the need for extra staff.

> From the character and construction of the Central Asylum itself, the
> cost of the staff is considerably greater than in ordinary lunatic
> establishments, as, in the total absence of mechanical restraint, or
> coercion of any kind, a full number of attendants is indispensable for
> the safe custody of the particular classes confined there. These circum-
> stances ... tended to raise the annual proportional expense of each
> patient to about £24, a sum much higher than in district hospitals for the
> insane.[59]

Because of the higher level of skill and experience required, higher
wages had to be offered to attendants/nurses to attract them to this
difficult work.[60] As in other asylums, there was a wide range of wages,
with the medical superintendent and the matron at the top of the
scale, and the women servants at the bottom. In 1852, for example, the
annual salary of the medical superintendent was £240, of the visiting
physician £150, and of the clerk £100. The most highly paid nurse, the
matron, came next, with a salary of £80, with ordinary nurses/
attendants earning between £12 (females) and £18 (males). The lowest
paid worker at this time was the housemaid, who earned £8 per year.[61]
By 1873, the medical superintendent was earning £360 and the matron
£95, with the attendants/nurses earning between £15 (females) and
£21 (males). In comparison with salaries and wages at other asylums
for the same year (1873), it is clear that while the top jobs were in line

with salaries elsewhere, the attendants were earning slightly more than those in district asylums.[62] There was also a higher ratio of staff to patients than in other asylums.

DIFFICULT AND DANGEROUS BEHAVIOUR

One of the questions that arises from the assertion that it was more costly to run a criminal lunatic asylum than an ordinary asylum is – were the patients dangerous or just difficult to manage? It is evident from the annual reports, that neither the inspectors of lunacy, nor the first medical superintendent, Dr G.M. Corbet, saw all of the Dundrum inmates as uniformly dangerous, either to the other inmates or to the public at large. However, descriptions of patients sometimes highlighted difficult behaviour, as in the report in 1855.

> As may be supposed, in an institution such as the Dundrum Asylum, many of the patients are at times highly excited and intractable: others morose and reserved, as if, in the sort of twilight intelligence they retained, their minds were engrossed with one train of ideas, or some painful remembrance of the past. Among others we have a remarkable case of character in a homicide who for five years, with only three exceptions, where he suddenly made short and angry observations, has maintained an unbroken silence … At the female side too, there is an infanticide, very taciturn and reserved, with a strong predisposition to self-destruction: her attempts are always with broken glass, which she endeavours to secrete.[63]

The first patient described in this extract did not really present any great difficulty, in management terms, as he may have been strangely silent, but he was rarely, if ever, violent. The second required a great deal of supervision, to guard her against herself. Today, we know that patients or prisoners on 'suicide watch' need twenty-four hour supervision. More difficult to predict and supervise are those who are occasionally violent towards others, individuals like the one described in the 1855 report.

> (A) convict from Spike Island, at the time deemed quite harmless (but who has since evinced a cold malignant disposition), stealthily getting behind one of his companions, whose verses and sarcasms give occasional annoyance, struck him on the head with a piece of iron he had secreted for the purpose, causing a large compound fracture, through which a considerable quantity of brain was discharged.[64]

The general tone of all the annual reports indicates that the most dangerous patients were those who had been transferred from the prison system. These were individuals who developed symptoms of mental disorder during their time in prison, and who were transferred to Dundrum because their difficult behaviour was linked to their mental state. In the annual report for 1861, Dr Corbet wrote:

> Were we to specify individuals of any particular class with whom we have a difficulty, these would be confined principally, if not wholly, to patients reported from the convict prisons as becoming insane.[65]

He went on to ask for extra security measures:

> Within the last twelve months, we thought it advisable to apply for the construction of some additional single rooms, to meet emergencies in regard to violent and refractory patients.[66]

As discussed earlier, Dr Corbet prided himself on his ability to keep order and discipline without any recourse to physical restraint. The building of additional single rooms would give more scope to confine difficult patients in solitary confinement. During the 1860s, the reports continued to emphasize the particular problems caused by convicts transferred from prison. In the 1864 report, we read:

> In previous reports we referred to the difficulty of managing convicts from Grangegorman prisons. The difficulty still exists. They are for the most part deranged to a certain extent (some few, however, have evidently been malingerers and acknowledged it themselves), but astute, wayward and uncertain; occasionally growing so ill at ease with themselves, as to desire to be sent back to their former servitude, where they are likely again to become fully as troublesome as they had been before.[67]

Some of these people were transferred back to the prison system, but this was only possible when they stopped showing any signs of mental disorder. Prison governors were reluctant to accept back individuals who had been troublesome in the past. Some of the patients took the situation into their own hands by attempting to escape, as happened in 1864.

> The escapes (three) were effected, one by a convalescent infanticide, and two by male convicts both reported sane, and whose period of imprisonment in one instance, not having a month to run, had all but expired.[68]

And in 1867, another convict managed to escape:

> The man who escaped was not, as reported by the Medical Officer, correctly speaking, insane, but a vicious person inured to crime. He got away twice and after the second escape was transmitted to Spike Island to undergo the remainder of his sentence.[69]

By the late 1860s, the presence of some dangerous inmates was acknowledged as a common feature of life within a criminal lunatic asylum, but there were differences of opinion as to its management. In England, a report in 1868 by the Commissioners in Lunacy on Broadmoor Criminal Lunatic Asylum, was highly critical of the methods being used by the medical superintendent, Dr Adolph Meyer, and his staff to contain violent inmates.

> Of the violent and even dangerous propensities of some of the patients placed in these wards, and of the generally unfavourable character of the rest, there is no doubt; but it is a matter of gravest doubt whether insane persons of the criminal class, having this disposition, should be treated differently from other patients suffering under mental disease.[70]

From the tone of the Commissioners' report it is clear that they were very unhappy with the treatment being meted out to some of those labelled as dangerous.

> It has been found, all but invariably, that by association with others, by some recreation or amusement, above all by regular daily outdoor exercise, improvement has been made in habits of the most inveterate, and in the most evil dispositions. No attempts of the kind are made at Broadmoor. If a patient exhibits violent conduct, he is for so many days, or portions of days, put into seclusion. If he is supposed to be, or has given proof of being, dangerous, he is isolated altogether … The seven men already adverted to, as held to be exceptional even in their class for dangerous violence, we found isolated in separate cells or cages, which some of them had not quitted for many months; rarely even walking in the airing courts under the restrictions imposed and one of them refusing altogether to do so.[71]

The tough regime implemented in Broadmoor might be explained by the fact that in 1866, Dr Meyer, the medical superintendent, had been attacked and seriously injured by a patient, who 'with a sudden yell, rushed forward and struck him on the head with a large flint slung in a handkerchief' during a Communion service.[72] Dr Meyer recovered from the blow, but he died prematurely in 1870. Against this background of violence directed against staff, the method of management in operation in the 1860s was justified and defended by the Council of Supervision at Broadmoor.

> Separation and seclusion are not practiced, in these cases, as means of treatment applied to a lunatic, but as means of safety; the element of lunacy is not so much to be considered as the elements of vice, low cunning, and the habits of convict life, all of which often exist in full force notwithstanding the disordered state of the intellect which has brought the individual to an asylum.[73]

The Broadmoor Council went on to justify the specific treatment of the seven violent men referred to by the Commissioners, by describing their record of crime and violence. They also refuted the allegation that there was a lack of amusement in general in the asylum:

> Each block, whether occupied by dangerous or ordinary patients, is provided with a bagatelle board, with books, newspapers, periodicals, cards, dominoes, drafts, as well as concertinas.[74]

It is probable that, as in Dundrum, many of the Broadmoor inmates had no interest in such amusements, which required literacy and some education. What is interesting is the fact that, during the 1850s and 1860s, the official story on the management of violence or disturbed behaviour in Dundrum was quite different to that being told about Broadmoor. However, this changed as the century progressed. By the 1880s, the orderly and safe situation in Dundrum had deteriorated.

DISPUTES AND ESCAPES

The deterioration in standards of control in the 1870s and 1880s was officially attributed to the lax style of management of Dr Isaac Ashe, formerly of Londonderry Asylum, who replaced Dr G.M. Corbet as medical superintendent in 1872. Ashe may have been a poor administrator, but his literary skills were excellent. The annual report from the inspectorate of lunacy for 1886 contained some of his extensive writings – a letter and a summary of cases as well as his report on Dundrum. In this report, Ashe expressed his views on almost every aspect of the management of criminal lunatics. These views reflected progressive medical opinion of the period and were fully in keeping with those expressed in earlier years by the inspectorate of lunacy. The following extract from the 1886 report is a good example of Ashe's philosophy:

It has been lately advanced that the main and primitive object of a criminal asylum was, and should be, a strict confinement of its inmates, and consequently that it ought to be regarded essentially as a gaol – thus rendering curative treatment secondary to secure incarceration. From this doctrine we dissent, our contention being that any person labouring under aberration of mind, who may have broken the law while so affected, or who after a criminal act becomes insane, ought to be treated as a lunatic; for in the first instance insanity condones the offence however punishable of itself, and in the second, entails a condonation during its existence – thus excluding such a convict from the category of common prisoners undergoing punishment after conviction.[75]

However, this rhetoric is contradicted in the letter that accompanied the report and in the description of the admissions during the year. The language used in this letter relates more closely to discourses of control than of care. In it, Dr Ashe refers to inmates as prisoners, often describing them as dangerous, and showing support for the 'elevation' of the boundary wall to improve security.

Dr Ashe also used his excellent writing skills to engage in extensive correspondence with the lunacy inspectorate with whom he was in almost continuous dispute during the 1880s. The disputes, often initiated by the visiting physician, Dr C.J. Nixon, included arguments about such diverse matters as the amount of money spent on bread, the price paid for a cow, the appointment of staff, and the circumstances of a number of escapes. Some of these complaints may have arisen from personal animosity between Dr Ashe and Dr Nixon, but others were based on facts showing mismanagement. For example, Nixon complained to the inspectorate that a man put forward by him for possible employment at Dundrum had not even received an interview. This man, who had been a coachman to a well-known dignitary, was later appointed, after the intervention of the lunacy inspectorate.

Dr Nixon also made a more serious complaint about the misuse by Ashe of public money, stating that he had used the services of the shoemaker and of the tailor at Dundrum, without paying for them. Ashe denied all charges and indicated that Dr Nixon was interfering in what was not his business. He also let the inspectorate know that he was deeply shocked at this questioning of his honesty and of his method of asylum management.[76] Other matters, on which Dr Ashe was questioned, came from the routine monitoring of the accounts by Dublin Castle. There were two specific incidents in which Dr Ashe was questioned by the Auditor General's office in relation to his handling of money. The first was a minor matter involving expenditure on bread. Ashe was questioned about special payments for different types of bread. He answered this query to the satisfaction of the Auditor General. The second was more serious as it ended up in court. This was a dispute that began when the land steward at Dundrum, William Phelan, bought a 'wild cow' at Dublin Castle market, without getting a proper license (in keeping with contagious diseases legislation). Dr Ashe said that he instructed Phelan to get the proper license but Phelan denied this. The court found both men responsible and they were each fined £3 plus £1 costs. The problem did not end there, as Ashe paid his fine and then charged it to the Dundrum account. The Auditor General was not happy with this and an enquiry began. Having been asked to give an account of the dispute, Dr Ashe wrote to the inspectors of lunacy, on 24 April 1888, denying any legal responsibility for Phelan's actions.

> On my own behalf I submit that, though his superior officer, I am in no sense his employer. He was not appointed by me, he was not my selection for the post, he is not paid by me, nor am I able to dismiss him, and he transgressed my express directions in regard of the transit of the cow. Therefore, I was not rightly held responsible by the bench for his action.[77]

Notwithstanding the fact that the Dublin Castle authorities were very unhappy about the payment of a personal fine from the public purse, the Attorney General agreed to it. The final correspondence on the file of the Chief Secretary's office, in relation to this dispute, tells the story eloquently. It is a letter from the Treasury to the under-secretary, sent in August 1888.

> In reply to your letter of 17th, I am directed by the Lord Commissioners of Her Majesty's Treasury to state that the practice pursued by the Medical Superintendent of Dundrum in charging fines and costs on himself and servant to the vote of his Department, without even, as it appears, obtaining the sanction by the Chief Secretary, is so extremely irregular that my Lords scarcely feel justified in giving their covering sanction to this transaction ... My Lords only sanction the amount (£4) in question, on condition that full warning is given to Dr Ashe that he will not be relieved of such a charge again if he incurs it without proper authority.[78]

Dr Ashe was winning the battles, but at this stage, it is highly likely, that he was losing the war. Another enquiry initiated by the inspectorate was about the escape of three female patients. It transpired that they had been helped by some female attendants who supplied them with keys and screwdrivers and allowed them to have a meal in the attendants' quarters before escaping.[79] Attendants who were suspected of helping or whose negligence led to inmates escaping were subject to an automatic fine of five shillings, a penalty deemed grossly inadequate by Dr Ashe. He referred to it in his description of an escape attempt in 1886.

> I am happy to be able to report that no escape of a permanent character has occurred in the past year: in one case a patient crossed the wall of the airing-court, having been undoubtedly helped over by some of his fellow-patients, notwithstanding that six attendants and some of the constabulary guard were on duty in the court at the time. That there was negligence on the part of the attendants and constabulary alike on this occasion, there can be, in my opinion, no possible doubt: and it is in reference to such cases as this that I have expressed the wish that I was empowered to inflict a somewhat heavier penalty than the trifling fine of five shillings now within my competence.[80]

This was just one attempt at an escape in that year. Another was more violent and involved a group of patients. The incident, as described by Dr Ashe, could have led to a large-scale escape:

> On the occasion above mentioned, a severe struggle occurred between the men in charge of the airing yard and a group of prisoners, sane or approximately so, who obviously took advantage of the opportunity to combine for aggressive purposes. Two of the attendants were knocked down and kicked, and incurred considerable risk of having their keys wrested from them ... There were but four men in charge of about one hundred prisoners in the yard at the time.[81]

Dr Ashe, like his predecessors, usually laid the blame for any violence or disruption in the asylum on 'sane' convicts and not on those whose insanity had been part of the cause of their crime. An example was a 27-year-old man from Nenagh, County Tipperary, referred to as T.B., convicted of burglary and sentenced to five years penal servitude. He was transferred from Mountjoy Prison 'on account of occasional outbreaks of violence and passion'. Ashe describes him as 'a habitual criminal of a very low moral type'. Another example was that of two brothers aged 25 and 30 from Galway, referred to as M.B. and P.B., who were sentenced also to five years penal servitude for violent assault on another brother: 'They are both suffering from delusional mania and are badly conducted and violent men.' One wonders how these violent men were being contained in an institution which, by its own admission, was understaffed and inadequately secured. Dr Ashe was worried enough about discipline to put his thoughts in writing to the inspectors in 1886.

> The presence of these sane prisoners, capable as they are of combination, organization, and conspiracy, is a source of constant anxiety and danger here ... I have been disappointed in an endeavour to have their ringleader, the notorious W. M. of prison history, again secluded within the walls of a prison ... It was discovered that this man was actually swearing in his comrades, sane and insane alike, to resist discipline and take the lives of the warders and others, myself included, who might have to enforce discipline among them. If such persons are to be confined here it will be a matter of urgency to make special structural provision for their safe-keeping.[82]

Ashe thought his problems could be solved by raising the peripheral wall. However, the inspectorate, spurred on by the complaints submitted by Dr Nixon, and the endless disputes over administrative matters, thought that the problems were more complex. They instigated an official inquiry in 1891, which resulted in the replacement of Dr Ashe by Dr George Revington, formerly of Manchester Asylum, in 1892.[83] At that stage, it was clear that Dundrum was grossly understaffed (in relation to Broadmoor) as well as being far from secure and, therefore, could not deliver the kind of treatment regime lauded in the early years of its establishment.

In the final decade of the century, a number of major changes were made at Dundrum. These changes coincided with the appointment of two new inspectors of lunacy – Dr G. Plunkett O'Farrell and Dr E. Maziere Courtenay. They included the replacement of Dr Ashe and sixty staff, the introduction of new pay and conditions for attendants, new systems of administration and record keeping, and a number of building alterations, aimed at improving security and comfort. In his first annual report in 1894, the new medical superintendent, Dr George Revington, did not hide his opinion of the former regime. He was scathing about almost every aspect of asylum management.

> The inefficient members of the former staff have been pensioned or dismissed, and no less than sixty appointments were made during the year ... The freedom from accidents, assaults, and escapes which has distinguished the year is unimpeachable evidence of the loyalty and ability of the new staff ... The kitchen is occupied by males only, and the indiscriminate intermingling of the sexes, which was one of the worst

> characteristics of the former administration, has been rendered
> impossible ... The absence of records and registers, and the existence of
> thousands of unclassified papers, rendered the work of the clerical
> department laborious in the extreme ... A small observation room has
> been provided on the female side, and bars and padlocks are gradually
> disappearing.[84]

His plans for the future included not just the old rhetoric about occupation and leisure but some new ideas on payment for work, formerly
regarded as therapeutic in itself, and some ideas on 'aftercare'.

> It is proposed to pay patients for work done, as at Broadmoor Asylum
> and to assist recovered patients to make a fresh start in life. I regard this
> 'aftercare' of patients as most important, and I believe that there will be
> fewer relapses ... By such methods I hope to alleviate the lot of the
> unfortunate class entrusted to my care, to promote their cure, abolish
> their belief that they are beyond sympathy, neglected and forgotten, and
> finally to disarm the spirit of hostility which exists between the patient,
> and what he terms his 'Keeper'.[85]

It is interesting that in his description of patients admitted during his
first year as medical superintendent, Dr Revington's words were not
very different from those of his predecessor. He too described a
number of male prisoners transferred from Mountjoy Prison in
phrases such as 'a dangerous character and a determined runaway' or
'a dangerous character, a marked criminal type' or 'a very dangerous
type of man', or 'a convict of the corner-boy type with congenital
mental defect'.[86] Two of the men, who appear to feature in these
descriptions, are also referred to in the male casebooks for the period.

One was Michael Mullins, a middle-aged man from Limerick who,
in 1868, was acquitted on the grounds of insanity for the murder of his
daughter. He was sent to Dundrum at the pleasure of the Lord
Lieutenant. Mullins insisted that he had been drunk at the time and
that he had fallen on the child, accidentally killing her.[87] In 1868, Dr
Jelston, the junior doctor at Dundrum, had him 'under close obser-
vation' but in spite of this, 'he never evinced the slightest evidence of
being insane, on the contrary he was a scheming designing rogue and
murderer'. However, because of his insanity conviction, he could not
be transferred to the prison system. Mullins escaped just a few months
after being admitted and remained free for five years. However, he
was brought back to Dundrum in 1873, when a local constable
recognized him in his home village. At that time, the medical verdict
was that Mullins 'is by his own confession a professional cheat, he is

extremely cunning and is apparently destitute of moral feeling'. His notes also record that 'he sleeps soundly'. Mullins was not a man to worry about his crimes. He was finally discharged to Limerick Asylum in 1899.[88]

Another man who was regarded as a difficult and dangerous person was C. Connell, a 31-year-old single man from Cork, convicted of rape in 1899. The prison surgeon at Mountjoy Prison (where Connell was first confined) said he was 'subject to attacks of acute mania, becoming violent and necessitating him being placed under restraint'. Dr Revington believed he was malingering in order to take advantage of the comparatively comfortable conditions in Dundrum and declared him sane. Connell went from Mountjoy to Dundrum, back to Mountjoy and then back to Dundrum within a few months. Revington agreed to keep him but described him as 'a regular corner boy of the worst description ... he doesn't work, is a malingerer, is sly and bad tempered'. However, by the following year he was 'suffering from hallucinations' and 'spends half the night beating the cell door with his sheets'. He was transferred to Cork Asylum in 1905.[89] Having examined the scant records of the few young men described as 'corner-boy' types, it is hard to know what was meant by such a description. People regarded as troublesome and dangerous were often transferred frequently between Dundrum and major prisons. The only hope of freedom was escape. For the well-behaved, sane or insane, there was the prospect of total discharge or transfer to a local asylum.

DISCHARGES

Because of the different legal conditions under which people were admitted to Dundrum, some were more easily discharged than others.[90] Those who had been found guilty of a crime and had spent time in prison before being declared insane, could be discharged completely, or transferred back to prison, if sanity returned. Those who had completed their sentences were freed, and those who had not were returned to prison. Those who were found insane before or during the trial, or who were found 'guilty but insane', could not be discharged without the specific permission of the Lord Lieutenant, even if they showed no signs of insanity. These were people held indefinitely 'at the pleasure of the Lord Lieutenant or of His Majesty (LLP or HMP)' – in Broadmoor they were known as 'Pleasure Men'.[91] These differences in discharge procedures led to long debates on the possibility of discharging certain people who were no longer insane and had repented of their crimes, but who were held indefinitely. In 1861, Dr White, the inspector of lunacy, wrote in the annual report:

> The act of the lunatic in nine cases out of ten, let it eventuate even in murder, is perhaps more a symptom or the result of disease than aught besides – the casual product of some passing excitement or strong delusion – when a party becomes thoroughly sane and continues so for a lengthened period, unless there be special reasons to the reverse, we feel justified in recommending the exercise of clemency; and, therefore do not yield to any abstract prejudice hostile to the liberation of a recovered criminal lunatic whose disposition and behaviour brought continually under our observation, have given satisfaction to the Resident Physician, Dr Corbet, and whose sanity has been conjointly certified by him and the Visiting Physician.[92]

The question of how just the system was became the subject of discussion within the inspectorate of lunacy very soon after the opening of Dundrum. In the 1855 report, Dr White indicated that he felt that confining a person in Dundrum beyond what would be called today the 'tariff time' for a crime, was unjust.

> The lunatic labours under a disadvantage in one respect; for, though acquitted of a moral crime, he may still become the penal sufferer by a more lengthened confinement.[93]

Dr White was ahead of his time, as this is an issue that has only recently been resolved at the European Court of Human Rights (ECtHR). The ECtHR has made it clear that indefinite confinement without review is indeed a breach of human rights. There were a number of examples in Dundrum of people who had never been sentenced (having been found unfit to plead at the time of the trial) and who were viewed by the medical staff as sane. These people were in a legal and medical limbo. They could not be transferred to their local asylum or to prison nor, indeed, be discharged. Other patients, acquitted of serious crimes, such as murder, on the grounds of insanity, felt that their indefinite sentences led to a longer period in confinement than necessary or just. One patient, rather unusually, made his feelings about the injustice of the situation known and was featured in the inspector's report for 1854.

> The individual in question, acquitted on the plea of insanity, complains that he has thereby been most unfairly and harshly treated; that he never was deranged; that the offence he committed was the result of the

hardship and injustice he suffered at the hands of another, and of his consequent anger and excitement; and that had he been tried regularly and found guilty, he would have escaped with a comparatively short imprisonment.[94]

Most people did not complain personally, but relied on their relatives to petition the Lord Lieutenant for their discharge or for their transfer to an asylum nearer their family. As will be discussed in later chapters, many of the women who killed children, and who gained their sanity very quickly after admission to Dundrum, were often among the first to receive a 'free discharge', and allowed to return to family members. Some of these are referred to in the 1861 report.

> Since the opening of the Central Asylum, the number of patients who have obtained free discharges amount to 28, and it is gratifying to us to be able to state that, up to this date, there has not been, as far as we are aware of, any instance of misconduct on the part of the persons so discharged.[95]

Others were transferred either to asylums or to prison, depending on their original legal status within the system. In the event of sanity being restored, convicts had to finish their sentences, and those found unfit for trial, had to return to court. In the 1864 annual report, the statistics given in 1861 are expanded with a slight difference in the number of free discharges. However, it is worth reading, as it gives the general picture of discharges in the early years of Dundrum. Of those admitted since 1850, 79 were discharged (57 males and 22 females) as follows:

> Of the 57 males, 22 were transferred to asylums, 26 altogether liberated, and 9 sent to prison, 5 of the latter for the remainder of their penal servitude, and 4 charged with murder, to stand their trial, having on their first arraignment been found incompetent to plead ... Of the 22 females, 9 were placed in the asylums of the districts to which we found them chargeable from birth, or residence; 12 were liberated, and 1 was remitted to prison.[96]

Some cases led to lengthy discussions on the legality of discharge and of transfer. One example of a legal wrangle over transfer was that of the Rae sisters – two women (aged 25 and 27) from County Down, who had been convicted of the manslaughter of their mistress in 1873 and sentenced to penal servitude for life. They were transferred from prison to Dundrum in 1876 because they both showed signs of mental disorder. In spite of discussions about possible transfer to an ordinary asylum in 1905, permission was refused and they died in Dundrum.[97] Part of the reason for the rejection of the appeal on their behalf was the fact that overcrowding at Dundrum had been put forward as an argument for their discharge. The Lord Lieutenant was not happy to have this as a legal precedent. Because they had not completed their sentences, it was felt that they could not be released or transferred to an ordinary district asylum. Others were luckier. It helped to have relatives who would petition the Lord Lieutenant for a pardon. As in other parts of the criminal justice system, it also helped to speed up discharge if the family could offer a sailing ticket and the promise of a new life outside of Ireland. Some of these stories will be explored in later chapters and it will become clear that for some people, the label 'criminal lunatic' did not necessarily mean that their lives were over. Many returned to normal life with their families and friends.

NOTES

1   Mark Finnane, 'Irish psychiatry, Part 1: The formation of a profession', in G.E. Berrios and H. Freeman (eds), *150 Years of British Psychiatry 1841–1991*, (London: Gaskell, 1991), pp. 306–13. David Healy, 'Irish psychiatry, part 2: Use of the Medico-Psychological Association by its Irish members – plus ça change!', pp. 314–20, in Berrios and Freeman, *150 Years*.

2   See reports on some meetings held in Ireland: Anonymous, 'Notes and News: The AGM of the Medico-Psychological Association 1885', *The Journal of Mental Science*, xxxi, 135 (October 1885), pp. 428–41; Anonymous, 'Notes and News: Irish (quarterly) meeting of the Medico-Psychological Association, December 1887', *The Journal of Mental Science*, xxiv (January 1888), pp. 649–50.

3   Isaac Ashe, 'Some observations on general paralysis', *The Journal of Mental Science*, xxii, 97 (April 1876), pp. 82–3.

4   G.W. Abraham, *Law and Practice of Lunacy in Ireland* (Dublin: Ponsonby, 1886), p. 13.

5   S.W. North, 'Insanity and Crime', *The Journal of Mental Science*, xxxii, 138 (July 1886), pp. 163–81, p. 166.

6   *Asylums Report*, HC 1874 (c. 1004) xxvii, 363, p. 256.

7   *Asylums Report*, HC 1851 (1387) xxiv, 231, p. 232.

8   J. W. Williams, 'Unsoundness of Mind, in its Medical and Legal Considerations', *Dublin Quarterly Journal of Medical Science*, xxxvi (Nov 1854), pp. 260–87, p. 260.

9   Ibid.

10 D. Yellowlees, 'Case of Murder during Temporary Insanity induced by Drinking or Epilepsy', *The Journal of Mental Science*, xxix, 127 (October 1883), pp. 382–7, p. 386.

11 P.M. Prior, 'Roasting a man alive: The case of Mary Rielly, criminal lunatic', *Eire-Ireland*, 41,1–2 (Spring/Summer 2006), pp. 169–91.

12 North, 'Insanity and Crime', p. 170.

13 Ibid., p. 171.

14 For discussion, see Roger Smith, *Trial by Medicine: Insanity and Responsibility in Victorian Trials* (Edinburgh: Edinburgh University Press, 1981), p. 10.

15 Oscar Woods, 'Notes of some cases of *Folie à Deux* in several members of the same family', *Journal of Mental Science*, xliii, 183 (October 1897), pp. 822–5.

16 M. J. Nolan, 'Case of *Folie à Deux*', *Journal of Mental Science*, xxxv, 149 (April 1889), pp. 55–61.

17 Oscar Woods, 'Criminal Responsibility of the Insane', *The Journal of Mental Science*, xl, 171 (October 1894); pp. 609–21.
18 Ralph Partridge, *Broadmoor: A History of Criminal Lunacy and its Problems* (London; Chatto and Windus, 1953), p. 1.
19 F. McAuley and J.P. McCutcheon, *Criminality: A Grammar* (Dublin: Round Hall Sweet and Maxwell, 2000), p. 646.
20 Criminal Lunatics Act 1800 (39 & 40 Geo 3 c. 94); Partridge, *Broadmoor*, p. 1.
21 For a full discussion of the case and of the many versions of the man's name, see R. Moran, *Knowing Right from Wrong: The insanity defense of Daniel McNaughtan*, (New York: The Free Press, 1981).
22 Ibid., p. 2.
23 For full discussion see H.I. Kaplan and B.J. Sadock, *Comprehensive Textbook of Psychiatry, 6th Edition* (London and Baltimore: Williams and Wilkins, 1995), pp. 2763–6.
24 Cited in C.M. Green, L.J. Naismith, R.D. Menzies, 'Criminal responsibility and mental disorder in Britain and North America: A comparative study', *Medical Science and the Law*, 31, 1 (1995), pp. 45–54, p. 51.
25 J.Q. La Fond and M.L. Durham, *Back to the Asylum: The future of mental health law and policy in the United States*, (Oxford: Oxford University Press, 1992), p. 217.
26 Green *et al.* 'Criminal responsibility', p. 48.
27 For discussion, see P. M. Prior, 'Mentally disordered offenders and the European Court of Human Rights', *International Journal of Law and Psychiatry* 30,6 (2007), pp. 546–57.
28 Criminal Lunatics Act 1800; Lunacy (Ireland) Act 1821 (1 & 2 Geo. 4 c. 33).
29 Trial of Lunatics (Ireland) Act 1883 (46 & 47 Vic c. 38), Section 2.
30 Third Interim Report of the Interdepartmental Committee on Mentally Ill and Maladjusted Persons, *Treatment and Care of Persons Suffering from Mental Disorder who Appear Before the Courts on Criminal Charges*, Pr 5l. 8275 (1978), pp. 4, 23, 24, 33, cited in McAuley and McCutcheon, *Criminality*, p. 698.
31 Criminal Law (Insanity) Act 2006 (Ireland 2006, No. 11).
32 Gibbons *et al.*, 'Guilty but insane', p. 468.
33 Ibid., p. 469; *RIC Return of Outrages for 1888*, p. 11 (NAI, CSO, ICR2); Dundrum, Female Casebook, 1893–1920s, p. 29, Case F772.
34 Woods, 'Notes of some cases'.
35 *RIC Return of Outrages for 1896*, p. 8 (NAI, Police Reports 1882–1921, Box 4).
36 Gibbons *et al.*, 'Guilty but insane', pp. 469–70.
37 Criminal Lunatics (Ireland) Act 1838 (1 & 2 Vic. c. 27).
38 Smith, *Trial by Medicine*, p. 34.
39 For similar discussions in England, see Partridge, *Broadmoor*; Walker, *Crime and Insanity in England, Vols. 1 and 2*.
40 *Asylums Report*, HC 1847 (820) xvii, 355, p. 362.
41 Ibid.
42 *Asylums Report*, HC 1864 (3369) xxiii, 317, p. 380.
43 Robert Menzies, 'Contesting criminal lunacy: Narratives of law and madness in west coast Canada 1874–1950, *History of Psychiatry*, xii (2001), pp. 123–56.
44 *Asylums Report*, HC 1849 (1054) xxiii, 53, p. 62.
45 *Asylums Report*, HC 1852–53 (1653) xli, 353, p. 366.
46 Joseph Robins, *Fools and Mad: A History of the Insane in Ireland*, (Dublin: Institute of Public Adminstration, 1986), p. 134.
47 *Select Committee Report on Lunatic Poor 1843*, HC 1843 (625) x, 439, Evidence: Appendix 1, p. 25.
48 *Asylums Report*, HC 1852–53 (1653) xli, 353, p. 367.
49 Ibid., p. 368–9.
50 *Commission of inquiry 1858*, HC 1857–58 (2436) xxvii.1, p. 25.
51 *Asylums Report*, HC 1865 (3556) xxi, 103, p. 125.
52 *Asylums Report*, HC 1867–8 (4053) xxxi, 303, p. 334.

53 *Asylums Report*, HC 1874 (c. 1004) xxvii, 363, Appendix F, p. 258.
54 Ibid., p. 256.
55 *Asylums Report*, HC 1854–5 (1981) xvi, 137, p. 156.
56 *Commission of Inquiry 1858*, HC 1857–58 (2436) xxvii.1, p. 16.
57 Ibid.
58 Ibid.
59 *Asylums Report*, HC 1852–3 (1653) xli, 353, p. 369.
60 *Asylums Report*, HC 1854–5 (1981) xvi, 137, p. 157.
61 List of staff continued in the internal report on Dundrum in the inspectors of Lunacy Report Book, 1852. (NAI OLA 6/1: Item 472).
62 *Asylums Report*, HC 1874 (c. 1004) xxvii, 363, Appendix F, Tables 14 & 15, p. 255–6 and Appendix C, Table 23, pp. 220–5. Please keep in mind that it is difficult to make direct comparisons, as attendants were paid different rates according to their experience and skills.
63 *Asylums Report*, HC 1854–5 (1981) xvi, 137, p. 156.
64 Ibid.
65 *Asylums Report*, HC 1861 (2901) xxvii, 245, p. 254.
66 Ibid., p. 255.
67 *Asylums Report*, HC 1864 (3369) xxiii, 317, p. 382–3.
68 Ibid., p. 377.
69 *Asylums Report*, HC 1867 (3894) xviii, 453, p. 489.
70 *Report by the Commissioners in Lunacy on Broadmoor Asylum*, HC 1868–69 (244) li. 477, p. 478. (Hereafter, *Commissioners Report on Broadmoor*).
71 Ibid., p. 478–9.
72 Partridge, *Broadmoor*, p. 70.
73 *Commissioners Report on Broadmoor*, p. 481.
74 Ibid., p. 482.
75 Report from Dr Ashe, included in the *Asylums Report*, HC 1886 (c. 4811) xxxiii, 559, p. 570.
76 Letter from Dr Ashe to the inspectorate of lunacy in 1889. Dundrum, *Letter Book 1878–88*.
77 Letter from Dr Ashe to the inspectorate of lunacy dated 24 April 1888 (NAI, CSORP, 1888/File number 17094).
78 Letter from the Treasury to the Under Secretary, Sir Joseph West Ridgeway, August 1888. (NAI, CSORP, 1888/ File number 17094).
79 Letters from Dr Ashe to the inspectorate. (Dundrum, Letter Book 1878–88).
80 Dundrum Annual Report by the Dr Ashe, included in the *Asylums Report*, HC 1886 (c. 4811) xxxiii, 559, p. 570.
81 Report from Dr Ashe to the Inspectorate of Lunacy, included in ibid., p. 680.
82 Ibid., p. 681.
83 *Asylums Report*, HC 1893–4 (c. 7125) xlvi, 369, p. 441.
84 Ibid., p. 437.
85 *Asylums Report*, HC 1893–4 (c. 7125) xlvi, 369, p. 439.
86 *Asylums Report*, HC 1895 (c. 7804) liv, 435, pp. 572–3.
87 *Asylums Report*, HC 1874 (c. 1004) xxvii, 363, p. 10.
88 Dundrum, Male Casebook, M. Mullins, 1868, no. M440, p. 62.
89 Dundrum, Male Casebook, C. Connell, 1899, no. M1016, p. 51.
90 See Appendix 1: Legal Basis for admission to Dundrum 1850–1900.
91 Partridge, *Broadmoor*, p. 3.
92 *Asylums Report*, HC 1861 (2901) xxvii, 245, p. 253.
93 *Asylums Report*, HC 1854–55 (1981) xvi, 137, p. 153.
94 Ibid., p. 154.
95 *Asylums Report*, HC 1861 (2901) xxvii, 245, p. 254.
96 *Asylums Report*, HC 1864 (3369) xxiii, 317, p. 377.
97 Dundrum, Female Casebook, Charlotte and Mary Rae, 1877, no. F503 and F704, pp. 9, 21, 155; NAI CRF 1910/ P1 (Patterson file containing Rae file, NAI CRF 1905/ R36).

PART II

The Stories

CHAPTER FOUR

Men who killed women

D R TERENCE B. BRODIE WAS an interesting man. In spite of the fact that he had murdered his wife, Molly, he was able to start a new life in South Africa as a professional man with a private income. His story is a good illustration of some of the arguments used in the late nineteenth century, by men who pleaded insanity to the charge of murdering a woman. Dr Brodie was the dispensary doctor in Spiddal, County Galway. At the age of 36, he shot his older wife (aged 43), a woman of independent means, without any obvious provocation.[1] The crime occurred on 12 July 1886. According to police records:

> [Mrs Brodie] was shot dead, at about twelve o'clock, noon, by her husband, Terence B. Brodie, who was at the time suffering from alcoholic insanity. The fatal wound was inflicted with a breech loading fowling piece, the shot penetrating the right eye, and lodging in the brain.[2]

The police description of the precipitating factor in the crime – 'alcoholic insanity' – was based on medical reports and the doctor's explanation of his action. He told the arresting officer that there was a plot against his life and that his wife made no effort to protect him from the people who were trying to kill him. As there was no evidence of any such plot, these thoughts were considered delusional. The tragedy was reported in the *London Times* newspaper on the following day.

> A report from Galway states that Dr Terence Brodie of Spiddal murdered his wife this morning in a fit of delirium tremens, and gave himself up to the police. He desired to be tried at the present assizes, and says he will meet his fate like a man.[3]

A week later, Dr Brodie was found 'unfit to plead' at the Galway Summer Assizes, with two medical witnesses testifying that he was suffering from 'alcoholic insanity'. When he was brought to trial in March 1887, he was found 'guilty but insane' at the time he committed the crime.[4] During the court hearings, Brodie's legal defence focused on his delusions and also on the fact that he had consumed a significant amount of alcohol in the days prior to the crime. Coleman Naughton, who worked for Brodie, told the court about both.

> I remember about six o'clock that morning seeing Dr Brodie sitting on the kitchen table ... He told me to go out in the yard and call in Danny McIntyre and Dan Lydon. I told him they were not in the yard at all – I knew they were not in the yard. He told me to go out again – saying 'don't you see them coming in the kitchen'... He was drinking heavy up to Thursday night before this.[5]

Brodie had also spoken about the plot on his life to the district inspector of the RIC in Spiddal, Frank M. Feely, on the day of his arrest. Feely recalled the conversation in his statement.

> He [Brodie] put out his hand to me to shake hands. I took it. He said 'There was a plot against my life'. I then said 'I want to caution you not to say anything' and I was about to finish the usual caution when he interrupted me and said, 'I am not going to criminate [sic] myself'. I then asked him to come to the Barrack which he did. On the way, he said 'There was a plot against my life. They wanted to bully me, but they could not. I want to charge Danny McIntyre with plotting against my life and James Tolan with being an accessory' ... He told me he had told his wife the previous day four times to send for the police to protect him[6]

The police and medical examiner interpreted this statement as evidence of paranoid delusions. However, other evidence presented to the court by a domestic servant, Bridget McDonough, pointed to the possibility of a different interpretation of events. Bridget made a damning statement, suggesting that the crime was part of a pattern of violence.

> I heard him on more than one occasion telling his wife that he would get rid of her. I recalled last Sunday fortnight – she had to hide herself from him on that day from his violence – I saw him chucking her about the yard on that day by the arms – I heard him say 'I would tramp on you'. I saw him violent to her frequently before that, she had to leave the house in January or February last to escape from his violence and I accompanied her.[7]

This evidence points to a history of domestic violence towards Mrs Brodie. Bridget had witnessed two serious incidents in the six months prior to the murder. However, Bridget was only a domestic servant in the house of a middle-class professional man and her word alone was not powerful enough. Evidence from another servant, Coleman Naughton, also showed Dr Brodie as a very controlling man, engaged in what could be construed as a deliberate act of domination and destruction.

> Before Dr Brodie got the gun, he called to Mrs Brodie to bring him up a glass of whiskey, which she did, and when she arrived on the lobby, I saw Dr Brodie with the gun on the lobby ... She went in with the whiskey into her own and Dr Brodie's bedroom and left the whiskey on the back window-seat, she then went over to the door and asked him would he take his whiskey? He was then on [sic] the lobby but he did not make any reply.[8]

Mrs Brodie's behaviour here is entirely consistent with what we know today about domestic violence. She obeyed her husband's instructions even when they were unreasonable, because of her fear of the consequences of disagreeing with him. On this occasion, the threat of violence was real – Dr Brodie was holding a loaded gun. Coleman Naughton recounted the actual conversation and movements that took place before the final act of violence.

> She [Mrs Brodie] then asked Dr Brodie would he let her down to her lunch? He said he would not – she asked him a second time, saying that she had left the teapot in the parlour when she had brought him up the whiskey and that she would come up again after lunch. He said no, two or three times. She asked him again and he replied that he would not until he liked. She then got a newspaper, went over to the front window and sat down. Dr Brodie still remained on the lobby. Mrs Brodie remained sitting at the window for about half an hour or three quarters and Dr Brodie remained outside on the lobby except once when he came in and walked straight out again ... He had the gun in his hand this time – when he went out on this occasion. He remained outside for about a quarter of an hour very silent. He then ran in and held the gun quite close to her face and fired the gun.[9]

Naughton went on to recount some of Brodie's words after he shot his wife.

> I saw her [Mrs Brodie] fall by degree from the window on the floor. While I was running over to catch the gun, I heard Dr Brodie say 'I have your life now, Molly, anyway'. After I caught the gun, he said 'I will shoot the whole bloody lot of you and myself afterwards'. I continued to try and take the gun from him, and he to hold it until I got as far as a turn on the stairs when he let go [sic] the gun.[10]

TERENCE BRODIE'S DEFENCE

W. Concannon, the lawyer acting on behalf of Brodie, cross-examined the witnesses in relation to Brodie's drinking. His intention was to link alcohol abuse with his client's violent behaviour. Coleman Naughton told the court that the doctor had been drinking heavily until the Thursday before the crime but added that that he saw 'no sign of drink' on him from that day onwards. Bridget McDonough conceded that he was usually drunk whenever he was violent towards his wife, but also said that he had stopped drinking some days before the crime.

> I never saw any dispute or violence except when he was in liquor. He was very drunk on the Sunday fortnight I have mentioned. He had been drinking for a fortnight up to the Thursday previous to the 12th inst.[11]

The argument being built up by the defence was based on medical literature of the time. There were two arguments about alcohol abuse. According to the first argument, a state of 'transitory frenzy' or 'temporary insanity' could be caused by the consumption of too much alcohol. As already discussed in an earlier chapter, 'hallucinations or delusions leading to dangerous violence' had already been linked to the 'insanity of intemperance' by psychiatrists such as Dr Yellowlees of Glasgow Royal Asylum.[12] The abuse of alcohol could lead to delusions causing the perpetrator of the crime to believe that the victim posed a threat to his or her safety.[13] The second argument was about 'delirium tremens', the term used to describe Dr Brodie's condition by the doctors who examined him after his arrest. According to this argument, the individual did not have to be drunk at the actual moment of the crime for the court to conclude that he was not responsible for his actions. The legal defence from a case in Newcastle Upon Tyne, England, in 1881, illustrates the point. This was the case of William Davis (aged 38) who had attacked his sister-in-law with 'intent to murder'.[14] Davis had previously been drinking heavily, but was sober at the time of the crime. His lawyer argued that he was suffering from 'delirium tremens', hence 'he was disordered in his senses, and would not be able to distinguish between moral right and wrong at the time he committed the act'. The final judgement in the case was that Davis was insane at the time of the crime. The legal outcome was summarized in *Cox's Criminal Law Cases 1877–82*:

> Drunkenness is no excuse, but delirium tremens caused by drinking and differing from drunkenness, if it produces such a degree of

madness, even for a time, as to render a person incapable of distinguishing right from wrong, relieves him from criminal responsibility.[15]

In Dr Brodie's case, there was no reported evidence that he believed
his wife to be involved in a plot to kill him, but the jury accepted the
argument that his alcohol consumption prior to the crime had relieved
him of responsibility for the murder. It handed down a verdict of
'guilty but insane'. Brodie was sent back to the Central Criminal
Lunatic Asylum for Ireland at Dundrum (where he had awaited trial),
to be held indefinitely 'at the pleasure of the Lord Lieutenant'.

The decision of the court may have been swayed by the fact that Dr
Brodie was not only a well-respected member of the community, but
also that his alcoholism could be explained by the terrible tragedies
that had happened to him just a few years earlier.[16] Born in 1850 in
Cork, Dr Brodie studied medicine at Queen's College, Galway (now
NUI, Galway). At the age of 24, he married Frances M. Eyre, the
daughter of John J. Eyre, owner of Clifden Castle in County Galway.
The wedding ceremony took place in the Clifden Catholic Chapel. The
newly married couple moved to Spiddal, a coastal village just west of
Galway city, where he worked as the Dispensary Medical Officer. In
late 1879, just six years after they were married, a series of tragedies
struck the Brodie family. At this time, they had three children (two
boys and one girl) and Mrs Brodie was pregnant with a fourth. The
two boys (aged 4 and 2) died of 'diptheria' in November. This was
followed by the death of mother of 'post-partum haemorrhage' in
early December and of the new baby of 'convulsions' nine days later.
The girl, Marguerite (known as Daisy), was taken to Dublin to be
cared for by her aunt, Maria Brodie.[17] Within the space of a few
months, Dr Brodie had lost his entire family. However, he maintained
his position as the dispensary doctor in Spiddal and in 1880, a year
after his wife's death, he married for a second time, this time in a
Church of Ireland in Dublin.

Brodie's new wife was Mary Jane (known as Molly) Bunbury.
Though her address at the time of her marriage was given as 6 Lower
Mount Street, Dublin, it is also likely that she spent some time at the
Manor House in Spiddal, which her family owned and where her two
widowed sisters were living at the time.[18] We know very little about
Molly, except that she came from a Protestant family, that she was
older than Terence and that she and her three sisters had a private
income from an inheritance of £2,000 invested on their behalf and
shared between them.[19] Dr Brodie and his new wife settled in Spiddal.
They did not have any children and Daisy, his daughter from his first

marriage, continued to live with her aunt in Dublin. Six years later, Molly Brodie was dead and her husband was confined to the Central Criminal Lunatic Asylum for Ireland at Dundrum.

From the time of his commital to Dundrum in 1887, Brodie never showed any signs of insanity. This was also a feature of other cases involving 'delirium tremens', such as that of William Davis (of Newcastle upon Tyne). His lawyer told the court that 'under proper care and treatment, he recovered in a week and was then perfectly sane'.[20] Two years after Brodie's admission, the medical superintendent recommended that he be released, stating that he had suffered only temporary insanity at the time of the crime and was now perfectly sane. After a lengthy correspondence between the Chief Secretary's office at Dublin Castle and various interested parties, Brodie was released in 1892 – having completed six years of confinement in Dundrum. The memorials, addressed to the Lord Lieutenant, show that the appeal for Brodie's release (with a view to emigration) was supported not only by his family and friends but also by the Bishop of Limerick (in 1889) and the Crown Prosecutor for Galway, Mr French (in 1892). They also show that his release was initially opposed by his dead wife's family (though they agreed to it later).[21] Her three sisters alleged that he had been cruel to his wife throughout their marriage and had tried to kill her before. They also argued that as there were no children in the marriage, he would be the sole heir to her estate. They asked that, if released, he be required to leave the country and to renounce claims to his dead wife's money – which would then revert to them. The following extract from a letter, written in May 1897, by a solicitor on behalf of Mrs Brodie's family, sets out some of the legal points in the case.

> My object in troubling you is this. One convicted of felony is civilly dead and from this state, a pardon only can release. I am acting for one of the murdered lady's sisters (all of whom have a reversion in a sum of £2,000, if he is either civilly or physically dead), of which he is at present receiving the dividend.[22]

The amount of money referred to in this letter was substantial. It was equivalent to approximately £150,000 of purchasing power at 2006 prices.[23] One of the interesting points raised in this letter is the legal limbo occupied by people confined to asylums. The laws on mental disorder, then as now, were very clearly aimed at protecting the financial interests of people who were deemed insane. It would have been legally unacceptable for a court to remove any financial rights from a person who was confined under any section of lunacy legislation. Therefore, any rights that Dr Brodie had to his wife's estate (including interest from this investment), remained intact because of his successful insanity defence. This would not have been the case, had he been found guilty of murder.

Brodie's three brothers (all medical doctors) put forward the opposite view, pleading for his discharge and indicating that Dr Brodie would emigrate, if released. Among the memorials asking for his release were two from Brodie himself. Writing in 1889, three years after his conviction, he said that he had been adequately punished by being confined to Dundrum – being obliged to 'consort with criminal lunatics of the lower grades of life', that he loved his wife and was repentant for his crime. He said he would like to start a new life, with his daughter, aged 15, from his previous marriage. In 1892, the presence of a child and the purchase of a sailing ticket by his brothers were noted in his file as points in favour of his release. The final memorial from Dr Brodie's solicitor in June 1892 seemed to clinch the deal.

> [The] petitioner is willing to leave the country permanently ... Petitioner has never ceased to regret the terrible crime of which he is admittedly guilty and by which he has deprived himself of the companionship of an affectionate wife for whom petitioner entertained no other feelings than those of respect and love ... He wishes now to atone so far as he can to his child for the deep wrong he had done to her and he proposes making this atonement if permitted to do so to the utmost of his power.[24]

While there is some indication on the Brodie file that the requests put forward by Mrs Brodie's sisters were considered, the Lord Lieutenant gave permission for Brodie's release without making any intervention with regard to his rights to inheritance. The final entry on his convict file is a letter from a solicitor, giving details of the proposed journey, with a copy of the ticket to the Cape enclosed, suggesting that his client needed ten days to buy 'an outfit' for the journey. Brodie was discharged in 1892 and emigrated to South Africa.

Dr Brodie built himself a new life in South Africa, getting a job as a 'railway medical officer' almost immediately after his arrival.[25] Certificates of his medical qualifications, issued to him by the Royal College of Physicians and Surgeons (in Edinburgh) and by the Medical Registry Office (in Dublin) in August 1892, were accepted by the South African authorities, and his license to practice medicine there was issued in October of the same year. He married for the third time in 1894, this time in a Wesleyan Church. He and his English-born wife had four children, two of whom died as infants. He established his own medical practice and, until his death, continued to work as a doctor in the community, with approximately a year of service in camps 'established by the British occupying forces for the women and children of Boer families uprooted from their farms' during the Anglo-Boer War.[26] It is unlikely that any facts from his past were known in his community. He died after a stroke in 1896, leaving his wife and their two children very badly off financially. We know this from a letter written by his widow to the colonial office, asking for the payment of fees which, she claimed,were due to her husband for the work he had done during the war. In this letter, she said that she was 'quite penniless and that her husband had lost everything during the war, which his private income had also ceased upon his death'.

WIFE-KILLING

Some general information on the killing of women by men will help in our understanding of men like Terence Brodie. Today, men outnumber women in general crime statistics throughout the world and this pattern does not change when the crime is related to a mental disorder. A similar pattern operates in relation to homicide in general, with more men than women convicted for murder and manslaughter. Although male-on-male homicide is more common statistically, the number of male-on-female homicides is significant.[27] Judging by the RIC records on reported crime, this pattern was well established in nineteenth-century Ireland, with most of the male-on-female homicides taking place within the family network. The victims included wives, mothers, daughters, aunts and sisters.[28]

It is extremely difficult to put exact numbers on these crimes, because of the problems surrounding crime statistics in nineteenth-century Ireland. From my own research and that of Conley, Finnane, Malcolm, O'Donnell and Wilbanks, it is clear that the majority of both perpetrators and victims of homicides were male and that in crimes where women were the victims, the perpetrators were likely to be male.[29] In other words, while men who killed men were in the majority, a substantial number of men killed women.[30] Because official crime statistics do not give the level of detail required to make an accurate judgement of how many men killed women, we have to rely on partial statistics derived from detailed police reports for some periods. RIC records on 'outrages reported to the constabulary office' reveal the names of over 100 men who killed their wives between 1838 and 1892 and almost the same number of men who killed other female relatives.[31] These victims included mothers, daughters, sisters, aunts and female in-laws. These records also show that many of the cases did not reach court and that, of those that did, very few of these men were executed. Some had the death sentence reduced to penal servitude for life, and many received short sentences or were sent to Dundrum as criminal lunatics.[32] One explanation of wife-killing is given in the report on Dundrum by the inspectors of lunacy for Ireland in 1855:

> The most frequent kind of homicide among the men is wife murder ... This fact, at first sight, might seem to argue less constancy, fidelity and tenderness with the male sex; but there are strong causes to explain away, or, at least, reduce the force of the conclusion; for it is well known, that, occasionally, among the first and most marked symptoms of the disease with lunatics may be reckoned a mistrust and aversion to members of their own family, and to those particularly with whom they had been united by the strongest ties of affection, and who, if physically weaker, in case any control is attempted, are most exposed to suffer from their violence.[33]

This comment reflects the medical argument that the killing of a wife or close relative could be symptomatic of a mental disorder – in other words, the crime was a manifestation of a pre-existing mental condition which showed itself in the pressurized environment of the home.[34] However, it is also a highly gendered and incorrect view of the situation. The 'most frequent kind of homicide' in Ireland was not 'wife-murder' – in fact, most homicide victims were male.[35] However, men who murdered their wives (or indeed any member of their family) had a higher than average probability of putting forward a successful insanity defence.

It would also be wrong to assume that the medical profession in Ireland suggested a direct link between insanity and the potential to kill. In fact, the opposite was true, as is evident in the writings of Dr Corbet, the medical superintendent at Dundrum. In the annual report in 1864, he wrote:

> As to the homicidal propensity among the insane, or a predisposition to kill for the mere object of killing, we apprehend it to be of the rarest occurrence. The act, when preconceived, appears to us to be almost uniformly directed against an individual alone, and to result from some lurking ideas or fancy of an actual or intended wrong.[36]

In other words, it is very rare for someone with a mental illness to kill and when it happens, it is usually not random. Rather, the victim is perceived by the perpetrator as a threat – real or imaginary. This is usual not only in cases where there is evidence of an existing mental disorder, but also in cases where the crime takes place during what the medical and legal professions called 'temporary insanity' or 'transitory frenzy'.[37] In these cases, where the impulse to kill or to commit a violent act was linked to alcohol consumption, lawyers and doctors did not always agree as to whether or not this removed or reduced responsibility for the crime. In relation to a case in Scotland in 1883, that of 'George Miller, age twenty seven, a native of the North of Ireland ... who had killed a man ... but could recall nothing that had occurred', Dr Yellowlees, of Glasgow Royal Asylum, commented as follows on his acquittal on the grounds of insanity:

> There can be little doubt as to the correctness of this opinion, though some may demur to the complete exculpation of a man who willfully drank to excess after so many warnings as to the dangerous condition which drinking induced. Hallucinations or delusions leading to danger-ous violence are of course frequent in the insanity of intemperance. Transient delusions of a like kind may follow even a single carouse.[38]

An exploration of the cases in which men had killed women while in a state of intoxication confirms the concern raised here by Dr Yellowlees. Often these were men who were known to be violent when they had drunk too much, yet they were excused of responsibility for their crimes on the basis of their alcoholic state. Some were acquitted completely, some were given short sentences and a few were sent to district asylums, having been found 'unfit to plead'. For example, James McMaster, a publican from Belfast, who killed his wife, Margaret, aged 30, 'while in a state of intoxication', was sentenced to twelve months imprisonment. The RIC report gave jealousy as the motive for the crime.[39] In the same year, John Sullivan, a rag gatherer from Cork, killed his wife, by stabbing her in the neck 'with a sharp pointed poker' during a quarrel. He too was 'under the influence of drink' and was acquitted.[40] Similarly, in 1884, John McCauley, a mechanic from Belfast, killed his 40-year-old wife, Catherine, after a bout of drinking. She 'died from the effects of injuries inflicted by her husband, who flung her down stairs, thereby fracturing her skull'. The police reported that though he had been drinking, he was 'not intoxicated' at the time of the crime. He was acquitted of her murder.[41]

All of these crimes highlight not only the link between intoxication and domestic violence, but also the relative leniency of the judicial system in relation to male violence against women. Does this show an acceptance of domestic violence (directed towards women) in the Irish courts? Conley thinks not. She quotes from a Limerick newspaper and from assizes reports to back up her claim. 'The *Limerick Reporter* used the headline "Shocking Outrage" for a story about a fisherman who had struck his wife in the head with a pewter pot.'[42] However, Conley does suggest that the involvement of alcohol in a violent attack made it less serious in the eyes of the law. 'Sane men who assaulted their wives received light punishment … As with recreational violence, drink was sometimes accepted as an excuse.'[43] It is clear that the concept of masculinity in nineteenth-century Ireland incorporated behaviour that was both violent and irrational. Though violence was not condoned, it was accepted as a likely outcome of male drinking patterns.

It is very difficult in retrospect to reconstruct the arguments used in many of these court cases, because of the loss of so many of the court records in the Custom House fire in 1921, and the selective coverage of cases in newspapers and other sources.[44] However, there are indications in police records that the men who got lighter sentences or were acquitted of murder were seen as neither dangerous nor deliberately cruel. For men regarded as dangerous or deliberately violent, two very severe outcomes were possible – an indefinite sentence to confinement in Dundrum as a criminal lunatic, or a sentence to execution by hanging. The crucial element in the decision to accept the insanity defence was the evidence presented to the court that the crime had taken place as a result of a 'transitory frenzy' during a period of 'temporary insanity', that could be a symptom of an existing mental disorder, or could be brought on by either intoxication or epilepsy.[45] I found no evidence of epilepsy as a cause of such a 'frenzy' in cases in which women were killed by their husbands or male relatives, but some in relation to intoxication (See Table 4.1). For example, Michael Glasheen, a farmer from County Tipperary was sent to Dundrum in 1883 for killing his thirty-five year old wife, Maria. According to the police report:

> She died from the effect of injuries inflicted by her husband Michael. The deceased who was in a delicate state of health was lying in bed when her husband came into the house under the influence of drink. He dragged her out of bed and violently assaulted her. Several slight wounds were found on her body as well as two large burn marks. These injuries combined with the shock to her enfeebled system caused almost immediate death. The outrage is solely attributable to drink.[46]

Table 4.1 *Wife killers found to be insane at the time of the crime*

Name	County	Weapon	Cause/diagnosis	In Asylum*
Patrick Morgan	Down	Unknown	Chronic mania	1867–91
Andrew Dolan	Leitrim	Knife	Delusions	1870
William Hackett	Tyrone	Brick	Insanity	1873
Daniel Collins	Cork	Hatchet	Insanity	1879
Michael Glasheen	Tipperary	Fists	Alcoholic frenzy	1883
John Carty	Tipperary	Stick	Insanity	1884
Dr Terence Brodie	Galway	Shotgun	Delirium tremens	1886–92
James Casey	Louth	Hammer	Delusions	1887
Michael Roache	Waterford	Razor	Insanity	1887
John Dwyer	Tipperary	Stone	Insanity	1887
Darby Lydon	Galway	Pitchfork	Insanity	1889
William Ivory	Westmeath	Gun	Insanity	1891
Allan Spiller	Antrim	Knife	Melancholia	1892–99
Alexander McMurray	Antrim	Hammer	Alcoholic frenzy	1893
Michael Fox	Longford	Fists	Dementia	1894
James McDermott	Fermanagh	Mallet	Insanity	1895
John McDermott	Roscommon	Fists	Delusions	1897
John Curren	Donegal	Blunt object	Insanity	1898

* Some went to Dundrum and some to district asylums.

Sources: Medical records (Dundrum), RIC records and individual convict files (National Archives of Ireland).

Here, we see the police report pointing the court towards an explanation of the crime which in other cases got the accused man off with a light sentence. However, the subsequent examination of her body indicated that this man was not only dangerous when drunk, but that this final act of violence against his wife was part of a pattern of continuous abuse also linked to his over-indulgence in alcohol. This led to the conclusion that he was dangerous, but not responsible for his actions. He was acquitted on the grounds of insanity and confined to Dundrum indefinitely. This verdict, which was worded differently to that handed down to Dr Brodie, had the same effect. The different verdicts reflect a change in the law after 1883. Before then, under legislation dating from 1821 and 1845, murderers could be 'acquitted on the grounds of insanity' – as happened in Glasheen's case. After the passing of a new law in 1883, the verdict became 'guilty but insane'- as happened in Brodie's case.[47] The outcome was the same – confinement in Dundrum indefinitely 'at the Pleasure of the Lord Lieutenant'.

Another common denominator emerged in reports on cases where the insanity defence was successful. This was jealousy as a motive for the fatal attack on a wife – jealousy based on an alleged infidelity. Guillais, in his analysis of crimes of passion in nineteenth-century France, suggests that:

> Sexual honour, symbolized by female purity, has always been the highest stake in power relations in our society. Men consider themselves responsible for the behaviour of their wives because that is where the essence of their moral honour lies.[48]

From this standpoint, murder could be seen as a socially acceptable method of restoring the balance to a relationship in which power has been challenged. Though Ireland does not have a tradition of 'honour-killing' by male relatives of women deemed to have brought shame on the family name, there is no doubt that some murders were 'crimes of passion'. However, the evidence suggests that it was not a common occurrence. More frequent were cases in which the jealousy was based on an infidelity for which there was no evidence. Legal representatives for men who had murdered their wives in a fit of false jealousy, used the insanity defence to avoid the death penalty.[49] In cases where it was accepted that the wife had not been unfaithful, the husband's jealousy was viewed as delusional and symptomatic of a mental disorder. In 1870, Andrew Dolan, a farmer from Leitrim, killed his wife by stabbing her with a knife. The police reported that 'he laboured under an unfounded suspicion of his wife's infidelity'.[50] Similarly, in 1887, James Casey, a baker from County Louth, killed his 60-year-old wife Mary Anne, on a public road near Ardee. According to the police report, 'her skull was fractured and she received other injuries which caused immediate death. The weapon used was an iron hammer. It is believed that jealousy was the cause of the crime.'[51] Dolan and Casey were found to be insane, and sent to Dundrum (see Table 4.1). These men, and others like them, were viewed with some leniency within Dundrum and pleas for clemency were often presented to the Lord Lieutenant by the medical superintendent. For example, in the report of 1855, one such man is referred to:

> The lunatic labours under a disadvantage in one respect; for, though acquitted of a moral crime, he may still become the penal sufferer by a more lengthened confinement. Amongst other instances under our cognizance, as illustrative of this view, we shall refer to … a man in the Central Asylum, who it was proved whilst labouring under maniacal excitement from jealousy towards his wife in consequence of her

supposed freedom of conduct, committed homicide. On recovery from his insanity he was brought to trial, when the fact was proved. This person is now quite sane, and has been so for some years.[52]

Some of these men were discharged home and some to district lunatic asylums, depending on their state of mind and the willingness of families to have them return home. The arguments used in pleas for clemency for these men were not entirely logical, as the original sentence had often been based on the premise that the act of violence based on 'insane' jealousy was a symptom of an underlying mental disorder. If this was the situation, as it proved to be with some patients in Dundrum, then the symptoms of insanity would not have disappeared completely, but would have surfaced later in life. The fact that they did not re-appear might indicate that they were not insane at the time of the crime and should have been convicted of murder.

MURDER AND MANSLAUGHTER

For some men, the fact that they had been drunk at the time of the crime did not sway the court towards leniency, with dire consequences. They were sentenced to death. In 1892, John Boyle, a labourer from County Tyrone, was found guilty of murdering his 30-year-old wife, Annie, and was sentenced to death. He was executed on 6 January 1893.[53] According to the police report:

> [The] accused returned to his home in an intoxicated state, about ten o'clock pm on 2nd November. The body of deceased was found next morning in the house with the skull and spine fractured and other marks of violence. The husband and wife had had frequent quarrels. He was of a fiery temper and it is said that deceased was sometimes in the habit of drinking.[54]

It was not unusual for men to be sentenced to death for killing a woman, although by the 1890s, when John Boyle appeared before the courts, the use of the death sentence had decreased greatly – from a high of sixty in 1848, to seventeen in 1851, sinking to six in 1854, and remaining in single figures for the remaining years of the century.[55] As the number of death sentence convictions decreased, so too did the number of executions. Many appeals for clemency to the Lord Lieutenant led to a reduction in the sentence from 'death' to 'penal servitude for life'. With the exception of the year of the Maam Trasna murders in 1883, when twelve men were hanged, executions were in single figures throughout the second half of the century.[56] This pattern was reflected in what happened to men who killed women. An analysis of prison and RIC records for the period 1850–1900 revealed at least ten men sentenced to death for this crime, only two of whom were executed.[57] Both of these men had killed their wives. One was John Boyle and the other was Dr P.H.E. Cross.

It is not clear from the records that exist on the case of John Boyle, why he was executed while others were not. Perhaps there was additional evidence of violence towards his wife. The second case in which an execution was carried out is clearer. This was a case of poison. Dr Cross, a retired army surgeon from Cork, who murdered his 49-year-old wife in 1887. According to the police report:

> Mrs Mary Laura Cross, aged 49 years, wife of Dr P. H. E. Cross, retired army surgeon, of Shandy Hall, Dripsey, died on 2nd June 1887 and was buried. In consequence of rumours afloat in the neighbourhood concerning suspicious circumstances attending her death, her body was exhumed on 21st July 1887 and the necessary parts removed for analysis. It was found on examination that the intestines contained a quantity of strychnine and arsenic and the medical evidence went to show that the deceased died from the effects of poison. It is believed she was poisoned by her husband in order that he might marry another lady, who became his wife shortly afterwards.[58]

Cross was tried at the Cork Winter Assizes in 1887 and was hanged on 10 January 1888.[59] The crucial element here seemed to be the use of poison, which implied premeditation and the intent to kill. Nineteenth-century courts were very unforgiving of those who used poison to kill or injure others. David Dripps, a farmer from Londonderry, was sentenced to death for poisoning his 75-year-old wife in 1873, as was Thomas Price, a labourer from Co. Tyrone, who killed his 66-year-old wife, using arsenic, in 1878.[60] The same sentence was passed on Catherine Delaney from County Tipperary, who also used arsenic to kill her 53-year-old farmer husband Michael, in 1884.[61] Fortunately for Dripps, Price and Delaney, the sentences were reduced to penal servitude for life.

Though it is likely that more than the two men referred to in the RIC records were executed for killing a woman in the second half of the nineteenth century, the number was probably a very low proportion of the 106 men who were executed during this period.[62] By this time, execution was only used for the crimes of murder or treason. As discussed earlier, only people (mostly men) who were regarded as having committed the most serious murders had the death sentence carried out, and very few domestic crimes made it into this category. Most of those sentenced to death appealed their sentence and had it reduced to penal servitude for life (see Table 4.2). Court and police records show at least eight cases in which this happened to men who killed their wives. The most famous of these men was William Burke Kirwan from Dublin, who killed his wife in 1852, and the others were William Slattery (1870), David Dripps (1873), Thomas Price (1878), Matthew Murphy (1884), Thomas Crozier (1886), Patrick Mooney (1891) and John Conran (1893).[63]

Table 4.2 *Wife killers convicted of murder and sentenced to death*

Name	County	Weapon/ Cause of death	Sentence	In Prison
William B. Kirwan	Dublin	Drowning	Reduced PS life	1852
William Slattery	Tipperary	Heavy instrument	Reduced PS life	1870
David Dripps	Londonderry	Poison	Reduced PS life	1873
Thomas Price	Tyrone	Poison	Reduced PS life	1878
Matthew Murphy	Kilkenny	Knife	Reduced PS life	1884–1904
Thomas Crozier	Fermanagh	Gun	Reduced PS life	1886–1906
Dr P.H.E. Cross	Cork	Poison	Executed 10.1.88	1888: 6 mths.
Patrick Mooney	Down	Pickaxe	Reduced PS life	1891
John Boyle	Tyrone	Fractured skull	Executed 6.1.93	1893: 2 mths.
John Conran	Wicklow	Gun	Reduced PS life	1893

Key: PS–Penal servitude in prison
Source: General Prison Board and individual convict records (National Archives of Ireland).

William Burke Kirwan achieved notoriety not only because he killed his wife, but also because he was leading a double life. 35-year-old Kirwan, an artist, lived with his 29-year-old wife, Sarah, 'in a fashionable part of Dublin' at 6 Upper Merrion Street. They had been married for over ten years and had no children.[64] He was also in a long-term relationship with Teresa Kenny, who lived in Sandymount with their seven children. Kirwan divided his time between the two women, spending some nights in Sandymount and some in Merrion Street. The situation became public in early September 1852, when Sarah was found dead among rocks on Ireland's Eye, an island off Howth. She and her husband had been picnicking there during the day, as they had often done before. Post-mortem results revealed that her death was caused by drowning but it was not clear whether or not her husband had played a part in her death. When the story of his relationship with Teresa Kenny became public knowledge, his fate was sealed. In spite of the fact that the evidence was circumstantial, Kirwan was found guilty of murdering his wife Sarah and was sentenced to death. The sentence led to extensive debates in legal and medical circles and to a media frenzy. Efforts to obtain a reprieve were unsuccessful but his death sentence was changed to transportation for life.

> And so, late in January 1853, the order went forth, and the wretched man ... received his sailing orders – to be transported for ever from his comfortable house, his children and his native land, to spend the rest of his life amid the grisly hardships of a convict settlement in Australia.[65]

In fact, Kirwan did not go to Australia. According to M. McDonnell Bodkin K. C., writing in 1918:

> The late Dr P. O'Keefe, formerly doctor of Spike Island prison, told a friend on mine that he accompanied Kirwan when, on his release, as the last prisoner on Spike Island (before it was turned to its present use), he proceeded to Liverpool, whence he sailed to America, with the intention of joining and marrying the mother of his children, whose name figured so prominently at his trial.[66]

The case caused great controversy not only at the time, but for many years afterwards. Richard Lambert, writing in 1935, regarded the sentence as a gross miscarriage of British justice, because of the use of circumstantial evidence to arrive at a murder conviction.

> For it proved that, in nineteenth-century Ireland, a man could receive and serve a life sentence for adultery, combined with suspicion of murder – neither of which offences, in themselves, does our law recognize as punishable crimes.[67]

Other cases did not receive the coverage of the Kirwan case and we have only police and court records to fall back on. What is clear from the sometimes scant police and court records is that each case was judged in its own merits and that the outcome was not predictable. In some cases in which less violence occurred, or where it was judged to have been accidental rather than deliberate, the verdict was often one of manslaughter or of assault, leading to a much lesser shorter sentence. Table 4.3 lists a selection of men referred to in *RIC Returns of Outrages*. The list is not comprehensive, but it shows the range of sentences handed down by the courts.

Table 4.3 *Wife killers convicted of manslaughter or assault*

Name	County	Weapon/ Cause of death	Sentence	In Prison
James McMaster	Antrim	Beating	12 mths. Prison	1868
James Crow	Monaghan	Kicking	12 mths. Prison	1869
Mr Longbridge	Antrim	Stick	4 mths. HL	1884
James Turley	Armagh	Stone	10 yrs. PS	1885
Charles Rehill	Fermanagh	Beating	15 yrs. PS	1885
Hugh Daly	Armagh	Kicking	PS life	1886
Terence Magovern	Cavan	Beating	15 yrs. PS	1889
Peter Molloy	Monaghan	Kicking	9 mths. HL	1889
William McVeigh	Antrim	Push, causing fall	12 mths. HL	1896
William J. McCann	Antrim	Knife	PS life	1898

Key: PS –Penal servitude in prison
      HL –Hard labour in prison

Source: General Prison Board and individual convict records (National Archives of Ireland).

In 1868, James Crow, a publican from County Monaghan, kicked his wife 'in the abdomen' and she died as a result of her injuries. He was sentenced to twelve months imprisonment.[68] In 1896, William McVeigh, from Belfast, was also sentenced to twelve months in prison, this time with 'hard labour' for killing his 28-year-old wife.

> A quarrel took place between them in the house of a friend, *in consequence of the deceased refusing to give her husband money*. Blows were exchanged and the deceased was knocked down and her head coming in contact with the fender, she received injuries which caused almost immediate death. *The parties had been at a wedding and were somewhat under the influence of drink at the time.*[69]

A more serious view was taken of men who had a history of violence towards their wives – men such as Charles Rehill and Terence Magovern. Rehill, a farmer from Dresternaw, County Fermanagh, was sentenced to fifteen years penal servitude for beating his wife to death in 1885. According to the police report:

> Anne Rehill, farmer's wife, aged thirty eight years, died from the effects of the bursting of a blood vessel in the liver, caused by a beating given by her husband, Charles Rehill. *Deceased lived on bad terms with her husband and received much ill-treatment from him.*[70]

A similar story emerged in the case of Ellen Magovern, killed by her husband in 1889. According to the police report:

> Ellen Magovern, farmer's wife, aged fifty years, was found dead in her bed on the morning of 31st October. Death had resulted from dislocation of the neck, caused by the head being forced violently backwards. It is believed the crime was committed by her husband, Terence Magovern. *They had lived unhappily for some years previously, and Magovern had on several occasions ill-treated his wife and subjected her to violence.*[71]

In some of the cases in which the death was judged to be more deliberate, if irrational, the defence fell back on the insanity plea, arguing that a sudden violent act was symptomatic of a previously existing mental disorder. Some of these men were sent to Dundrum and others to a district asylum pending a place in Dundrum. A few had already spent time in an asylum, while the majority lived at home with their families, showing little or no sign of madness.

An exploration of these cases reveals that at a time when dangerous lunacy legislation was being widely used to confine people (especially men) who showed any signs of violence, in a district asylum, some individuals escaped the long arm of the law and did not come to public attention until they killed someone. John Carty, a butcher from County Tipperary, had been in a lunatic asylum for a time but had been released some years before he killed his 40-year-old wife, Mary, in 1884. According to police reports, he 'must have suddenly got a return of his malady, as apparently without any reason, he attacked his wife with a stick in their own house, and fractured her skull'.[72] Three years later, John Dwyer, a farmer from Thurles, killed his 47-year-old wife, Margaret. He too had spent some time in an asylum. The police reported:

> [Mrs Dwyer] left her home accompanied by her husband, John Dwyer, and when in a lonely place, about a mile distant from the house, it is believed that the husband attacked her and killed her by breaking her neck and battering her head with a stone. The accused was of unsound mind. Some weeks previously, he was discharged from a lunatic asylum, where he had been confined for an attempt on his own life.[73]

The fact that this man had attempted suicide, seemed also to convince the court of the unsoundness of his mind. This was a common feature of other cases also. A suicide attempt was seen as symptomatic of a mental disorder and was often used as the basis for committal to a district asylum. Some men made suicide attempts after the crime, though not always successfully. For example, in 1890, William Ivory, a farmer from County Westmeath, killed his 40-year-old wife, Anne, and then tried to kill himself. As can be seen from the police record, this was linked to insanity.

> [Mrs Ivory] died from a gunshot wound in the head, inflicted by her husband. After perpetrating the crime, the accused attempted to drown himself in an adjoining river, and also cut his throat with a razor, inflicting wounds of a serious nature. It is believed that he was at the time of unsound mind.[74]

Another example of a wife-killing accompanied by a suicide attempt and preceded by a period of confinement in a district asylum is that of Michael Fox, a labourer from County Longford, who killed his 59-year-old wife, Bridget, in 1894.

> [Mrs Fox] was beaten by her husband, with an iron bar and also with a heavy club, and received injuries to the brain, from the effects of which she died abut two hours afterwards. The accused subsequently attempted to commit suicide by striking himself on the head with a hatchet and cutting his throat with a razor. He dangerously wounded himself and had to be sent to hospital, where he was detained until he was fit to be placed under arrest. It is believed that he was insane when he committed the crime. In June 1893, he was sent to Mullingar Asylum as a dangerous lunatic and was released in the following December.[75]

All four men, Carty, Dwyer, Ivory and Fox, were found to be insane at the time of their crimes and were ordered to be confined indefinitely as criminal lunatics.

Some of these men were sent first to a district asylum, then to Dundrum and later back to their local district asylum. By the last quarter of the nineteenth century, Dundrum was becoming very over-crowded. Attempts to move people out to district asylums were only successful if the person was quiet and easy to manage. For example, in 1887, after a complete review of all the patients in Dundrum, twelve men and three women were transferred to their local district asylums and again, in 1891, twenty-eight men and eleven women were transferred. All were described as insane and as 'fit subjects for a lunatic asylum'. Other descriptions included 'quiet and harmless', 'hardworking', 'slightly depressed', and 'too demented to work'.[76] The majority of those transferred had spent over twenty years in Dundrum, so it is clear that court decisions to sentence a person as a criminal lunatic often led to a life-time in confinement. These transfers made way for the admission of men like Carty, Dwyer, Ivory and Fox who, unless they had the means and the education to argue their way out of there, were likely to remain locked away from society for most of their adult lives.

Table 4.4 *Matricide: Male killers convicted of murder or manslaughter*

Name	County	Weapon/ Cause of death	Sentence	In Prison
John Heaney	Antrim	Fall caused by push	4 mths. In prison	1885
John Ahern	Cork	Hammer	5 years PS	1888–95
Rev. G. Griffith	Kerry	Gun	Death, reduced to PS life	1893
Michael McCann	Antrim	Fists/beating	14 years PS	1900

Key: PS –Penal servitude in prison
Sources: General Prison Board and individual convict records (National Archives of Ireland).

MATRICIDE

There is something particularly shocking about a son who kills his mother. Police records from the nineteenth century show that this crime was fairly rare – as it continues to be today. An analysis of RIC records for the period 1838–1900 revealed that out of sixty-six men who killed women, eight had killed their mothers, one a stepmother and one a mother-in-law.[77] All of the men seemed to live with their mothers, a fact showing their financial interdependence. In most cases the place of residence was the family farm. Two of the mothers were in their fifties, but the others were in their seventies. Of the eight cases examined for this discussion, four were found to be insane at the time of the crime and sent to Dundrum on an indefinite sentence, one was sentenced to death but had the sentence later reduced to penal servitude for life, two received prison sentences and one committed suicide (see Tables 4.4 and 4.5).

The death sentence was passed in the only case in which a gun was involved. It was different to the others in a number of other ways also – the family was fairly prosperous, the mother was quite young, and the perpetrator of the crime was a clergyman. The crime happened on the 23 June 1893 in Tralee, County Kerry. According to the police report:

Mrs Lucy Griffith, widow, aged fifty four years, was shot by her son, the Rev. George C. Griffith, Protestant clergyman, in the drawing room of their house, sometime between eleven o'clock and twelve o'clock noon. The accused fired three shots from a revolver into the head of the deceased. Two of the bullets were found in the skull, and the third, which appeared to have been fired when the deceased was on the floor, was found embedded in the carpet of the room, under her head. The accused and his mother seemed to have lived on the most affectionate terms, and the crime would appear to have been committed when the former was suffering from temporary insanity. It is stated there had been lunacy in the family and that the mind of the accused became affected owing to his pecuniary difficulties.[78]

From this report, it appears that though the family was fairly well-off, living in a house with a 'drawing room' and 'carpet', the Rev. Griffith was in some kind of unspecified money trouble – recorded by the police as 'pecuniary difficulties'.

As usual, the police report gave a possible motivation for the crime. In this case, it pointed towards 'unsoundness of mind', as there was evidence of insanity in the family and it was widely believed, at the time, that heredity was the most powerful factor in the transmission of mental disorder. Griffith was tried at the Tralee Summer Assizes of 1893, but the jury did not reach a verdict and he was tried again at the Cork Winter Assizes later that year. The jury's indecision is understandable when one reads the account of the trial in the *Journal of Mental Science*.[79] While the defence built up a picture of a man who could be described as insane, the judge was not convinced that his mental state removed legal responsibility for the crime.

One witness said that his 'habits as a boy were very eccentric' and that 'he was quiet and depressed and did not care for companionship'. Another witness said he heard Griffith talking to himself one night about a month before the crime. 'He was gesticulating and after a time jumped up and washed his hands and then proceeded to make his bed. He always made his own bed and washed his hands fifteen times a day.' The local doctor, Leslie Crosbie, who had been called to see Mrs Griffith two days before she died, also noticed some strange behaviour on the part of her son. He told the court that he thought Griffith was 'getting softening of the brain'. The final word on his mental state was given by the expert witness, Dr Oscar Woods, medical superintendent at Cork District Asylum. When asked if he considered that the facts he had heard about the defendant's behaviour pointed to insanity, he told the court:

I consider that they are evidence all through life of an exceedingly unstable mind, and that he was on the border line of sanity and insanity for many years. I consider there is in this case some hereditary predisposition which would act as a predisposing cause, liable to be set aflame by a comparatively slight exciting cause.[80]

Dr Woods was not allowed to give an opinion on whether or not Griffith was responsible for his actions at the time of the crime, because the judge felt that this was the question the jury had to try. According to the report on the case in the *Journal of Mental Science*, the judge said that:

Every man was presumed to be sane by the law, because if they were to excuse misconduct or crime committed upon persons on the suggestion merely that they were not in that state of mind that would make them morally responsible, all society would be at an end, unless it was made out on sufficient evidence to warrant them in coming to that conclusion ... The question was not whether he exhibited eccentricities or peculiarities of manner. The question was whether on the 23rd June he knew he was doing what was wrong or not ... Did he know at the time he put this revolver to his mother's head and fired it – did he know that he was doing wrong?[81]

The jury finally agreed a verdict of guilty of murder, but recommended the prisoner to mercy 'on the ground of his weak intellect'. Griffith was sentenced to be hanged. The possession and use of a gun was viewed as evidence of deliberate intent. The date for the execution was set for 9 January 1894, but fortunately for the Rev. George, the sentence was commuted to penal servitude for life. We don't know what happened to him after this. If Dr Woods was correct in his prediction, he may have ended his days in an asylum.[82] If not, he may have been freed after a few years in prison.

In contrast to Griffith, John Heaney, from County Antrim, who killed his 70-year-old mother, Margaret, in 1885, got a very light sentence, as her death was viewed as accidental. Margaret, a charwoman, died from the effects of an assault by her son. According to the police report:

It would appear that a dispute arose between the mother and son, and that she remonstrated with him regarding his idleness and intemperance and struck him. He thereupon pushed her out of the house causing her to fall and fracture her thigh bone.[83]

Heaney was sentenced to just four months imprisonment. A longer sentence was given to John Ahern, from Cork, who killed his 60-year-old mother, Julia, in 1888. He was also lucky, as the crime had an element of cruelty and was linked to alcohol consumption – a combination of characteristics that could have led to a finding of temporary insanity. Julia, who worked as a housekeeper, died from a wound to the head received from her son.

> An altercation arose between them, and the son, who was under the influence of drink, flung a hammer at his mother. The wooden handle struck her on the head, inflicting a wound which proved fatal.[84]

Ahern was sentenced to five years penal servitude. Heaney and Ahern and their mothers lived in the kind of family arrangement that was very common in post-Famine rural Ireland – the single son living on the family farm with an ageing parent.

Table 4.5 *Matricide: Male killers found to be insane at the time of the crime*

Name	County	Weapon/Cause of death	Diagnosis/ cause	In Asylum*
Patrick McCarthy	Cork	Hatchet	Imbecility	1869–91
Edmund Hart	Kilkenny	Knife	Insanity	1890
John Kean	Longford	Knife	Deaf and dumb	1892
James Mitchell	Galway	Suffocation	Insanity	1892

* Some went to Dundrum and some to district asylums.

Sources: Medical records (Dundrum), RIC records and individual convict files (National Archives of Ireland).

Four of the men who killed their mothers did find their way into an asylum – via the prison system (see Table 4.5). Two of the killings were particularly gruesome and there is some indication in the files that the men were intellectually disabled as well as having a mental disorder at the time of the crime. Edmond Hart, a labourer from Kilkenny, killed his 75-year-old mother, Mary, in 1890. According to police records, '[Edmund] was at the time in a state of insanity. The body of the deceased was disemboweled, a portion of the thighs mutilated, the face disfigured and partly eaten away by the accused.'[85] This case was tragic in a number of ways. First of all, Hart showered horrific abuse on his mother. However, she had not been the cause of his anger. According to the report in the *Kilkenny Journal*, he was a fisherman who also worked on his wife's family farm. His anger knew no bounds when his mother-in-law sold the farm. He threatened to kill her or the landlord. However, nobody predicted that he would do it, least of all his mother.[86] Equally shocking, was the crime of James Mitchell, from County Galway, who killed his 70-year-old mother, Mary, in 1892. She was described in police records as a farmer and we can assume that her son worked and lived on the farm. The description in the police report was graphic.

> At about six o'clock am [on 20th September] the accused came to the police barrack at Castleblakeney and stated that he had killed his mother. The police proceeded to the house and found the body of the deceased lying on a bed. Her tongue had been torn out and was lying on her neck. It was found that death was due to suffocation, caused by blood flowing into the lungs. The accused is believed to have been insane when he committed the outrage. He had previously been very kind to his mother and lived on the most friendly terms with her.[87]

Both Hart and Mitchell were sent to Dundrum as criminal lunatics, as were also Patrick McCarthy and John Kean. McCarthy, from Clonakilty, County Cork, killed his mother, who was a widow, in 1868. We don't know, from the records, what age this woman was, but we know that she owned a farm and 'died from the results of frightful injuries inflicted on her head with a hatchet' by her son Patrick. Because he was one of the patients transferred from Dundrum in the 1890s, we can track his asylum career. He was described in medical notes variously, as 'very treacherous and violent', 'quiet, amiable and stupid' and as suffering from 'imbecility or moral insanity'. The phrase 'moral insanity' was often used to describe individuals of 'weak intellect' who could not distinguish right from wrong. Patrick McCarthy remained in Dundrum until 1891 (twenty-three years in confinement) when he was transferred to Cork District Asylum. He was described then as 'quiet, [with] chronic dementia'.[88]

Just as McCarthy was leaving Dundrum, another man who had killed his mother was about to be admitted. This was John Kean, from County Longford, who killed his 70-year-old mother, Catherine, in 1892. She was also described as a farmer. At the time of the crime, she had refused to give her son money for clothes. He was described as 'deaf and dumb and said to be not quite sane'. He attacked his mother 'with a shoemaker's knife and inflicted several incised and punctured wounds about her face and head'.[89] This woman had probably done her best for this son, whose disability would have marked him out as outcast in a society that had little tolerance and no support services for men like Kean. Unfortunately for her, as she became frail, he became powerful, with terrible consequences for both of them.

Some men decided that they could not face the world after committing a crime that shocked even themselves. They committed suicide. As we have seen already, this was not unusual in cases where men killed their loved ones. However, not all of them were successful in their efforts. One man who did succeed was no stranger to violence. Unlike most of the other men described here, this man was probably only in his twenties and it was not the first time he had hit his mother. His name was Thomas Hall Cinnamond, a farmer from Muckamore, County Antrim, who killed his 56-year-old mother in 1900. According to the police report:

> The son quarrelled with his mother because his dinner was not ready when he returned from Belfast. She left the house and he ran after her, caught her by the arm and pulled her round. She fell, and he kicked her while she was lying on the ground. She became unconscious and died shortly afterwards from an effusion of blood on the brain. When the offender found that his mother could not live, he showed great remorse and at once committed suicide by shooting himself through the head with a gun. It appears that the offender, who was a man of violent temper, had frequently quarrelled with his mother and assaulted her on previous occasions.[90]

Anyone reading this report will see all the elements of domestic violence that continue to feature in the abuse of women by their male relatives. It is very difficult for a woman to admit to being abused by her son. Like many other women who kept silent about domestic violence, she died a violent death at the hands of her abuser.

FEIGNING MADNESS

Men who continued to show signs of mental disorder after their crimes, were probably the truly 'mad' who 'deserved' to be sidetracked from the prison system, as they were not responsible for their actions. However, this could not be said for many of those whose violence had occurred during a bout of 'temporary insanity' or 'transitory frenzy' and who appeared completely sane within a short period after the crime. These were men like Dr Terence Brodie, John Logue and Allan Spiller, whose delusions at the time of the conviction persuaded the juries of their insanity, but who were released within six or seven years of their crime, having been perfectly sane for most of their time in confinement. The problem with temporary delusions was that the authorities (medical or legal) were not always sure what these delusions represented. Were they part of a chronic condition that preceded the crime – leading to the conclusion that the homicide was a manifestation of insanity? Were they transitory – connected to the actual situation surrounding the homicide but caused by alcohol or epilepsy? Were they a clever ploy to explain an act of temporary cruelty – a form of words that would lead to a medical recommendation for an acquittal from responsibility?

Some of these explanations were considered in the case of Dr Terence Brodie. The court came to the conclusion that his delusions were transitory but real and that they were connected to the consumption of alcohol. Two other cases that appear in convict records are equally controversial – these are the cases of Allan Spiller and John Logue.

Allan Spiller, a 26-year-old Presbyterian salesman from Belfast, killed his wife and two children – by cutting their throats with a razor and assaulting them with a hammer in 1892. According to the police report:

> Mrs Elizabeth Spiller, aged twenty seven years, and her children, James Alexander, aged three years, and Annetta Hampton, aged one year and nine months, were murdered in their residence. The accused enticed the deceased persons into a garret, where he cut their throats with a razor and assaulted them with a hammer, inflicting wounds which caused immediate death. He then surrendered himself to the police, and admitted his guilt, stating that he would have committed suicide, but that cowardice prevented him. The accused has been out of employment and appears to have committed the fatal act through fear that his wife and children would become destitute and dependent on the charity of others.[91]

According to his medical record at Dundrum, Spiller was depressed until his trial and hoped that he would 'be found guilty and hanged for his crime' as he had 'no wish to live'. At his first trial in July, he was found 'unfit to plead', but later was found 'guilty but insane' and admitted to Dundrum to be held indefinitely. Spiller made a dramatic recovery of his sanity and within a year of his confinement, he was described by the medical superintendent, Dr George Revington, as being 'sociable and a good worker' and 'a fair wicket keeper'. By then, he had convinced medical staff that he was not responsible for his crime. The medical notes are sympathetic:

> [T]he anxiety of trying to support his family ... family troubles between his wife's people and himself, want of sleep and sufficient nourishment, all these worries in a delicate constitution ... caused an attack of homicidal melancholia.[92]

In 1899, Spiller was described by Dr Revington as 'a pleasant, fairly well educated man, possessed with a certain amount of ability and far superior to the penal class of asylum patients. He presents no symptoms of insanity.' In fact, Spiller, like Brodie was one of the few educated patients in Dundrum. Though he was just a 'salesman' and not a member of any profession (as Brodie was) he obviously came from a background of some priviledge. He was also a good cricket player – a skill that endeared him to the staff. Spiller had no history of mental disorder and was considered sane for most of the time he spent in confinement. After seven years in Dundrum, he was discharged to relatives. Perhaps Spiller was truly insane at the time of his crime, and perhaps he was not. However, he was certainly helped by the fact that his education and social manners were more like those of the medical staff than those of the other criminal lunatics.

Another example of a miraculous return to sanity was more controversial at the time. John Logue, a 28-year-old policeman from Woodford, County Galway, shot his ex-girlfriend and her mother in 1902. The girl, Lizzie, survived but her mother died. The precipitating factor was the news that Lizzie was about to marry someone else. According to the police report:

> Maria McCormack, publican, aged 50 years, was shot by Constable John Logue RIC in the following circumstances. About 11.30 pm, the Constable came to Mrs McCormack's door and asked to see her. Mrs McCormack went outside the door to speak to him. Hearing their voices raised in altercation, Eliza McCormack, daughter of above named, went out, and immediately Logue fired six shots from a revolver at them. Two of the bullets entered Mrs McCormack's abdomen and she died about two hours afterwards. Three bullets struck Eliza McCormack, one passing through the right arm and two others through the breast, but she recovered from the injuries. The motive for this crime was that Mrs McCormack had refused to sanction Logue's addresses to Eliza McCormack, and the last named was about to marry another man.[93]

Logue was arrested and brought to Galway Prison while awaiting trial. While there, he engaged in such bizarre behaviour that a doctor was called to see him on a daily basis. The report of the prison medical officer, Dr Kinkead, on 3rd September gives us an idea of this behaviour:

> He would reply to no questions nor would he speak, seemed to have some difficulty standing. On being let down on his bed he did not fall flat, but at first his head and shoulders were raised, then he sank down with his forehead on the pillow, then he half raised himself and

appeared to follow with his eyes some object at the end of the cell, then lay down, then raised himself, and his eyes moved as if again following [an] object, then lay down again. His breakfast untouched was in the cell.[94]

Three days later, Logue continued to worry the authorities. Dr Kinkead wrote of his visit on 6 September:

Logue reported violent last evening and during [the] night. Attacked men in charge. A third man had to be placed in cell. [He] did not sleep at all. On my visit I found him being held in bed by two men. Breathing hurried, pulse rapid and weak, eyes turned towards right, pupils regular, does not speak.[95]

Logue continued to become more violent and Dr Kinkead visited him daily. On 8 September, he wrote:

Getting more restless and more violent. Taking some tea and beef tea. Giving him nutrient enemas. He gets violent every 10 minutes. Eyes rolling, swallows, struggles violently and kicks. Makes efforts to get out of bed. It has taken three men to restrain him.[96]

Dr Kinkead's complete report was sent to the Chief Secretary's office in Dublin Castle, with a request for a visit from Sir George O'Farrell, inspector of lunatics and a member of the General Prison Board. O'Farrell, accompanied by Dr Stewart Woodhouse, visited Logue on 13, 14 and 15 September and concluded that he was feigning insanity. They based this conclusion on a number of facts which they outlined in their report to the prison: the fact that the onset of the condition was sudden, that Logue presented the symptoms of different forms of mental disease, that the paralysis in his legs disappeared within two days, and that his physical health was improving. He was visited again in mid-October by O'Farrell and Woodhouse, who again concluded that 'he appears perfectly rational'. They did agree that he was 'very nervous, flushes, and is easily startled'. In spite of their reports, which were presented to the court, Logue was found 'guilty but insane' at the Sligo Winter Assizes on 4 December 1902, and sent to Dundrum.[97] He later admitted to medical staff in Dundrum that he had indeed been acting a part.

I feigned insanity. Sir George O'Farrell and Dr Woodhouse were twice down in Galway to see me. They said I did it badly, but I did not know how to do it well. I knew nothing of insanity and had nothing to go on. I refused food, did not speak for seven weeks, tried to remain awake, shouted, jumped out of bed, threw myself about, attacked the warders [and] struggled with them as long as I was able to. I did not need to hurt them. There was never anything wrong with my mind but I wanted to save my life.[98]

Logue's behaviour was completely normal after admission to Dundrum. Dr Revington, medical superintendent, said of him: 'He is a very quiet and most respectable man and is very anxious to get on well here. I have no doubt that he is and always was perfectly sane.' After five years of confinement, he was conditionally discharged to his sister, Bridget, in County Donegal. After his discharge, there was a lengthy correspondence between the office of the Lord Lieutenant and various people speaking on behalf of Logue. The official focus was on his behaviour. The local RIC sent yearly reports, saying he was doing well and keeping temperate, although he 'fell out with' lots of people, including his two sisters and a clergyman who had vouched for him. Logue's focus was on the issue of compensation, which he claimed for the loss and damage to his clothes and his bicycle while he was in Dundrum.

The correspondence between Logue and the lunacy inspectorate about his property, showed a man who found it difficult to take 'No' for an answer. Dr Revington, the medical superintendent in Dundrum at the time of Logue's confinement, had kept his clothes and bicycle in the store-room as a favour to Logue. In the normal course of events, the property of patients was returned to their family, at the time of admission. Logue did not wish his mother to know about his crime or his punishment, a wish that was respected. One of the letters written by Logue to Dr Revington in 1908 shows something of his temperament.

> As regards your not accepting liability for the state of my belongings, I hold a written document from James McDonough stating that he has a distinct recollection of your telling me in the shoemakers-ship, 'Make your mind easy about those clothes of yours, Logue. I will keep them safe for you'. Have you done so? Constable John Ferris is prepared to state that you sent him to seek storeage [*sic*] in Dublin without my knowledge or consent. Two officials in Dundrum heard me request your permission to have my clothes kept in the shoe-shop in order to look after them. This you declined to do. I also asked you to have them sent to Prescotts to be cleaned etc. This you also declined to do ... I shall for reasons already stated accept £5 compensation for damages to top coat suit and bicycle, and take all as they are.[99]

Logue's clothes were delivered to him in Malin Head, County Donegal, the cost of 'conveyance' having been paid by the inspectorate of lunacy.

The correspondence as to compensation for what appears to be moth-damage to one jacket and slight rust to his bicycle, does not indicate that he got his £5. Other correspondence in his convict file in 1909 shows that Logue got into a dispute with the sister, who had taken legal responsibility for him on discharge, and with the local priest. His second sister, Kate, signed an undertaking in June 1909 to 'keep watch over him' and to report any potential for dangerous behaviour – an indication that his other sister, Bridget, had refused to continue with this responsibility. Fortunately for his family and for others with whom he was in dispute, Logue got married in February 1911 and emigrated to the US two months later. One wonders if he turned up again in the criminal justice system or the mental health system in his country of adoption. From reading the files on this man, it is clear that he was a very difficult character. Whether or not he was mentally ill is open to question.

The case of John Logue brings us to the end of this chapter on men who killed women. What we have learned is that while most victims of male killers were male, a significant number of them were female. Women were most at risk from men who were closely related to them either by marriage or birth. The range of outcomes for the killer was wide. Some cases never went to trial, due to lack of evidence, and of those that did, less than 50 per cent led to convictions.[100] Because official crime records do not give a sufficient level of detail to do a complete analysis of the verdicts, we have to rely on a snapshot taken from RIC reports for two years for which this detail is provided – 1868 and 1884.[101] In 1868, six men were arrested for killing women. Four of these men killed their wives. The fifth had killed his mother and the sixth his aunt. Only one of the six, Patrick McCarthy from County Cork, who killed his mother, was found to be insane and sent to Dundrum as a criminal lunatic. Three were acquitted and two got twelve months imprisonment.[102] In 1884, the situation was similar. Of the six men who killed women, four killed their wives, one his stepmother and one a neighbour (in a land dispute). Two were sent to Dundrum, two were acquitted, one was sentenced to four months in prison with hard labour and one was sentenced to death. Those acquitted or given short sentences were usually judged to have been involved in an argument which escalated into an attack. The man sentenced to death, Matthew Murphy from County Kilkenny, had cut his estranged wife's throat as she lay asleep in her own home. His sentence was later reduced to penal servitude for life and he spent twenty years in prison.[103]

These and other cases have formed the basis for the discussion in this chapter. As a final word, we can say that the killing of women by men was clearly not an unusual crime in nineteenth-century Ireland. Murder is never an acceptable crime, but at a time when political unrest and disputes over land were given the highest priority in the criminal justice system, domestic violence, leading sometimes to death, was not high on the agenda of either the police or the media. This is not surprising, as it continues to be part of the 'dark figure' of crime.

NOTES

1 There is some dispute about Mrs Brodie's age. While 43 is the age given in the *RIC Return of Outrages*, the death register gives her age at death as 60. This would make her over twenty years older than her husband. (Pearce E. Rood, Personal communication.)

2 *RIC Return of Outrages for 1886*, Homicides (NAI, CSO ICR2), p. 8.

3 *London Times*, 13 July 1886. This reference and other facts, brought to my attention by Pearce E. Rood, are gratefully acknowledged.

4 Court Report of Galway C. and P. Crown Assizes 1887, (Hereafter, Galway Court Report), Verdict statement, 16th March 1887 (NAI, 1C-19–153).

5 Galway Court Report, Witness statement of Coleman Naughton on 15th July 1886.

6 Galway Court Report, Witness statement of Frank Feely on 15th July 1886.

7 Galway Court Report, Witness statement of Bridget McDonough on 15th July 1886.

8 Galway Court Report, Witness statement of Coleman Naughton on 15th July 1886.

9 Ibid.

10 Ibid.

11 Galway Court Report, Witness statement of Bridget McDonough on 15th July 1886.

12 D. Yellowlees, 'Case of Murder during Temporary Insanity induced by Drinking or Epilepsy', *The Journal of Mental Science*, xxix, 127 (October 1883), pp. 382–7.

13 Anon., 'Psychological Retrospect', *The Journal of Mental Science*, xxviii, 121 (April 1882), pp. 119–25; S.W. North, 'Insanity and Crime' *Journal of Mental Science*, xxxii, 138 (July 1886), pp. 163–81.

14 *Cox's Criminal Law Cases*: Report of cases in all courts of England and Ireland (London: John Crockford, Law Times Offices), Vol. xiv: 1877–82, pp. 563–4.

15 Ibid., p. 563.

16 This account of Dr Brodie's life is based on an unpublished study by Pearce E. Rood. Personal communication 2007.

17 Pearce E. Rood. Personal communication, 2007.

18 Information on the Bunbury family supplied by Pearce E. Rood. Personal communication 2007.

19 As noted already, there is some dispute about Molly's age. Based on police records she was likely to have been seven years older than Terence, but based on the register of deaths, she may have been over twenty years older than him.

20 *Cox's Criminal Law Cases*, p. 563.

21 Information on convict appeals which includes material on Terence Brodie (NAI, CRF, Misc. 1420/ 1897).

22 Letter addressed to the Governor of Dundrum, 26 May 1887 in a file on convict appeals, which includes material on Terence Brodie (NAI, CRF, Misc. 1420/ 1897).

23 Calculated from data by Lawrence H. Officer, *Purchasing power of British Pounds from 1264 to 2006*, available on www.measuringworth.com.

24 Memorial from solicitor for Dr Brodie in June 1892, in a file on convict appeals, which includes material on Terence Brodie (NAI, CRF, Misc. 1420/ 1897).

25 This account of Dr Brodie's life is based on an unpublished study by Pearce E. Rood. Personal communication, 2007.

26 Information supplied by Pearce E. Rood. Personal communication 2007.

27 A. V. Merlo and J. M. Pollock, *Women, Law and Social Control*, (Boston, MA: Allyn and Bacon, 1995), Chapter 11.

28 *RIC Return of Outrages 1838–1921* (NAI, CSO ICR1; NAI, CSO ICR2; NAI, Police Reports 1882–1921, Box 4); Carolyn A. Conley, *Melancholy Accidents* (Lanham MD: Lexington Books, 1999).

29 Conley, *Melancholy Accidents*; Mark Finnane, 'A decline in violence in Ireland? Crime, policing and social relations, 1860–1914', *Crime, History and Societies*, 1, 1 (1997), pp. 51–70; Elizabeth Malcolm, *The Irish Policeman, 1822–922: A Life* (Dublin: Four Courts Press, 2005); Ian O'Donnell, 'Lethal Violence in Ireland, 1841–2003', *British Journal of Criminology*, Journal no. 45 (2005), pp 671–95; William Wilbanks, 'Homicide in Ireland', *International Journal of Comparative and Applied Criminal Justice*, 20, 1 (Spring 1996), pp. 59–75.

30 For example, see Conley, *Melancholy Accidents*, Table 4.1, p. 92.

31 *Return of Outrages 1838–1921* (NAI, CSO ICR1; NAI, CSO ICR2; NAI, Police Reports 1882–1921, Box 4). As noted already, the RIC records give this level of detail from 1868 only and do not include the Dublin area. For statistics on the same data, see Conley, *Melancholy Accidents*, p. 68.

32 Most of the examples of crimes used here are from RIC records, supplemented by information from convict record files, newspapers and court material.

33 *Asylums Report*, HC 1854–5 (1981) xvi, 137, p.155.

34 C. Lockhart Robertson,'A case of homicidal mania, without disorder of the intellect', *The Journal of Mental Science*, ix, 47 (October 1863), pp. 327–43.

35 Conley, *Melancholy Accidents*, Table 4.1, p. 92.

36 *Asylums Report*, HC 1864 (3369) xxiii, 317, p. 379.

37 Anon., 'Psychological Retrospect'; North, 'Insanity and Crime'; Yellowlees, 'Case of Murder'.

38 Yellowlees, 'Case of Murder', p. 386.

39 *RIC Return of Outrages for 1868* (NAI, CSO ICR1), Homicides, p. 5.

40 *RIC Return of Outrages for 1868* (NAI, CSO ICR1), Homicides, p. 8.

41 *RIC Return of Outrages for 1884*, Homicides, p. 3, and *1885*, p. 18 (NAI, CSO ICR2).

42 Conley, *Melancholy Accidents*, p. 69.

43 Ibid., p. 70.

44 *Cox's Criminal Law Cases*, 1843–1900; M. McDonnell Bodkin, *Famous Irish Trials* (Dublin: Blackhall Publishing, 1997 [1918]).

45 North, 'Insanity and Crime'; Yellowlees, 'Case of Murder'.

46 *RIC Return of Outrages for 1883* (NAI, CSO ICR2), Homicides, p. 10.

47 Lunacy (Ireland) Act 1821 (1 & 2 Geo 4 c. 33); Central Criminal Lunatic Asylum (Ireland) Act 1845 (8 & 9 Vic c. 107); Trial of Lunatics (Ireland) Act 1883 (46 & 47 Vic c. 38). For more detail, see Appendix 1.

48 J. Guillais, *Crimes of Passion: Dramas of Private Life in Nineteenth-Century France* (Oxford: Polity Press, 1986), p. 25. According to Article 324, line 2 of the Penal Code in France, a husband who murdered his wife or her lover when he caught them *in flagrante delicto* had committed excusable murder.

49 For discussion on a case (Matthew Murphy) in which the plea was not successful, see Conley, *Melancholy Accidents*, p. 63.

50 *RIC Return of Outrages for 1870* (NAI, CSO ICR1), Homicides, p. 10.

51 *RIC Return of Outrages for 1887* (NAI, CSO ICR2), Homicides, p. 5.

52 *Asylums Report*, HC 1854–55 (1981) xvi, 137, p. 17. No name or identifying information was given on this man.

53 *Death Book (Male) 1852–1932* (NAI, GPB CN 5).

54 *RIC Return of Outrages for 1892* (NAI, Police Reports 1882–1921, Box 4), Homicides, p. 5.

55 See Table 1.1: Sentences passed on criminal offenders in Ireland, 1845–51, in chapter 1; *Criminal Tables for 1852 (Ireland)*, p. 436. HC 1852–53 [338] lxxxi. 347; Carroll-Burke, *Colonial Discipline*, pp. 30–1.

56 *Death Book (Male) 1852–1932* (NAI, GPB CN 5).

57 *RIC Return of Outrages 1838–1921* (NAI, CSO ICR1; NAI, CSO ICR2; NAI, *Police Reports 1882–1921*, Box 4); *Death Book (Male) 1852–1932* (NAI, GPB CN 5); This figure does not include the Dublin area, as the same level of detail was not available in the DMP records. However, as crime in the Dublin area was as high if not higher than in other areas of the country, it is likely that many more men met the same fate.

58 *RIC Return of Outrages for 1887* (NAI, CSO ICR2), Homicides, p. 10.

59 *Death Book (Male) 1852–1932* (NAI, GPB CN 5).

60 *RIC Return of Outrages for 1873* (NAI, CSO ICR1), Homicides, p. 4; and *for 1878*, p. 5.

61 *RIC Return of Outrages for 1884* (NAI, CSO, ICR2), Homicides, p.11; NAI, PEN 1898/ 121 (Delaney).

62 Record of executions 1850–99 in *Death Book (Male) 1852–1932* (NAI, GPB CN 5).

63 *Death Book (Male and Female) 1852–1932* (NAI, GPB CN 5); *RIC Return of Outrages for 1850–1900* (NAI, ICR 1–3 and Police Reports 1882–1921, Box 4).

64 R.S. Lambert, *When Justice Failed* (Essex Street, London: Methuen, 1935), p. 162.

65 Ibid., p. 224.

66 Ibid., p. 84.

67 Lambert, *When Justice Failed*, p. 224.

68 *RIC Return of Outrages for 1868*, Homicides, p. 6.

69 *RIC Return of Outrages for 1896*, (NAI, CSO, ICR2), Homicides, p. 8. Italics in original report.

70 *RIC Return of Outrages for 1885*, (NAI, CSO, ICR2), Homicides, p. 5. Italics in original report.

71 *RIC Return of Outrages for 1895*, (NAI, CSO, ICR2), Homicides, p. 4. Italics in original report.

72 *RIC Return of Outrages for 1884*, (NAI, CSO, ICR2), Homicides, p. 11; *RIC Return of Outrages for 1885*, Homicides, p. 19 (NAI, CSO ICR2).

73 *RIC Return of Outrages for 1887* (NAI, CSO ICR2), Homicides, p. 13.

74 *RIC Return of Outrages for 1891* (NAI, CSO ICR2), Homicides, p. 13.

75 *RIC Return of Outrages for 1894* (NAI, Police Reports 1882–1921, Box 4), Homicides, p. 6.

76 Transfers from Dundrum to District Asylums 1891 (NAI, CRF Misc. 392/ 1891).

77 *Return of Outrages 1838–1921* (NAI, CSO ICR1; NAI, CSO ICR2; NAI, *Police Reports 1882–1921*, Box 4); *Death Book (Male) 1852–1932* (NAI, GPB CN 5). This figure is not complete, as details on crimes are only available from 1868, and the data does not include the Dublin area, as the same level of detail was not available in the DMP records.

78 *RIC Return of Outrages for 1893* (NAI, Police Reports 1882–1921, Box 4), Homicides, p. 11.

79 Oscar Woods, 'Criminal Responsibility of the Insane', *The Journal of Mental Science*, xl, 171 (October 1894), pp. 609–21.

80 Ibid., p. 615.

81 Ibid., p. 616.

82 Ibid., p. 619.

83 *RIC Return of Outrages for 1885* (NAI, CSO ICR2), Homicides, p. 3.

84 *RIC Return of Outrages for 1888* (NAI, CSO ICR2), Homicides, p. 11.

85 *RIC Return of Outrages for 1890* (NAI, Police Reports 1882–1921, Box 4), Homicides, p. 5.

86 *Kilkenny Journal*, 16th July 1890, cited in Conley, *Melancholy Accidents*, p. 60.

87 *RIC Return of Outrages for 1892* (NAI, Police Reports 1882–1921, Box 4), Homicides, p. 8.

88 *RIC Return of Outrages for 1868* (NAI, CSO ICR1), Homicides, p. 8; Transfers from Dundrum to District Asylum 1891 (NAI, CRF, Misc. 392/ 1891).

89 *RIC Return of Outrages for 1892* (NAI, Police Reports 1882–1921, Box 4), Homicides, p. 6.

90 *RIC Monthly Return of Outrages for Sept. 1900* (NAI, Police Reports 1882–1921, Box 4), Homicides, p. 6.

91 *RIC Return of Outrages for 1892* (NAI, Police Reports 1882–1921, Box 4), Homicides, p. 3.

92 Dundrum Male Casebook Allan Spiller, 1892, patient no. M851, p. 25.

93 Extract from *RIC Return of Outrages for 1902*, contained in the convict record file on John Logue [NAI, CRF 1911/ L16 (Logue)].

94 Report from Galway Prison in the convict record file on John Logue [NAI, CRF 1911/ L16 (Logue)].

95 Ibid.

96 Ibid.

97 Extract from the Medical Officer's Journal in the convict record file on John Logue [NAI, CRF 1911/ L16 (Logue)].

98 Dundrum Male Casebook John Logue, 1902, patient no. M1091, p. 179.

99 Letter from Logue, 25 February 1908, in convict record file on John Logue [NAI, CRF 1911/ L16 (Logue)].

100 Conley, *Melancholy Accidents*, Table 4.1, p. 92.

101 *RIC Return of Outrages for 1868* (NAI, CSO ICR1); *RIC Return of Outrages for 1884* (NAI, CSO ICR2).

102 *RIC Return of Outrages for 1868* (NAI, CSO ICR1).

103 *RIC Return of Outrages for 1884* (NAI, CSO ICR2).

CHAPTER FIVE

Women who killed children

MARGARET RAINEY WAS A 19-year-old single Episcopalian servant from Belfast, who in 1891, was found 'not of sound mind or capable of pleading' in relation to the murder of her illegitimate child, and was sent to Dundrum. She had delivered the baby (a girl) safely, with the doctor present, in lodgings arranged by her sister. This sister, Jane, had also arranged for the baby to be sent to a nurse soon after its birth, to allow Margaret to take up a position 'in service'. However, Margaret was not happy with this arrangement. She would have preferred to keep the baby at home, but her mother refused to accept her. On the night of the crime, Margaret had been left alone with the baby for a short period. At around eleven o'clock that night, she alerted a neighbour, saying that her baby had been 'stolen by a person or a dog'.

Sadly, they found the baby dead in the yard next door. The medical opinion was that it had died as a result of injuries sustained from a fall, probably from an upstairs window. Margaret denied having thrown the baby through the window and insisted that it had been stolen. She was sent to Dundrum where her initial diagnosis was dementia. This diagnosis changed over time, so that by 1893 (two years later), she was assessed by Dr Revington, medical super-intendent, as 'weak-minded rather than insane'. She was discharged in 1894 to her sister Jane, who had supported her throughout her ordeal.[1] Margaret was a typical example of the single women sent to Dundrum for killing a child. She was just one of the many women referred to by the inspectors of lunacy when they wrote in 1854 of the frequency of infanticide among female patients in Dundrum and of the possibility of discharge.

> We have no record of a female killing her husband, the most common mode of destruction among women being infanticide … One patient alone, a respectable married female, who destroyed her infant, whilst labouring under puerperal mania, has been liberated since the date of our last report.[2]

As discussed in an earlier chapter, statistics on crime across time and place point to the fact that women are much less likely than men to engage in criminal behaviour.[3] However, there is one area of crime where women are highly visible – that of child murder. The victims range in age from newborn to adolescence though the most vulnerable age is immediately after birth.[4] Here, the focus is on women who killed one or more children in the second half of the nineteenth century. These women and their families were experiencing the impact of changes in many aspects of social and economic life, changes brought on by the decline in population following the Famine of the 1840s, the consolidation of British rule as reflected in the expansion of institutional responses to law and order problems, and the growing political discontent of large sections of the population.[5]

In the discussion that follows, we will see how economic hardship, combined with social stigma, could lead to a situation of extreme violence between a mother and her child. In the case of an illegitimate child, this violence was often seen as the solution to the social and economic problems caused by its birth. However, then as now, this was not the end of the story. Child-killing by a mother, when it becomes public knowledge, is regarded as one of the most incomprehensible of actions. In the words of Dr F.T. MacCabe, Medical Officer of the Prisons Board in 1886 – it is 'a perversion of the maternal instinct'.[6] It requires a public response that allows for some form of severe punishment for those deemed fully responsible for their actions and an element of clemency for those who are not. In Ireland, as elsewhere, the societal response to the killing of a child by his or her mother was quite complex. This response depended on the age of the child and the mother's circumstances. Unmarried mothers who killed their new-born infant were viewed with great compassion, while mothers (usually married) who killed older children were viewed with horror and disbelief.

Most of the Irish statistics that are comparable to other countries relate to what most writers refer to as infanticide. Before discussing these statistics, let me sound a note of caution on the use of this word.[7] The term 'infanticide' appears in nineteenth-century official government reports and in medical and legal texts, but strictly speaking, there was no crime of infanticide in England until 1922 or in Ireland until 1949.[8] The crime was a specific one which referred to the death of a new-born child (clarified in 1938 in England to mean under twelve months), caused by his or her mother. If certain conditions could be proved to exist, such as the presence of temporary insanity, the woman could be convicted of infanticide. This conviction was a form of manslaughter, rather than of murder. By redefining it as a new crime, the court excluded the possibility of the death sentence, which still remained on the statute books for murder in both countries. However, though the legal crime of infanticide was not yet in existence, homicide records kept by the police, distinguished clearly between child victims under the age of twelve months and those over this age. Statistics on child victims under twelve months of age were used as statistics on infanticide.[9] For the purpose of the discussion here, I will use the term 'new-born child murder' in relation to these children, except where the term 'infanticide' appears in the original primary source or is used by another author. This is in keeping with current academic literature on the subject.[10] It is more of a legal than a factual distinction, as both terms refer to the same crime, with the proviso that infanticide can only be committed by a mother.

A previous study by Connolly suggests that, when compared with England, Ireland had lower rates of both illegitimacy and of infanticide during the nineteenth century.[11] However, according to McLoughlin, friends and family members (of the mother) often went to great lengths to conceal the birth and death of an unwanted child and that this was reflected in the low rate of reporting of the crime to the authorities.[12] Because of this under-reporting, it is very difficult to be certain of the extent of the murder of new-born babies or of older children in Ireland. This non-reporting of suspicious infant deaths, however, was not peculiar to Ireland, as shown by historical research on Germany and England.[13] Commenting on England, Knelman writes that 'the disappearance of children does not seem to have been of particular interest among the poor, whose rate of reproduction was perhaps greater than was felt necessary by the rest of society'.[14] Of course, we know that the killing of babies was not confined to lower income women, but those with money may have had a different way of dealing with an unwanted child. These women placed a child with a 'nurse', whom they paid to care for it discretely. Some of these 'nurses' cared for more than one child, a practice that was not bad in itself, but one that led to abuse, because of the secrecy involved and the money to be made. Some unscrupulous women engaged in what became known as 'baby farming' – the care of large numbers of children in circumstances that were far from ideal. Some of these children were placed in care by their mothers and others by workhouse managers.

What was of concern to those interested in child protection was the fact that because these children were either illegitimate or poor (or both), untoward or unexpected deaths did not arouse attention or suspicion. During the 1860s, there was an outcry against 'baby-farming' in England, as the newspapers became involved in a campaign to publicize details of poor conditions, neglect and suspicious deaths in some of these 'care' homes. Some of the 'nurses' were suspected of deliberately causing the death of one or more children, while others were suspected of neglecting children in a way that caused injury and death. The public debate revealed indifference, if not collusion, between mothers and the nurses with whom unwanted infants were placed. How else might one explain the lack of investigation when the babies died?[15]

Returning to the Irish situation, the best estimates of infanticide are those compiled by O'Donnell from police records and judicial statistics.[16] He suggests that the highest level of 'baby-killing' (victims under one year) was during the period 1851–60, an average annual rate of 18.3 per million of the population. This represented 49 per cent of the average annual rate for all homicides for that period. This pattern is consistent with (though lower than) the pattern for England in the mid-nineteenth century, where infanticide (victim under one year) accounted for 61 per cent of all homicide victims.[17] O'Donnell also found that in Ireland, the rate of baby-killing declined rapidly after the Famine, as did the overall homicide rate, so that by 1891–1900, the average annual rate for baby-killing was 4.4 per million of the population, representing 19 per cent of the average annual rate for all homicides during that period.[18] Debates on the reasons for the decline in this crime include theories about the influence of the Famine and of religious belief on illegitimacy, the impact of improvements in child health, and changing attitudes to children within Irish society.[19]

An exploration of the records of women who appeared before the Irish courts for child murder during the nineteenth century, shows that they could be dealt with in either of two ways. In the first half of the century, they could either be found guilty of murder or manslaughter and sentenced to death, transportation or imprisonment, or they could be found 'unfit to plead' or insane at the time of the crime and sent to a district asylum. In the second half of the century, for women found guilty of murder, the death penalty remained a possibility. For those convicted of manslaughter or whose death sentence was commuted, penal servitude (in prison) replaced transportation. Some judges also opted to use the lesser conviction of concealment of birth – under Section 60 of the Offences Against the Persons Act 1861.[20] This latter sentence was only applicable to women who had recently given birth and carried with it a much less punitive sentence. The opening of the Central Criminal Asylum at Dundrum meant that women found 'unfit to plead' or insane at the time of committing the crime, were sent there, rather than to a district asylum. As with men who killed women, discussed in the last chapter, the verdict handed down to women tried for the murder of a child changed in 1883. Before 1883, the verdict was 'acquitted on the grounds of insanity'. After this year, it became 'guilty but insane'. The outcome remained the same for both verdicts – an indefinite sentence in Dundrum at the pleasure of the Lord Lieutenant.[21] In the next section, we will discuss some of the women who were found to be insane at the time of their crime and sent to Dundrum, leaving the women convicted of murder and manslaughter until later in this chapter.

CHILD KILLERS IN DUNDRUM

An exploration of medical records at Dundrum, from the time of its opening in 1850 to the end of the century, reveals that one of the clear patterns of crime to emerge in relation to female patients is the frequency of child-killing among those sent there for involvement in a murder. Tables 5.1 and 5.2 give a brief outline of some of the social characteristics of these women – their age, marital status, religion, county of origin and diagnosis. Some of the information given here was verified in a number of sources, but some women featured in only one source. This has to do with the delicate nature of an insanity conviction, and the different methods of record keeping between the prison system and the asylum system. Because all of the patients in Dundrum had been indicted for a crime, their names were (and still are) in the public domain. Their cases were reported fully in court records and some made it to the newspapers. However, once inside Dundrum, there was no requirement on the administration to keep individual files on patients (as there was for convicts doing penal servitude). The best source of information is often the convict record file, containing correspondence that took place between, or on behalf of, an individual patient and the office of the Chief Secretary for Ireland, which handled all the appeals for early discharge. However, unlike ordinary convicts, these patients could be discharged on the recommendation of the medical superintendent of Dundrum, backed up by the inspectors of lunacy, without any intervention on the part of the patient or his or her family. In some cases, this was a very short procedure, leaving a small 'footprint' for the researcher.

Existing records suggest that women who killed a new-born child during a period of temporary insanity, and who regained sanity quickly in Dundrum, were recommended fairly quickly for discharge.

Table 5.1 *Women who killed a new-born child (age under 1 year)*
and found to be insane at the time of the crime

Name	Age	Religion	Marital status	Diagnosis	In Asylum*
Mary Glass	21	Catholic	Single	Congenital idiot	1868–1902
Kate Connor	18	Catholic	Single	Chronic mania	1888–1902
Mary Finnegan	31	Protestant	Married	Chronic mania	1889
Agnes Rennie	31	Protestant	Married	Melancholia	1889
Margaret Rainey	19	Episcopalian	Single	Dementia	1891–94
Mary O'Flaherty	34	Catholic	Married	Melancholia	1892
Ellen Byrne	26	Catholic	Single	Puerperal insanity	1893–94
Hannah Sullivan	17	Catholic	Single	Dementia	1895–96
Ann McDonnell	38	Catholic	Married	Melancholia	1900–1910

* Some went to Dundrum and some to district asylums

Sources: Medical records (Dundrum), RIC and convict record files (National Archives of Ireland).

Each case had, of course, to go before the Lord Lieutenant, but as outlined in the report of the inspectors of lunacy in 1866, great 'clemency' was shown by his office. The inspectors wrote that, in England, an acquittal of homicide on the grounds of insanity was equivalent to a sentence of imprisonment for life, whereas in Ireland, the Lord Lieutenant has 'several times extended his clemency to such persons' and 'no evil consequences' had emerged from their early discharge. They give the example of a young mother who 'in a paroxysm of puerperal mania, destroys her infant', but who recovers quickly, realizing her crime and her loss. They ask 'is it not better if she goes to her family?'[22]

Women who did not recover their sanity were kept in Dundrum if their behaviour was difficult to control, but they were discharged to their local district asylum if they became calm and easily managed. In Table 5.1, we have information on nine women who were regarded as infanticide cases – women who had killed a new-born child. Margaret Rainey, mentioned at the beginning of this chapter, was one of these women. Another young single woman in the same predicament was Hannah Sullivan, a 17-year-old Catholic servant from County Cork. She was indicted for the murder of her new-born child in 1895 and was found 'guilty but insane'. According to Dundrum medical records, she killed the baby 'by cutting off its head in a loft of her master's premises at Tralee'.[23] Hannah herself said that it was an accident, that she did not know what was happening, as she did not realize she was expecting a child. She also said that the baby's head had got caught in the toilet seat as she gave birth. Hannah may have been telling the truth when she said that she did not realize that she was giving birth, as this was a story repeated by other young unmarried women whose babies died in suspicious circumstances. In all of these cases, the young woman was alone at the time of the birth.

Similar stories were told by young English women tried for new-born child murder. Margaret Arnot writes of Elizabeth Cornwall, a 38-year-old servant from London, who delivered her baby in a 'chamber pot' in her employer's house in 1847.[24] She left the baby in the pot until the next day, when she emptied it into a 'slop pail' and threw it into the 'water closet'. Elizabeth's crime was discovered only when she told a friend about her actions and the distress she was feeling. When she found herself before the court, accused of murder, she told the judge, 'I never saw it, as it came from me in the chamber utensil, so it remained'.[25] She also said that she did not know she was pregnant. While this may seem unlikely for someone of Elizabeth's age – she was thirty eight at the time – it could be true for 17-year-old Hannah Sullivan. As Arnot suggests, the denial of a pregnancy is one way of avoiding the responsibility of deciding what will happen when the baby is born, an event that would destroy the character and life chances of women such as Elizabeth and Hannah. Luckily for Hannah, she was treated with compassion in Dundrum and, after showing no signs of insanity, she was discharged to her mother after one year in detention.[26] The official view of the medical staff involved in the forensic psychiatric services of the time is reflected in the annual reports on Dundrum by the inspectors of lunacy. In 1854 they wrote:

> Great commiseration is, no doubt, due to many who come within this category; for we can fully imagine how shame and anguish must weigh on an unfortunate and betrayed female, with enfeebled system, what strong temptations induce her to evade the censure of the world in the destruction of the evidence of her guilt, by a crime that outrages her most powerful instinct, maternal love of offspring. The thought of such a fearful exposure no doubt may lead to some sudden and impulsive act, for which, as generally happens, she is judged with the utmost leniency.[27]

This extract also reflects one of two contradictory views of women who killed their infants. These two views are discussed thoroughly by Mark Jackson, in his study of new-born child murder in eighteenth-century England.[28] One view saw the woman as a wicked murderer, and the other saw her as a virtuous victim attempting to protect her honour. The job of the court was to decide which type of woman stood before it. If the first, she deserved to be severely punished. If the second, she deserved to be cared for. Jackson argues that as the eighteenth century drew to a close in England, the humanitarian approach gained some ground and led to debates on 'temporary insanity' linked to childbirth and the emergence of the diagnosis of 'puerperal insanity'.

In the Dundrum medical records examined for this discussion, the diagnosis of puerperal insanity was used only in relation to one of the women found to be insane at the time she killed her infant (see Table 5.1). This was Ellen Byrne, a twenty-six-year-old single prostitute (a Catholic) from Dublin, whose case was covered in the newspapers as 'the Goldenbridge infanticide'. Ellen had drowned her baby in the canal. She said that she had been refused entry to the South Dublin Union and that she had tried to give the baby away but, when she did not succeed, she left the baby at the side of the canal, hoping someone would find it and care for it. She was found 'guilty but insane' and sent to Dundrum in 1893. In her medical notes, she was described as a 'nervous and delicate subject, greatly emaciated and run down constitutionally through her mode of life, privation and drink' and later as 'a bloodless emaciated girl, looks like a mere child, is the subject of advanced phthisis (tuberculosis)'. As well as being physically debilitated, she was 'depressed, apathetic and emotional' at the time of her admission to Dundrum. She was diagnosed as having 'puerperal insanity' and died in 1894 – within a year of admission.[29]

INSANITY AND CHILDBIRTH

The debate on the impact of childbirth on a mother's mental state and the possibility of it leading to irrational behaviour, including violence, was part of a wider debate on female insanity.[30] This debate was based on assumptions about the female psyche that included characteristics such as passivity, emotional instability and irrationality.[31] All of these characteristics were seen as highly related to the reproductive cycle, leading to periods of vulnerability to mental disorder. The period before and after childbirth constituted one of these vulnerable points in time. One of the most influential Irish doctors writing on 'mental disorders of pregnancy and childbed' in the mid-century was Dr Fleetwood Churchill, who wrote in the *Dublin Quarterly Journal of Medical Science* in 1850. He set the tone for his essay by elaborating on the complexity of the relationship between mind and body.

Man is a compound being, with the interdependence of mind and matter so finely adjusted, that, so long as the balance is preserved, the action of the machine is as perfect in its nature as wonderful in its results. But the very nicety of this balance, the very intimate and accurate relation between the body, or especially the brain, and the mental development, appears occasionally to lead to the disturbance of the latter. The cords are so fine and so tense that an excess of vibration in the one extremity induces discord in the other.[32]

Having made the general point about the delicacy of the inter-relationship between mind and body, Churchill went on to elaborate his theory in relation to women.

If this be the case with men, who are possessed naturally of a firm and vigorous constitution – if a very slight deviation from bodily health distorts or upturns their mental operations, how much more exposed must women be to such disturbances, who, in addition to the causes common to both, possess a more delicate organization, more refined sensibilities, more exquisite perceptions, and are, moreover, the subjects of repeated constitutional changes and developments of a magnitude and importance unknown to the other sex.[33]

Women, therefore, are not only more 'delicate' and more 'sensitive' than men, but they also have more physical changes to contend with throughout the various stages of their lives. There was nothing new about this view of women, but Churchill used it to set the scene for his next argument, which made the connection between insanity and physical conditions related to reproduction.

These functions are menstruation, conception and pregnancy, parturition and childbed, and lactation. That functions of such great consequence ... should exert an influence upon the mind of the female, cannot be a matter of surprise, and a little inquiry will show us that the mental condition does correspond to these changes by an increased sensitiveness and by a greater liability to disturbance; and further, that this disturbance may amount to incoherent action or insanity.[34]

This kind of argument formed the intellectual background for legal and medical decisions made in relation to women involved in crime during the nineteenth century. In his article, Dr Churchill went on to discuss this theory with special reference to 'puerperal mania', drawing evidence from the writings of internationally renowned 'alienists' or 'mad-doctors' of the time. The concept of 'puerperal mania' was often put forward in cases of new-born child murder, but the link was not made directly in the medical literature until the second half of the century. The highly influential British psychiatrist, Dr Henry Maudsley, discussed the association between menstruation, pregnancy and the homicidal tendency in an essay on homicidal insanity in the *Journal of Mental Science* in 1863.

> Irregularities of menstruation, as recognised causes of nervous disorder, may act on different parts of the nervous system in different persons, in one giving rise to hysterical convulsions or hysterical mania, in another to epilepsy, and in another to suicidal or homicidal impulse. A woman who was in the deepest despair because she was afflicted with the thought of murdering her children ... perfectly recovered on the return of her menses ... Morbid impulses notably spring up during pregnancy.[35]

Examples of this argument had already appeared in the very early reports on Dundrum. For example, in the annual report for 1852 we read:

> In the Asylum at Dundrum there are a few cases, which we trust may soon become subjects for your Excellency's benevolent consideration: amongst others, that of a young woman, of respectable condition, and the mother of three children, who, from fright at her last confinement, was attacked by puerperal mania, and destroyed her infant. She is now, and has been for about eighteen months restored to reason; her husband and family are urgent for her liberation.[36]

This argument was also used in evidence to the Royal Commission on Capital Punishment in 1866, as part of the debate on the appropriateness of the death sentence for women who had killed their children.[37] The Home Office in England, in 1864, had adopted the policy of advising that the death penalty be commuted in all cases where a mother had been convicted of murdering her new-born baby (under one year old).[38] This policy was also extended to Ireland, and women who were found guilty of the murder (of a new-born child) and sentenced to death had no difficulty in having their sentences commuted to penal servitude for life. However, it was much easier to be lenient towards these women if their crime could be linked to insanity. As argued by Dr F.T. MacCabe, Medical Officer of the General Prisons Board in his 1886 report to the Chairman of the Board, on women in the prison system for new-born child murder:

> If Puerperal Mania could be ascertained to have existed in any of these cases, that circumstance would totally alter their aspect from a medico-

legal point of view, as it is well known that in Puerperal Mania no symptom is more constant than a perversion of the maternal instinct leading to the destruction of the infant.[39]

The debate on 'puerperal mania' as a cause of violence towards new-born babies, made it possible for courts to excuse a woman of responsibility for her action in killing her child. However, when this happened, the woman was sent to Dundrum as a criminal lunatic, where she awaited her fate at the pleasure of the Lord Lieutenant. Some of these women, like Margaret Rainey and Hannah Sullivan, were discharged within one or two years of committing their crimes. Others were destined to spend many years within an asylum, either in the Central Criminal Asylum at Dundrum or in their local district asylum. These were the women who were diagnosed as having chronic mental disorders – mania, melancholia, dementia and insanity related to overindulgence in alcohol.

CHILD MURDER AND CHRONIC INSANITY

In the inspector's report on Dundrum for 1854, the difficulties surrounding the detention of women sent to them for child murder were discussed.

> Unless the deed is accompanied with, and followed by distinct symptoms of insanity, the difficult question presents itself to us: is such a person – sane immediately after the act, sane at trial, and sane on admission – to remain for life – or, if not for life, for what period – the inmate of an asylum, and the associate of lunatics?[40]

As in the case of other patients in Dundrum, the decision of the court to excuse individuals from responsibility for a crime on the grounds that they were suffering from temporary insanity at the time, did not mean that these people continued to be of unsound mind after conviction. Not all of the female patients who had killed children were suffering from a temporary insanity such as 'puerperal mania'. In fact, many were judged to have a chronic condition that simply manifested itself at the time of the crime – a theory expounded by Dr C. Lockhart Robertson, of the Sussex Lunatic Asylum, in the *Journal of Mental Science*.[41] His arguments are reflected in the medical notes of some of the Dundrum women who killed one or more of their children (for diagnoses, see Tables 5.1 and 5.2). These women never recovered their sanity and continued to be incarcerated in Dundrum or in another asylum until they died. Some of them had killed new-born children and some had killed older children. For example, Mary Glass, a 21-year-old single Catholic girl from County Antrim, was found 'unfit to plead' in 1868 in relation to the murder of her new-born child.[42] Mary was judged to be a 'congenital idiot' – in other words, she was intellectually disabled. She had the added disadvantage of having her mother in Dundrum (we don't know for what crime). She spent thirty-four years in Dundrum and was then transferred to Antrim district asylum in 1902. This seems an inordinately long time in confinement as a criminal lunatic for a crime that usually attracted a more compassionate approach. While one might conjecture that the presence of Mary's mother in Dundrum delayed her transfer to the less restrictive and less stigmatizing environment of the district asylum, this was not the case, as she died in 1873.[43]

Another woman whose time in Dundrum was longer than average was diagnosed as suffering from melancholia for most of her time there. This was Ann McDonnell, a 38-year-old Catholic married woman from County Sligo (see Table 5.1).[44] Ann was married at the age of 20 and had eight children. When a ninth child was born, she suffered an attack of 'acute melancholia' and killed the baby by drowning it in a nearby river. She was indicted for murder and found 'guilty but insane'. Ann spent ten years in Dundrum before being discharged to her husband in 1910. She was sane at the time of her discharge.

Table 5.2 *Women who killed a child (age over 1 year) and found to be insane at the time of the crime*

Name	Age	Religion	Marital status	Diagnosis	In Asylum*
Johanna Doyle	40	Catholic	Married	Chronic mania	1888–95
Sarah McAlister	33	Catholic	Married	Melancholia	1892
Catherine Wynn	35	Catholic	Married	Melancholia	1893–1911
Mary Jane Simpson	45	Presbyterian	Married	Melancholia	1893–1901
Mrs Sadlier	30s	Catholic ?	Married	Mania	1896

* All, except Ellen Sadlier, were in Dundrum

Sources: Medical records (Dundrum), RIC and convict record files (National Archives of Ireland).

Some women with a chronic condition were never released from Dundrum. One of these was Mary O'Flaherty, a 34-year-old Catholic married servant, who had given birth to six children. Five of her children died young from natural causes. When her sixth baby appeared to be delicate also, she drowned it. The baby was just eight months old. Her medical notes state that 'for the last seven years, she had neglected her religious duties and now, fearing the death of her remaining child, she thought she was doomed'. She made up her mind to drown herself and the baby but, unfortunately for her, she survived. She was found to be insane at the time of the crime and sent to Dundrum in 1892. She remained there until her death and though her husband came regularly to see her, 'she took no pleasure in his visits'.[45]

Two women, who killed more than one child, were regarded by medical opinion as suffering from chronic conditions. They were Sarah McAlister, a 33-year-old Catholic married woman from County Antrim, who poisoned the youngest two of her six children in 1892, and Catherine Wynn, a 35-year-old Catholic married woman from County Sligo, who drowned her three children in a bath of boiling water in 1893.[46] Sarah McAlister denied killing her children, but admitted that she tried to kill herself because she had learned of her husband's unfaithfulness. According to her medical notes, she continued in her efforts to commit suicide: 'we have great trouble getting her to eat food ... she wants to starve herself'. Catherine Wynn had also tried to kill herself by putting her head into the same bath of boiling water that she had used to drown her children. Neither of these women recovered their sanity.

There are other women who were found to be insane at the time of their crime but about whom we know very little, because they were admitted directly to district asylums and did not appear in Dundrum records. For example, an English barrister, Michael J. F. McCarthy, writing in 1901 on 'religious insanity', referred to a Mrs Sadlier from County Tipperary, who killed her four daughters aged between five months and four and a half years, in 1896. She cut their throats with a razor.

> Their heads were almost severed from their bodies ... Her words were, as sworn to by the Sergeant at the inquest: 'Well, I killed the four children in order that they may be with the Almighty God, as I consider they were not capable of committing sin. I hope they were not. They were not up to the age of reason. I strove to destroy them before they would fall into the same sins that I had committed'.[47]

McCarthy selected this case to highlight the evils of religious fervour, but his account is verified in RIC records, which tell us that Mrs Sadlier appeared to 'suffering from religious mania', though she had never shown any signs of insanity before she killed her children. She was sentenced and remanded and later 'removed to Limerick district asylum by order of the Lord Lieutenant'.[48] Like Mary O'Flaherty, Sarah McAlister and Catherine Wynn, she never recovered mentally from this tragedy.

What is interesting for our discussion here is that these women were deemed 'mad' rather than 'bad' and were thus excused of responsibility for this most terrible crime. In her study of folklore surrounding child murder, Anne O'Connor suggests that for women who killed more than one child, repentance was the key to being accepted by society. If a woman knew that she had done wrong and was sorry for it she could be forgiven. Otherwise she left herself open to being completely ostracized as evil.

> In our examination of child murderess traditions, the figure of a Satanic woman who would destroy her own child/children or that/those of another woman without repenting of such an act, has emerged. This figure has been seen to resemble the witch-midwife character in her diabolical association and evil deeds.[49]

Accounts of women sent to Dundrum reveal that it was not quite as simple as that. Many women did not repent of their crimes, as they did not appear to understand the gravity of their actions. However, they were not treated as evil. In fact, many were excused of responsibility on the grounds of insanity and were cared for rather than punished. However, care in an asylum, while better than confinement in a prison, was still characterized by loss of liberty and rejection by society.

A MURDER CONVICTION

Although many women pleaded insanity to the charge of child murder, it was possible for some women to be sentenced to death. According to convict records, nineteen women were sentenced to death for this crime in the period 1864–1902, a sentence that was never carried out.[50] Only three women were executed in Ireland during the second half of the nineteenth century, and all had been involved in the murder of a man.[51] Roger Smith, in his study of nineteenth-century trials in England found similar patterns of sentencing for child murder. For example, he estimated that between 1849 and 1864 there were thirty-nine convictions for child murder by a mother, but that very few were executed for the crime, the last hanging for infanticide in England being that of Rebecca Smith in 1849.[52] Smith had committed a particularly horrific crime. According to her own confession, she had killed seven of her eleven children with rat poison.[53]

Table 5.3 *Women convicted of the murder of a child and sentenced to death*

Name	Age	Marital status	County of origin	Sex & Age of child (if known)	Mode of death	In prison
Mary Darby *	25	Single	Tyrone	Boy 16 mths.	Battered	1866–86
Anne Aylward*	28	Single	Kilkenny	Girl 18 mths.	Drowned	1871–86
Ellen Carroll*	?	Single	Kilkenny	New-born	Unknown	1872–84
Ellen Davey*	20	Single	Tipperary	Girl 12 days	Drowned	1873–86
Anne Jane Mills*	18	Single	Antrim	New-born	Drowned	1874–79
Mary Russell*	34	Single	Cork	Girl 4 weeks	Drowned	1878–86
Mary Brennan*	40	Widow	Leitrim	Boy 4 weeks	Strangled	1879–86
Mary Ellen Pritchard*	20	Single	Antrim	Girl 5 minutes	Smothered	1880–86
Catherine Robinson*	28	Single	Tyrone	Girl 6 weeks	Exposure	1881–86
Margaret Slavin*	40	Single	Fermanagh	Boy 11 days	Smothered	1881–86
Margaret Halloran*	36	Single	Kerry	5 months	Smothered & Drowned	1882–87
Eliza Smith*	19	Single	Monaghan	14 days	Smothered & Drowned	1882–87
Kate Kelly/Keogh*	33	Single	Dublin	Twins 7 days	Drowned	1883–88
Jane McDowell	28	Single	Down	New-born	Unknown	1889–91

* Women named on correspondence between the General Prison Board and the Lord Lieutenant in 1886

Sources: General Prison Board, RIC and convict record files (National Archives of Ireland).

It is clear from Irish official reports and correspondence in relation to women who killed children (especially those who had killed a new-born child) that government policy was to avoid the execution of women, if at all possible. In cases of child murder, the death sentence was invariably commuted to penal servitude for life. In fact, as will be seen in the cases discussed here, some served only five years in prison, though others were in prison for twenty years (see Table 5.3).[54] After discharge, some went home to their families and some emigrated directly from prison to the US.[55] This policy of helping ex-prisoners to emigrate will be explored in a later chapter.

Before discussing individual cases of women convicted of child murder, we will look at a particular policy debate that took place in the 1880s, which affected a number of the women whose stories are told here. This was the debate on the use of the death penalty in cases of infanticide. The Home Office policy of commuting the death sentence to penal servitude for life, for infanticide cases, was in place from 1864 in both Ireland and England.[56] However, the death sentence was still being handed down to some women, a situation that was thoroughly debated during the deliberations of the Royal Commission on Capital Punishment in 1866.[57] Many of the witnesses who appeared before the commission were unhappy with the use of the death sentence for infanticide.

The law was not reformed after this commission, but there was an official intervention from Dublin Castle during the 1880s aimed at rectifying any anomalies in the sentencing of women who had killed new-born children. In 1886, the Lord Lieutenant's office requested a report from the General Prisons Board on all women prisoners who had been sentenced to death for killing a child since 1864.[58] This provided an opportunity for those in the prison system who considered their sentences unjust, to place their arguments in writing before the highest authority in the land. The two most powerful voices in this debate were the General Prison Board's Chairman, Charles F. Bourke, and Medical Officer, Dr F.T. MacCabe. Bourke was later (in 1890) to take up the cause of prostitutes in Waterford and Athlone who complained that they were being arrested for merely walking on the streets of their towns. He let it be known to the local police that they were overstepping the mark by arresting these women when they were not committing any crime, pointing out that prostitutes were entitled to the 'protection and liberty accorded to other of Her Majesty's subjects'.[59]

Obviously, Bourke had a special interest in the plight of women within the prison system, an interest that was clear in the correspondence in 1886 between the General Prison Board and the office of the Lord Lieutenant. Based on a report written by Dr F.T. MacCabe on fifteen women, eleven of whom were still in prison having been found guilty of murdering a child and sentenced to be hanged, he raised two major concerns about the legal treatment of these women (see Table 5.3). The first issue was that of the great variation in the final sentences handed down to these women. All were initially sentenced to death, but when this was commuted, some were sentenced to as little as twelve months penal servitude, while others – 'for crimes that appear to be far less heinous' – were sentenced to life long imprisonment 'without any appearance of hope'. The second issue raised was that Ireland seemed out of step with other countries in Europe in its punitive approach to infanticide. Not only were these women sentenced to death and later condemned to imprisonment, but they were also rejected by their families and communities.[60]

As a result of the discussions that took place in 1886, and the decision of Lord Aberdeen, the Lord Lieutenant of Ireland at the time, nine of the eleven women in the prison system for killing a child (most of whom were new-born) were released immediately, with the remaining two in prison until they had completed either five or seven years from the date of their conviction (see Table 5.3). In spite of this intervention, the death sentence continued to be handed down for child-murder (including the murder of a new-born) for a further sixty years. According to a memorandum prepared by the office of the Chief Secretary in 1902, when the question of executing a woman was again high on the agenda, another five women had received the death penalty for 'infanticide' since 1884.[61] The lack of a specific legal crime of infanticide (which required new legislation) left the court with no option but to continue with the death sentence in some cases, as this was the automatic corollary of a murder conviction.

Returning to the debate in the 1880s, we see the effect of the enquiry by the Lord Lieutenant in the stories of some of the women whose cases were brought to his attention.[62] These women had been languishing in prison, having had their death sentence commuted to penal servitude for life, with very little hope of release. We look first at the stories of three single women who were found guilty of child murder, sentenced to death, had their sentences reduced to penal servitude for life, and were released before completing their sentences. The reason for focusing on single women, to start this discussion, is that they were in the majority among women convicted of the murder of a new-born child. As shown in Table 5.3, all except one of the eleven women brought to the attention of the Lord Lieutenant in 1886 were single. One of these women was Anne Aylward, a 28-year-old single woman, from County Kilkenny, who was convicted of the murder of her eighteen-month-old baby girl in 1871. The date for her execution was set for 17 August of that year. Her sentence was reduced to penal servitude for life, of which she served fifteen years. In one of her petitions to the Lord Lieutenant, Anne requested to be discharged so that she could begin a new life in a country in which she was not known.

> (That the) petitioner having now served nearly fifteen years imprisonment has to her credit in the prison a gratuity which would enable her to enter on an industrious course in life, in a strange country where she is unknown, and though now forty three years of age is strong and

active and being a good laundress would be well able to earn her bread.[63]

Anne was discharged directly to Liverpool dock in 1886, where she boarded a boat for New York, having been given her ticket and payment for her work while in prison.

Another woman in prison in 1886 was Mary Russell, a 34-year-old single woman from County Cork. She was convicted of the murder of her four week old baby girl in 1878 and was sentenced to be hanged on 26 August 1879. The baby's body was found on the slope of a railway line near a river on 16 December and a post-mortem showed that she had been drowned. This was a very common method of killing a young child in Ireland and in England during the nineteenth century.[64] Half of the fourteen women whose names appear in Table 5.3 used this method to kill a child. Two of the women – Eliza Smith and Margaret Halloran – had smothered the baby first, while others had held the baby face-down in shallow water near a ditch or a river. The symbolic meaning of water in ending the life of a new-born child cannot be ignored, but there is no evidence of any ritual surrounding these drownings.[65] It is likely that drowning was merely an easy way of killing a baby and of disposing of a body. According to Knelman, drowning was only one of the causes of death in new-born children. Others were exposure, starvation, injuries to the head from falls, poison and strangling.[66] The manner of killing a baby obviously depended on how young it was, where it was born, who knew of its existence, and the opportunities for hiding the body available to the mother.

While many young women who found themselves pregnant outside of marriage resorted to having the baby in a bedroom or an outhouse, Mary Russell, delivered the baby in a 'lying-in' hospital and had been discharged just three days before the child's death.[67] The nurse, who had attended her, remembered Mary and the clothes the child had on when she was found. Mary's family supported her through the ordeal, a feature that was quite unusual in situations like this. Her sister, Kate, said that Mary had lived with her in November and December and that 'she never was with child'. Her brother, Michael, did his best to supply her with an alibi, and her parents petitioned on her behalf. She was found guilty of murder and sentenced to death in 1879. Her sentence was commuted to penal servitude for life, and she was sent from Cork Prison, where she had been held before conviction, to Mountjoy Female Prison to serve her time.[68]

Her parents submitted memorials requesting clemency in 1880 and in 1882. They pleaded her case on two grounds – technical and humanitarian. The technical grounds were concerned with the manner in which evidence was gathered by the police. Some of this evidence was based on conversations between Mary and a policeman, while she was awaiting trial. Her parents alleged that the information gained from these informal conversations should not have been used in the trial – because Mary was very vulnerable at the time and may have incriminated herself. The second grounds used for the appeal was common in cases such as this – that she should be discharged on humanitarian grounds as she was 'very delicate'.[69] The memorial in 1882 also stated that if released, 'arrangements will be made by the family of the unfortunate girl to send her out of the country'. Mary was finally released home to her family in Bandon, in 1886, after spending seven years in prison.[70]

In spite of the policy not to use the death penalty unless absolutely necessary, a decade later, 28-year-old Jane McDowell, from Downpatrick, was convicted of the murder of her child, with the date of her execution set for 25 April 1889. Jane came from a poor but respectable Presbyterian family. She was illiterate but was a 'reliable' and 'hardworking' domestic servant, according to her previous employers. In a report on her character written by W.H. McArdle of the town inspector's office, Belfast, the blame for her downfall was attributed to the father of her child.

> Her character was good up to about seven years ago at about which time she began to keep company with a man named Hugh Campbell, a guard in the employment of the Belfast and County Down Railway company. She had a child to this man which is now about seven years of age and which is at present with the convict's mother. After this child was born, she still continued to keep company with Campbell and if reports speak true, he is the father of the child which the convict murdered and for which she is undergoing her present sentence.[71]

Jane's sentence was reduced to penal servitude for life, of which she served only two years. She was discharged home to her parents in 1891. This was one of the shortest periods of detention for this crime. Jane was probably lucky to have been convicted at a time when the Lord Lieutenant was committed to the early release of women found guilty of killing a new-born child. She also had the ongoing support of her family and her minister of religion, Rev. William Gordon. Jane sent and received a stream of letters to and from her family and her minister during her two years in prison.[72]

The common characteristic of these three women who received the death sentence – Anne Aylward, Mary Russell and Jane McDowell –

seems to be their age. They were regarded as old enough and rational enough to know what they were doing and, therefore, fully responsible for their crimes. Nine of the fourteen women listed in Table 5.3 as having received the death sentence, were over the age of twenty-five. It must have been very shameful for these women, some of whom were respectable servants in established households, to face the world with an illegitimate child. This was especially shocking when a woman was older and expected to be able to look after herself. The story of Margaret Slavin, the oldest woman to be sentenced to death for the murder of a new-born child, is illustrative of the kind of situation faced by a female servant who became pregnant by her employer. Margaret, whose prison photograph shows that she was a beautiful woman, was a 40-year-old single Catholic woman from County Fermanagh.[73]

In a letter from the RIC inspector's office in Enniskillen, she was described as a 'good and honest servant' who had worked for three years as a domestic servant to a Mr Scholes of Derryheely, before taking up a position in Brookboro with a Mr Maguire. She worked 'in service' for seven or eight years with this man. In April 1881, she gave birth to an illegitimate son in Enniskillen workhouse. She had the baby baptised as John Maguire. We can only assume from this that the father of her child was her employer. The question of sexual activity between servants and masters was a very tricky one. Although servants, in theory, were protected by law from 'summary dismissal', female servants were often dismissed when it was discovered that they were pregnant. Someone like Margaret could expect to be dismissed from her job, if marriage was not a possibility.[74] However, we do not know if she was the victim of a rape or if she hoped for a respectable relationship with this man. What we have is poignant evidence of hardship during the last hours of her baby's life. From the statement to the police given by Mary Jane Fox, a nurse at the workhouse, we learn that Margaret left there eleven days after the birth of her son.

> On last Wednesday morning, the 13th April, the prisoner Margaret Slavin left the workhouse about 10 o'clock in the morning. She came to bid me goodbye ... Between the time she was confined and Wednesday morning I had frequent opportunities of seeing the child and I believe it was a healthy child. While I was assisting to dress the child on the morning of the 13th, the prisoner told me not to be too exact in putting too many pins in it, that a stitch of a needle would do as well.[75]

From this account, it appears that the baby was perfectly healthy and that Margaret was not visibly upset when she left the workhouse.

However, within two hours, someone had reported her to the police. According to RIC Constable Thomas Springan:

> From information I received, I proceeded about 11.50 am in the direction of the Model School ... I met the woman now present, named as Slavin. She was coming towards the town on foot. I perceived that she had a bundle under her left arm. I stopped her and asked her what she had, pointing to the bundle. She replied that it was clothes ... I then took the bundle from her and examined it. I discovered that it contained the body of a male child ... The body of the child was warm but lifeless when I examined it. I saw marks on the head and neck of discolouration and some spots of blood on the child's pinafore.[76]

Margaret denied killing the child, but a post-mortem showed that 'the child's death was caused by asphyxia, produced by pressure on the neck'.[77] Margaret was convicted of murder on 11 July and sentenced to be hanged. The sentence was later commuted to penal servitude for life and Margaret spent five years in Mountjoy Prison, before being discharged in 1886. Like many other ex-convicts, she sailed from Dublin to Boston on 16 August 1886. During her time in prison, she only wrote one letter – to a priest, Fr Stackett in Enniskillen. She had no visitors nor did she receive any letters.[78] This was not unusual, as many women who had exposed their families to the shame of illegitimacy and murder were left to fend for themselves during their time in detention. It did not help the woman that she may have killed the child in order to avoid the familial shame that would follow the birth of a 'bastard child'.[79] The abandonment of women who became pregnant outside of wedlock was highlighted by Charles F. Bourke, Chairman of the Prisons Board, in his letter to the Dublin Castle authorities in 1886.

> In most countries of Europe (at any rate) women of this class who happen to fall, are not excommunicated immediately from the society of their equals, and have therefore less temptation to conceal birth, or to commit infanticide. But in this country, a girl who is unfortunate in this particular ... is at once discarded by her parents and disowned and isolated from all humane society and driven homeless in the wide world.[80]

Of course, this was not the case with everyone. Some women, like Mary Russell and Jane McDonnell, had strong family ties and communicated by letter with their families throughout their time in Mountjoy Prison. Both of these women returned to their families on discharge from prison. They may have emigrated after that, but they did not go directly from prison.

PAUPER MOTHERS

Poverty featured very strongly in the stories of women found guilty of murdering a new-born child. Most of these women were single. Some came from domestic service and others from family farms, but what binds their stories together is the abject poverty in which they found themselves as pregnancy advanced. Not only were they abandoned by their families, they were also rejected by the men who were responsible for the pregnancies. Because of this, they turned to the State for help. However, having had their babies in a workhouse infirmary, they often had to leave there with no means of supporting themselves.

The women whose names are listed in Table 5.4 are just a few of those who found themselves in this predicament. We only know about them because they were in prison in 1886 at the time of the Dublin Castle enquiry. In court, these women did not deny killing their children, but they tried to frame their accounts of the events leading up to the death in such a way as to make the action understandable. One such account is that of Ellen Davey, a 20-year-old single mother, who killed her baby in 1873. She had the baby, a girl, in the workhouse in Tipperary, where she spent three weeks recovering from the birth.

Table 5.4 *Pauper women convicted of the murder of a child (baby born in workhouse)**

Name	Age	Marital status	Workhouse where baby was born	Sex and age of baby	In prison
Mary Darby	25	Single	Dungannon	Boy 16 mths.	1866–86
Mary Brennan	40	Widow	Sligo	Boy 4 weeks	1879–86
Kate Kelly/Keogh	33	Single	Naas	Twins 7 days	1883–88
Margaret Halloran	36	Single	Listowel	Boy 5 months	1881–86
Catherine Robinson	28	Single	Omagh	Girl 6 weeks	1881–86
Margaret Slavin	40	Single	Fermanagh	Boy 11 days	1881–86
Ellen Davey	20	Single	Tipperary	Girl 12 days	1873–86

* Women named on correspondence between the General Prison Board and the Lord Lieutenant in 1886

Sources: General Prison Board and convict record files (National Archives of Ireland).

I left the Tipperary Poor House on last Thursday. I took the child with me ... On Saturday last I was near Dundrum and a woman found me with the child and got me a lodging in a neighbour's house. I lodged there with the child on Saturday night and on the next day I left the house ... I went about two or three miles of the road and the Devil corrupted me and I threw my little child onto one side of the river ... None of my people knew I was that way. After I threw away my child I found my way and went home to my Father ... My mind was astray when I drowned my little child ... I may lay the blame of all of this on the soldier, David [surname unreadable]. I have no more to say, where is the good?[81]

We do not know who the soldier was or if he was ever taken to court, but Ellen was sentenced to death. Her sentence was commuted to twenty years penal servitude, a shorter sentence than most women received for this crime. It is not clear why Ellen was not sentenced to penal servitude for life, as the characteristics of her crime, and of her situation, were paralleled in other cases which received the longer sentence. As with other crimes, judicial responses often depended on the perceived attitude of repentance of the offender for the crime and the level of culpability attributed to her. Unfortunately, some of these circumstances remain hidden from the researcher. Ellen spent twelve years in prison and was one of the women released in 1886.

Quite a different story, but one also dominated by social isolation and poverty, is that of Mary Brennan, a widow from Manorhamilton, County Leitrim, who in 1879 at the age of forty, was convicted of the murder of her four-week-old son. Mary had nine children from her marriage, but her husband had died five years before the birth of the dead child. According to the reports in her prison file, she 'led a blameless life', but she got herself into the unfortunate position of being in debt to a moneylender 'who seduced her'. Two months before the baby was due, she and three of her children – a girl aged ten, a boy aged eight and a girl aged five – went into the Sligo Workhouse. She stayed for one week after the child was born and then left, on foot, with her children and the baby, with the intention of going home to Manorhamilton – a distance of seventeen miles. The children recalled that as night fell, they stopped to sleep behind a ditch. They saw their mother taking the baby 'into the next field' and they heard it 'moaning'. They then continued on their way next day without the baby. She later told the prison doctor, Dr F.T. MacCabe, that she had intended leaving the baby at the door of the father, but 'became afraid'.

The baby's body was found in a bag in a lime kiln near the road. According to the post-mortem report, it had head and neck injuries 'inflicted before death'. Mary was sentenced to death, but her sentence was reduced to penal servitude for life. She spent seven years in prison, during which time she learned to read and write. She was finally discharged directly to Liverpool docks in 1886, with a gratuity of £8.10.4 for her work while in prison – approximately £640 at 2006 prices.[82] Her record tells us that she emigrated immediately to Philadelphia on the SS British Princess. It is likely that some of her children were in Philadelphia, although she had received no letters or visits from them or any other members of her family during her seven years in Grangegorman Prison.[83] This was a story not only of poverty, hardship and social isolation, but also one of rape. Mary Brennan and her children had been abandoned by her family and by her community in a way that was bound to lead to tragedy. Her exploitation and rejection by the father of the murdered baby went unpunished, a situation that was not unusual in this traditional patriarchal society. Having no means of support made her vulnerable to men like the moneylender into whose grip she fell, with dire consequences for herself and her children.[84]

Other women, who were poverty stricken, resorted to prostitution, but this too had tragic consequences for many women who became pregnant to men who had no interest in them or their children. We have already discussed Ellen Byrne, a 26-year-old single prostitute from Dublin, who drowned her baby in the canal after she had been refused entry to the South Dublin Union. Ellen's health, both mental and physical, was completely shattered by her way of life and by the death of her baby. She only lived for a year after being found 'guilty but insane' of the murder of her baby. Like other pauper women who survived on the streets and in the workhouse, Ellen had no support network of any kind.[85]

We do not have any statements from either Mary Brennan or Ellen Byrne, but the words of another woman reflect similar experiences of poverty and abandonment. Jane Quigley, from County Roscommon, was acquitted of infanticide in 1896, as the court judged that the baby was probably dead at birth. She told the police:

> I had it (the baby) on Sunday night about 9 p.m. There was no one in the house at the time but myself. I had it in the room, on the bare floor. I was lying on the floor at the time. It was a round lump. I threw it out through the window of the room on to the garden. It was the shape of a child. There was a head and legs and hands on it. It was not alive for there was no stir out of it. I rolled a wisp of hay around it before I threw it out. I told no one about it since until I am telling you now. I got up on

Tuesday following and I am up every day since. I should not have it by
rights for two months more. I mean the child. The father is James Leonard
from near Creggs. He had connexion with me in my own house against
my consent only once. No other man ever had any connexion with me.
I never saw the child since I threw it out of the window.[86]

It is important to remember when considering the women who came
before the courts for child murder, that it is highly likely that they
represented only a small proportion of actual killings. Dympna
McLoughlin argues that the child deaths that came to the attention of
the police were likely to be the violent deaths. In other words, those
that occurred as a result of neglect or 'overlaying' were likely to be
covered up by friends and reported as 'accidental' by officials.[87] This
was true not only in Ireland, but elsewhere. Ellen Ross writes of the
efforts made to stamp out infanticide in London in the 1890s, when
coroners and medical officers questioned every case of 'suffocation'
and 'overlying' to see if it might be a case of deliberate killing.[88]

O'Donnell's estimate of 'baby-killing' (victims under one year),
point to a high level of this crime during the middle of the century –
49 per cent of all homicides during the period 1851–60 – and to a
much lower level both numerically and as a proportion of homicides
by the end of the century. By the last decade (1891–1900), the average
annual rate was 4.4 per million, representing 19 per cent of the
equivalent rate for all homicides during the same period.[89] These were
the official statistics, based on convictions, but there is no doubt that
there were other deaths that were never counted.

CHILD MURDER BY FATHERS

Among officially reported deaths, there were some that were caused
by fathers and other relatives of the mother. Police reports indicate
that if a man was involved in the murder of a new-born child, it was
almost always as an accomplice of a woman. When men acted alone,
it was usually in relation to older children. Four men who appeared in
Dundrum reports had killed a child. Two of these were mentioned
already. Allan Spiller, a Presbyterian salesman from Belfast, cut the
throats of his wife and two children while they lay sleeping in 1892.
He was found to be insane at the time of the crime, having been
driven into a melancholic state by worries brought on by unemploy-
ment. He was well liked by the medical staff at Dundrum and was
discharged to friends in 1899, having recovered his sanity almost
immediately after the court case.[90] This was quite a different story to

that of the women who killed more than one child during a period of 'temporary insanity'. Sarah McAlister (who killed two children) and Catherine Wynn (who killed three children) never recovered their sanity.[91]

The second man who killed a child and who appeared in Dundrum reports many times was Michael Mullins, a 50-year-old Catholic from Limerick. According to Conley, Mullins was a tramp, who had already been in prison for assaults on women.[92] He was found 'guilty but insane' for the murder of his 21-month-old daughter in 1868. Mullins told the medical superintendent at Dundrum that he had accidentally fallen on his child when drunk. However, police records tell a different story. 'Police found the drunken Mullins banging the child's body against a wall. He had also stabbed her repeatedly.'[93] Mullins was regarded as more dangerous than insane in Dundrum but, even after escaping for a while, he spent the rest of his life in an asylum – in Dundrum from 1868 to 1899 and in Limerick District Asylum from 1899 until his death.[94] There are records of two other men who had killed a child during a period of insanity, but we know little of the circumstances due to the difficulties in tracing their records. They were recorded in the inspector's reports on Dundrum as J. B., a 50-year-old from Monaghan, and P. G., a 27-year-old shopkeeper from Roscommon. Each had murdered his child in 1885, was found 'guilty but insane' and continued to show signs of insanity after admission.[95]

Of course, we know that these were not the only men who killed a child in nineteenth-century Ireland. As with other types of domestic abuse, the level of violence against children often only became apparent when a violent or suspicious death occurred. As Conley points out, some children were more vulnerable to physical abuse than others – stepchildren and illegitimate children.[96] It is likely that children with disabilities were also vulnerable to neglect and violence. One particularly horrific case, in which a 13-year-old boy with intellectual disabilities was killed by his entire family, will be discussed in the chapter on family murders.[97] Others remain for future research.

Another aspect of child–killing that is not explored here is that of deaths caused in institutions or in 'baby-farms'. Though there were no scandals on the scale recorded for England in the 1860s, there is evidence of children being neglected, and even starved, by people into whose care they had been placed.[98] Conley writes of a case in Kildare, where an orphanage run by the Rev. George Cotton, a Protestant Minister, was found to be a place of neglect and abuse, rather than of care and kindness.[99] As with domestic violence, institutional abuse did not come to the attention of the authorities until a suspicious death occurred. It was often hidden in an institutional setting where a missing child might not be notified to the police as quickly as a child missing from a family. My own research on convict files threw up no evidence of a conviction for child-killing in an institution or a foster home in Ireland. However, this is not to say that it did not happen. Further research on deaths occurring among unwanted children placed in the care of individual 'nurses' or of institutions would, no doubt, uncover the truth.

To conclude this chapter, we can summarize some of the main themes. Child murder, especially that of new-born infants, was high in the first half of the century. It decreased numerically and in proportion to total homicides in the second half. Most of the crimes were committed by single women who had given birth to an illegitimate child. The death penalty remained on the statute books for child murder until 1949, when the Infanticide Act was passed in Ireland. Though no woman was executed for this crime during the second half of the century, the death penalty remained a possibility unless a woman could be excused of responsibility for her crime on the basis of temporary insanity. While 'puerperal mania' was the most acceptable diagnosis for a successful insanity plea, other types of mental disorder were also put forward, especially in cases where two or more children had been killed. For women who were found 'unfit to plead' or 'guilty but insane', their fate lay in the hands of the medical staff at the Central Criminal Asylum at Dundrum. Those who recovered their sanity quickly and who had supportive family networks – especially those who corresponded regularly with the lunacy inspectorate – were discharged within two or three years of committing the crime. For others, who did not regain sanity, the future lay within the asylum system. Women convicted of murder and sentenced to death did have their sentences reduced to penal servitude for life. Many spent between ten and twenty years in prison – in Mountjoy and Grangegorman Female Prisons. After discharge, some returned home to their families and many emigrated directly to the US.

The practice of sentencing women to death for infanticide continued until the mid-1940s in Ireland. In preparation for the passing of the Infanticide Act 1949, officials from the Department of Justice reported that twelve women had been sentenced to death for the murder of a new-born child since 1922, but that in the years 1946, 1947 and 1948, of the eighteen women brought before the courts for the murder of infants, none were sentenced to death. The most common legal approach, by then, was the use of Section 60 of the Offences Against the Persons Act (24 & 25 Vic c. 100), which allowed for the lesser conviction of 'concealment of birth', if the child was newly born.[100] From 1864, in Ireland (as in England), the death sentence was merely an empty threat, as neither the government nor the judiciary wished to carry out an execution on a woman who had killed a new-born child.

NOTES

1 NAI, CRF, 1894/ R.10 (Rainey); Dundrum, Female Casebook, M. Rainey, 1891, no. F838, p. 65; Dundrum, Physician's Book, p. 226.
2 *Asylums Report*, 155, HC 1854–55 (1981) xvi, 137, pp. 153.
3 K. Daly, *Gender, Crime and Punishment* (New Haven, CT: Yale University Press, 1994); Shani D'Cruze (ed.), *Everyday Violence in Britain 1850–1950: Gender and Class* (Harlow: Longmans/Pearson, 2000); Frances Heidensohn, *Women and Crime*, 2nd Edition (Basingstoke: Macmillan Press, 1996); A. Morris, *Women, Crime and Criminal Justice* (Oxford: Basil Blackwell, 1987); Ulinka Rublack, *The Crimes of Women in Early Modern Germany* (Oxford: Clarendon Press, 1999).
4 Robert Bluglass, 'Infanticide and Filicide', in R. Bluglass and P. Bowden (eds), *Principles and Practice of Forensic Psychiatry* (Edinburgh: Churchill Livingstone, 1990); Peter C. Hoffer and N. E. Hull, *Murdering Mothers: Infanticide in England and New England 1558–1803* (New York: New York University Press, 1981); Mark Jackson, *New-born Child Murder: Women, Illegitimacy and the Courts in Eighteenth-century England* (New York/Oxford: Oxford University Press, 1993); Judith Knelman, *Twisting in the Wind: The Murderess and the English Press* (Toronto: University of Toronto Press, 1998); Ellen Ross, *Love and Toil: Motherhood in Outcast London 1870–1918* (New York/Oxford: Oxford University Press, 1993).
5 Roy F. Foster, *Modern Ireland 1600–1972* (London: Penguin Books, 1988); Leslie A. Clarkson and E. Margaret Crawford, *Feast and Famine: A History of Food and Nutrition in Ireland 1500–1920* (Oxford: Oxford University Press, 2001); William E. Vaughan, 'Ireland c.1870', in W. E. Vaughan (ed.), *A New History of Ireland: V, Ireland under the Union, 1, 1801–1870* (Oxford: Clarendon Press, 1989), pp. 726–802.
6 Letter from Dr MacCabe to the Chairman of the Prisons Board, 30 June 1886 in NAI, CRF Misc. 1888/no. 1862.
7 For further discussion see, Jackson, *New-born Child Murder*, pp. 6–7.
8 Clarice Feinman, *Women in the Criminal Justice System* (Westport, CT: Praeger, 1994).
9 See, for example, *Criminal and Judicial Statistics for Ireland 1868*, HC 1868–69 (4203) lviii. 737, p. 751.
10 Margaret Arnot, 'Understanding women committing new-born child murder in Victorian England', in D'Cruze, *Everyday Violence in Britain 1850–1950*, pp. 55–69; Jackson, *New-born Child Murder*.
11 Sean Connolly, 'Illegitimacy and pre-nuptial pregnancy in Ireland before 1864: the evidence of some Catholic parish registers', *Irish Economic and Social History*, 6 (1979), pp. 5–23.
12 Dympna McLoughlin, 'Infanticide in nineteenth-century Ireland', in Angela Bourke *et al.* (eds) *Field Day Anthology of Irish Writing, Vol. 4: Irish Women's Writing and Traditions* (Cork: Cork University Press, 2002), pp. 915–22.
13 Knelman, *Twisting in the Wind*; Rublack, *The Crimes of Women*.
14 Knelman, *Twisting in the Wind*, p. 124.
15 For discussion of baby-farming and infanticide, see Knelman, *Twisting in the Wind*, pp. 160–73.
16 Ian O'Donnell, 'Lethal violence in Ireland, 1841–2003', *British Journal of Criminology*, 45 (2005), pp. 671–95, Figure 1, p. 677.

17 Bluglass, 'Infanticide and Filicide', p. 524.
18 O'Donnell, 'Lethal violence', p. 677.
19 Liam Kennedy, 'Bastardy and the Great Famine: Ireland 1845–1850', *Continuity and Change*, 14, 3 (1999), p. 429–52; O'Donnell, 'Lethal violence'.
20 Offences Against the Persons Act 1861 (24 & 25 Vic c. 100).
21 See Appendix 1: Legal basis for admissions to Dundrum 1850–1900. For discussion, see P. Gibbons, N. Mulryan, A. McAleer and A. O'Connor, 'Criminal responsibility and mental illness in Ireland 1850–1995: Fitness to plead', *Irish Journal of Psychological Medicine*, 16, 2 (1999), pp. 51–6, p. 52; P. Gibbons, N. Mulryan and A. O'Connor, 'Guilty but insane: the insanity defense in Ireland 1850–1995', *British Journal of Psychiatry*, 170 (1997), pp. 467–72, p. 447; Pauline M. Prior, 'Crime, mental disorder and gender in nineteenth-century Ireland', in I. O'Donnell and F. McAuley (eds), *Criminal Justice History: Themes and Controversies from Pre-Independence Ireland* (Dublin: Four Courts Press, 2003), pp. 66–82.
22 *Asylums Report*, HC 1866 (3721), xxxii. 125, p. 146.
23 Dundrum, Female Casebook, H. Sullivan, 1895, no. F946, p. 145.
24 Arnot, 'Understanding women', pp. 55, 60.
25 Cited in ibid., p. 60.
26 Dundrum, Female Casebook, H. Sullivan, 1895, no. F946, p. 145.
27 *Asylums Report*, HC 1854–55 (1981), xvi. 137, p. 155.
28 Jackson, *New-born Child Murder*, pp. 111–28.
29 Dundrum, Female Casebook , E. Byrne, 1893, no. F874, p. 93; Gibbons *et al.*, 'Guilty but insane', p. 469.
30 Elaine Showalter, *The Female Malady: Women, Madness and English Culture 1830–1980* (London: Virago Press, 1987).
31 Ibid., Roger Smith, *Trial by Medicine: Insanity and Responsibility in Victorian Trials* (Edinburgh: Edinburgh University Press, 1981), p. 143.
32 Fleetwood Churchill, 'On the mental disorders of pregnancy and childbed', *The Dublin Quarterly Journal of Medical Science*, xvii (February 1850), pp. 38–63, p. 39.
33 Ibid.
34 Ibid.
35 Henry Maudsley, 'Homicidal Insanity', *Journal of Mental Science*, ix, 47 (October 1863), pp. 327–43, p. 340.
36 *Asylums Report*, HC 1854–55 (1981) xvi. 137, p. 155.
37 *Report of the Royal Commission on Capital Punishment 1866, together with the Minutes of Evidence and Appendix*, HC 1866 (3590) xxi. 1.
38 Ellen Ross, *Love and Toil: Motherhood in outcast London 1870–1918* (New York/Oxford: Oxford University Press, 1993), p. 187.
39 Letter from Dr MacCabe to the Chairman of the Prisons Board, 30 June 1886, in NAI, CRF, Misc. 1888/no. 1862.
40 *Asylums Report*, HC 1854–55 (1981) xvi, 137, 155.
41 C. Lockhart Robertson, 'A Case of Homicidal Mania, without Disorder of the Intellect', *The Journal of Mental Science*, vi, 34 (July 1860), pp. 385–397, p. 395.
42 Dundrum, Female Casebook, M. Glass, 1868, no. F351, p. 5; Gibbons *et al.*, 'Criminal Responsibility', p. 53.
43 Gibbons *et al.*, 'Criminal Responsibility', p. 53.
44 Dundrum, Female Casebook, A. McDonnell, 1900, no. F1052, p. 189.
45 Dundrum, Female Casebook, M. O'Flaherty, 1892, no. F853, p. 77. Place of origin and date of death unknown.
46 Dundrum, Female Casebook, S. McAlister, 1892, no. F861, p. 81; C. Wynn, 1893, no. F868, p. 85.
47 M.J.F. McCarthy, *Five Years in Ireland 1895–1900* (Dublin: Hodges, Figgis and Company, 1901), pp. 190–91.
48 *RIC Return of Outrages for 1896* (NAI, Police Reports 1882–1921, Box 4), Homicides, p. 11.

49 A. O'Connor, *Child Murderess and Dead Child Traditions: A comparative study* (Helsinki: Academia Scientiarum Fennica, FF. no. 249, 1991), p. 103.

50 Letter of 1 July 1886 from the Chairman of the Prisons Board to the Lord Lieutenant, Dublin Castle, in NAI, CRF, Misc. 1888/no. 1862; Report to the CSO on females sentenced to death since 1881, in NAI, CRF, 1902/ D76 (Daly).

51 Honora and Bridget Stackpoole in 1853, Margaret Sheil in 1870. (NAI, GPB CN5: Death Book 1852–1930).

52 Roger Smith, *Trial by Medicine: Insanity and Responsibility in Victorian Trials* (Edinburgh: Edinburgh University Press, 1981), p. 147.

53 Ross, *Love and Toil*, p. 187.

54 Reports from the General Prison Board, in NAI, CRF, Misc. 1888/no. 1862.

55 For example, see: NAI, PEN, 1886/105 (Aylward) and NAI, PEN, 1886/239 (Pritchard).

56 For discussion on England, see Ross, *Love and Toil*, p. 187.

57 *Report of the Royal Commission on Capital Punishment 1866*, HC 1866 (3590) xxi. 1.

58 Correspondence contained in NAI, CRF, Misc. 1888/ no. 1862.

59 Correspondence contained in NAI, CSORP, 447/1891: For discussion, see Conley, *Melancholy Accidents*, pp. 122–3.

60 Letter of 1 July 1886 from the Chairman of the Prisons Board to the Lord Lieutenant, Dublin Castle, in NAI, CRF, Misc. 1888/no. 1862.

61 Memorandum of 19 December 1902, from the Chief Secretary's Office on the file of Mary Daly, who was executed in 1903, in NAI, CRF, 1902/ D76 (Daly).

62 Letter to the General Prisons Board containing the decision of Lord Aberdeen, Lord Lieutenant of Ireland, in NAI, CRF, Misc. 1888/ no. 1862.

63 Petition to the Lord Lieutenant of Ireland on 12 May 1886, included in NAI, CRF Misc 1888/no. 1862; See also NAI, PEN, 1886/105 (Aylward).

64 See Knelman, *Twisting in the Wind*, Chapter 5.

65 For discussion on ways of viewing child murder, see O'Connor, *Child Murderess*.

66 Knelman, *Twisting in the Wind*, p. 148.

67 A 'lying-in' hospital was a maternity hospital intended principally for the wives of poor industrious men. Some accepted single women.

68 NAI, PEN, 1886/145 (Russell).

69 Memorials for Mary Russell, in NAI, CRF, Misc. 1888/no. 1862.

70 NAI, PEN, 1886/145 (Russell). Information on Mary also included in NAI, CRF, Misc. 1888/no. 1862.

71 Letter of 19th April 1889 from W. M. McArdle to the Superintendent of Grangegorman Prison, in reply to a request for a report in NAI, PEN, 1891/20 (Mc Dowell).

72 Details of correspondence in NAI, PEN, 1891/20 (Mc Dowell).

73 Information contained in NAI, PEN 1885/142 (Slavin) and in NAI, CRF, Misc. 1888/no. 1862.

74 Jackson, *New-born Child Murder*, p. 49.

75 Deposition of Mary Jane Fox, made on 13 April 1881, in NAI, CRF, Misc. 1888/no. 1862.

76 Deposition of Constable T. Springan, made on 13 April 1881, in NAI, CRF, Misc. 1888/no. 1862.

77 Deposition of Dr Baptist Gamble, made on 13 April 1881, in NAI, CRF, Misc. 1888/no. 1862.

78 Information contained in NAI, PEN 1885/142 (Slavin).

79 For discussion of issues, see Kennedy, 'Bastardy and the Great Famine', and Jackson, *New-born Child Murder*, p. 48.

80 Letter from Chairman of the Prisons Board to the Lord Lieutenant, Dublin Castle, in NAI, CRF, Misc. 1888/no. 1862.

81 Copy of statement from the court case in NAI, CRF, Misc. 1888/no. 1862.

82 Calculated from data by Lawrence H. Officer, *Purchasing power of British Pounds from 1264 to 2006*, available on www.measuringworth.com.

83 NAI, PEN, 1886/ 240 (Brennan).
84 Ibid. Information also contained in NAI, CRF, Misc. 1888/ no. 1862.
85 Dundrum, Female Casebook , E. Byrne, 1893, no. F874, p. 93.
86 Roscommon C. and P., Crown Files at Assizes 1896–97, Witness statement on 19 October 1896, the Winter Assizes 1896. (NAI, File no. 1C-64–72).
87 McLoughlin, 'Infanticide', pp. 917–19.
88 Ross, *Love and Toil*, p. 188.
89 O'Donnell, 'Lethal violence', pp. 671–95.
90 Dundrum Male Casebook, S. Spiller, 1892, No. M851, p. 25.
91 Dundrum, Female Casebook, S. McAlister, 1892, no. F861, p. 81; C. Wynn, 1893, no. F868, p. 85.
92 Conley, *Melancholy Accidents*, p. 77.
93 *RIC Returns of Outrages 1868*, cited in Conley, *Melancholy Accidents*, p. 77.
94 Dundrum Male Casebook, M. Mullins, 1868, No. M440, p. 62: *Asylums Report*, p. 105, HC 1874 (c. 1004) xxvii. 363.
95 *Asylums Report*, HC 1886 (c. 4811) xxxiii. 559, p. 682.
96 Conley, *Melancholy Accidents*, p. 78.
97 Oscar Woods, 'Notes of a Case of *Folie à Deux* in Five Members of one Family', *Journal of Mental Science*, xxxiv, 148 (January 1889), pp. 535–9.
98 See Knelman, *Twisting in the Wind*, pp. 157–80.
99 Conley, *Melancholy Accidents*, pp. 79–81.
100 Minister's papers, Dáil, Infanticide Bill 1949. (NAI, JUS/90/8/218).

CHAPTER SIX

Women who killed men

MARY RIELLY FROM GALWAY appears to be the only woman in nineteenth-century Ireland to use the insanity defence successfully for having killed a man. Other women who had committed this crime were judged by the courts to have committed culpable murder, for which they received the death sentence (often reduced to transportation or penal servitude for life), or manslaughter, for which they were sent to prison for varying lengths of time (see Tables 6.1 and 6.2).

Academic literature on crimes committed by women highlight the relative absence of women from statistics on the murder of adults.[1] When they do become involved in this crime, their victims are usually spouses or close relatives. Even then, their contribution to the statistics on spousal or family murders is low, when compared with their male counterparts. As discussed in an earlier chapter, many more men kill their wives, than women kill their husbands. Theoretical explanations of the low female rate of adult homicide include notions of weakness and of compliance.[2] This weakness usually derives from a lack of opportunity and of physical strength and it leads to a state of fear of retaliation from those with more power (physical and legal), epitomized in male figures in both private and public spheres. The compliance may derive from fear in some cases, but it may also be based on realistic judgements on the impact of criminal behaviour on the woman herself and on her children. The loss of a mother to the criminal justice system, now as in the past, leads almost certainly to the placement of children under the protection of the State, which often means a lifetime of institutional rather than of family care.

Taking these considerations into account, what is sometimes seen as passive compliance by a female may, in fact, be a very active behaviour patterns aimed at securing her own safety and that of her children from an aggressive spouse and a powerful State. When this safety zone is breached in such a way as to indicate that compliance is no longer working as a strategy protecting her and/or her children from abuse, then she may take control of the situation by planning the destruction of the aggressor. In this event, extreme care has to be taken

Table 6.1 *Women convicted of murdering a man and sentenced to death*

Name	County	Victim	Weapon/ Cause of death	Sentence	In Prison
Mary Ann McConkey	Monaghan	Husband	Poison	Death. Executed 1/5/41	1841
U. Berhagra	Tipperary	Husband	Unknown	Death, reduced to transportation for life	1846
Peggy Crumeen	Donegal	Father-in-law	Unknown	Death, reduced to transportation for life	1847
Honora Stackpoole	Clare	Cousin	Beating	Death. Executed 29/4/53	1852: 8 mths
Bridget Stackpoole	Clare	Cousin	Beating	Death. Executed 29/4/53	1852: 8 mths
Margaret Shiel	King's County	Neighbour	Pistol	Death. Executed 27/5/70	1870: 3 mths
Elizabeth Buchanan	Londonderry	Husband	Pistol & Knife	Death, reduced to PS for life	1881–91
Catherine Dooley	Queen's County	Cousin	Blunt instrument	Death, reduced to PS for life	1884–98
Catherine Delany	Tipperary	Husband	Poison	Death, reduced to PS for life	1884–98
Mary Brophy	Cork	Brother	Knife	Death, reduced to PS for life	1886–95
Mary Daly	Queen's County	Husband	Hatchet	Death. Executed 9/1/1903	1902–03
Annie Walsh	Limerick	Husband	Spade & Fork	Death. Executed 5/8/1925	1925

Key: PS Penal servitude in prison
      HL Hard-labour in prison

Source: Transportation data-base, General Prison Board, RIC and convict records (National Archives of Ireland).

to ensure that the act of destruction will not fail. This may result in a series of premeditated actions which are later seen by the court as evidence of culpability for murder. Feminist theorists argue that, because women are usually physically weaker than their male aggressors, this planning is essential and should be conceptualized as a self-defence strategy rather than as the offensive act of murder.[3]

One of the methods used in the past by women to kill a man – that of poisoning – requires a great deal of premeditation. It was used frequently in nineteenth-century England, but if discovered, led to severe punishment by the court and the government. For example, of the nine women found guilty of murder by poisoning in the time-span 1862–82, six were executed. During the same period, only seventeen women had met this fate – out of a total of ninety-two condemned to death for all forms of homicide.[4] These statistics come from a report on women prisoners sentenced to death, prepared for the Home Secretary in 1882, just four years before a similar report in Ireland, discussed in the previous chapter.[5]

Of course, many women do not plan their crime. It happens as a result of an escalation of violence within a family or a community. Alcohol is sometimes involved in these violent altercations, and the weapons used are those available in the domestic or working situation. Just as poison denotes premeditation, so too does the use of a gun. However, in many cases in nineteenth-century Ireland and England, the weapon was a spade, a knife, a hatchet or an oil lamp (see Tables 6.1 and 6.2).[6] The use of these farm and household implements often persuaded the court that the crime was not planned and led to a verdict of manslaughter or assault rather than to one of murder.

Women in nineteenth-century Ireland were engaged in very similar crimes to those reported elsewhere in the academic literature. They had a much lower rate of participation in crime than men. Their highest visibility in crime statistics was in relation to crimes against property and when they did murder, their victims were usually children.[7] However, women did kill adults – men and women. Here, the focus is on women who killed men. While it is not possible to give an overall figure for the nineteenth century, it can be said that convict records and *RIC Returns of Outrages* reveal the names of at least thirty-two women who killed a man between 1840 and 1900 (see Tables, 6.1, 6.2, 6.3). Some killed husbands, some brothers or other relatives, and some killed neighbours.

Of the cases explored in this chapter, ten women were found guilty of murder and sentenced to death during the period 1840–1900. Four of these women were actually executed, the others having had their sentences reduced to penal servitude for life. In the first two decades of the twentieth century, two women were found guilty of murder (in each case the victim was a husband) and both were executed (see

Table 6.2 *Women convicted of manslaughter or assault for killing a man*

Name	County	Victim	Weapon/ Cause of death	Sentence	In Prison
Margaret Brosnan	Kerry	Husband	Knife	20 years PS	1879–90
Kate Shea	Kerry	Bailiff	Stone	18 mths. HL	1879
Margaret Kelly	Armagh	Husband	Stool	6 mths. HL	1880
Ann Morris	Tyrone	Cousin	Gun & kicks	12 mths. Prison	1880
Mary Lavelle	Mayo	Husband	Spade & pitchfork	PS life	1881–92
Catherine Lavelle (15)	Mayo	Father	Spade & pitchfork	10 years PS	1881–88
Margaret O'Neill/Neill	Galway	Cousin	Stone	14 years PS	1885–95
Mary Shufflebottom	Antrim	Neighbour	Oil lamp	6 mths. HL	1889
Lizzie Barr	Antrim	Stranger	Knife	3 years PS	1894–96
Mary Bingham	Mayo	Husband	Deep cuts to head	4 mths. HL	1889
Mary Walsh	Mayo	Son-in-law	Deep cuts to head	4 mths. HL	1889
Johanna Nolan	Kerry	Son (age 15)	Asphyxia	5 years PS	1891
Margaret Mingle	Monaghan	Stranger	Knife	12 mths. Prison	1891
Mrs Roache	Waterford	Husband	Oil lamp	5 years PS	1892
Maria Hughes	Queen's County	Husband	Hatchet	10 years PS	1893
Lizzie McAuliffe	Cork	Stranger	Umbrella point	4 mths. Prison	1894

Key: PS Penal servitude in prison
　　　HL Hard labour in prison

Sources: Transportation data-base, General Prison Board, RIC and convict records (National Archives of Ireland).

Table 6.1). Sixteen women and a 15-year-old girl were found guilty of manslaughter or assault and sentenced to imprisonment – sometimes with the additional condition of penal servitude or hard labour – for periods of time ranging from four months to life (see Table 6.2). As with men who killed women and women who killed children, the severity of the sentence depended on the circumstances of the death and the responsibility for the crime attributed to the woman offender. Six of the women selected for discussion here were arrested for the crime, but were either acquitted or discharged due to lack of evidence (see Table 6.3). Finally, only one woman was found 'guilty but insane' for murdering a man. This was Mary Rielly, whose case will form the final part of this chapter. There may have been other women for whom the insanity defence was used but, for the moment, they remain invisible. This is mainly due to the fact that records for some cases are very scant, following the destruction of a substantial proportion of court files in the fire at the Custom House in Dublin in 1921.

Table 6.3 *Women who were arrested for the murder of a man, but not convicted*

Name	County	Victim	Weapon/ Cause of death	Verdict	Year
Margaret Maher	Tipperary	Father-in-law	Push	Unknown	1857
Isabella Dixon	Tyrone	Father	Poison	Unknown	1860
Judy Mullin	Mayo	Husband	Gun	Discharged	1880
Sabrina Murray	Galway	Father-in-law	Push	Acquitted	1886
Catherine Murray	Antrim	Husband	Saucepan	Discharged	1890
Bridget Cunningham	Roscommon	Brother	Beating	Acquitted	1896

Sources: General Prison Board, RIC and convict records (National Archives of Ireland).

HUSBAND MURDER

As can be seen from Table 6.1, a number of women were found guilty of murdering a man in nineteenth-century Ireland. The death penalty was the automatic sentence for this crime but, as with other murders, women could make an appeal for clemency to the Lord Lieutenant. Whilst husbands featured as victims in murders committed in the second half of the century, no woman was executed for this crime. Only three women were executed between 1850 and 1900 (Honora and Bridget Stackpoole and Margaret Shiel), and these were for murders involving disputes over land, rather than over domestic matters. Before looking at their crimes, we will explore a very interesting case in the 1840s, in which a woman who poisoned her husband was executed.

Mary Ann McConkey, a Protestant from Monaghan, was convicted of murder on 20 March 1841.[8] Her husband, Richard, had died after eating a meal of green vegetables, which his wife had cooked for him.[9] Two other people had been in the house at the time, Mary Ann Johnson and her father George McMeehan. Only George had eaten from the same plate as Richard and he was violently ill later that day. Though the post-mortem did not establish what kind of poison was used, it confirmed that the death was due to poisoning. There was no evidence that Mrs McConkey had bought poison, but her fate was sealed when the court was told that she had begun a relationship with a younger man, James Smith, who lived nearby, over a year before her husband's death. According to witnesses, she had moved out from her home and lived with Smith 'in a state of criminal intercourse for three months'. The court also heard that she had recently given birth to a baby, whose father might not be her husband. Mary Ann Johnson gave evidence suggesting that Mrs McConkey intended to leave Monaghan with her lover.

> Prisoner said there was £10 in the house and if she could get it, she would go away with Smith. Witness said to her if she did that, she would leave her husband very lonely and Prisoner said 'she would give him a pill [that] would put him off the walk'.[10]

Memorials sent from the townspeople of Monaghan to the Lord Lieutenant on Mrs McConkey's behalf were signed by traders, clergy, bankers, doctors and the governor of the gaol. They pointed to the circumstantial nature of the evidence against her, the questionable character of one of the witnesses, and the questionable truth of some of the allegations about her relationship with her husband.[11] The requests for clemency fell on deaf ears and Mary Ann was executed on 1 May 1841. There would not be another execution for this crime for sixty years.

The next woman to be executed in Ireland for the murder of her husband was Mary Daly (aged thirty-six) who was hanged on 9 January 1903. She was followed by Annie Walsh (aged thirty-one), who was hanged on 5 August 1925. Annie was the last woman to be executed in Ireland.[12] Both of these women had lovers who had planned and carried out the murder of their husbands. Unlike the case of Mary Ann McConkey, which had not implicated anyone else in the crime, the cases of Daly and Walsh led to four executions. Daly's lover, Joseph Taylor (aged twenty-six) and Walsh's lover, Michael Talbot (aged twenty-four), were also hanged.

The stories of these women are mentioned here to highlight the fact that the judiciary viewed this as a rare crime. Though women did kill their husbands in the second half of the nineteenth century, the Irish courts judged that very few had deliberately planned and carried out the killing in order to move into a new relationship. One such woman was convicted of murder and sentenced to death. This was Catherine Delany, a 46-year-old Catholic farmer's wife from County Tipperary, who had four children. She had poisoned her husband in April 1884.

> Michael Delany, farmer and builder, aged fifty three years, died from the effects of arsenical poison administered to him by his wife, Catherine Delany, who it is alleged wished to get rid of him, as she was anxious to marry some one else.[13]

Her trial was delayed as was her date of execution, all of which gave her time not accorded to many accused of murder. At her trial in the summer of 1885, she was found guilty and sentenced to be hanged on 18 July. Luckily for her, the execution was postponed for a month, giving her more time to present an appeal. The debate on the use of the death sentence for women was at its height during the 1880s in Ireland and in England, but it is difficult to know if this debate affected the fate of Delany. Though the *RIC Return of Outrages* indicated that she had a lover, nobody else was arrested for the crime, so perhaps there was some doubt as to her motive for poisoning her husband. Catherine's petition for mercy was successful and her sentence reduced first to penal servitude for life and later to twenty years. She spent thirteen years in prison and, during that time, she kept in constant contact by letter with her solicitor and with her four children. They had emigrated to the US and settled in Providence, Rhode Island. Catherine sent and received a very high number of letters, a situation that was extremely unusual, as most prisoners received very few letters. She did not hesitate to ask for special permission to write extra letters. For example, in 1890 she wrote six and received four. These letters show that in spite of the fact that she had killed their father – allegedly to marry another man – her children did not abandon her. They wrote to her all through her time in prison, submitted twelve memorials (one per year) requesting her release and, finally, sent her a sailing ticket and some money to enable her to join them in the US.

However, Catherine's plan to settle in the US did not materialize. When she was discharged in 1898, she boarded a ship for the US at Queenstown, County Cork, but she was sent back to Ireland, as she was refused entry to Boston by the US Immigration Commission.[14] Though no explanation for this refusal is given on her file, it is likely to be connected to the fact that she had poisoned her husband. Though her punishment was severe both in terms of her long term of imprisonment and the isolation from her children, Catherine was lucky not to have been hanged.

Another woman, who had been found guilty of the murder of her husband, also escaped execution. This was Elizabeth Buchanan, aged around forty, from County Londonderry who, in 1881, shot her

80-year-old husband (an army pensioner) during a quarrel. Elizabeth had gone to the police and told them that her husband had shot himself. However, the police did not believe her from the moment they found the body, as shown in the report in the *RIC Return of Outrages*:

> When the police arrived at the scene, they found Buchanan quite dead, with his face cut and disfigured. They inquired for the weapon, with which the act was committed, whereupon Elizabeth Buchanan took a small pistol from her pocket, and stooping as if to take it from the floor, gave it to them. She made several contradictory statements.[15]

Obviously, this was not a well planned murder, if it was planned at all, as it was very obvious to the doctor who carried out the post-mortem that her husband could not have shot himself.

> The doctor who examined the deceased stated that it was impossible that the wounds could have been self inflicted. It was proved that death had been caused by blows from some sharp instrument. A lead pellet was found, which appeared to have been fired at the neck of the deceased after death.[16]

Elizabeth was convicted of murder and sentenced to death. The date for her execution was set for 23 August 1881.[17] However, the jury 'recommended her to mercy' and her death sentence was commuted to penal servitude for life because of her 'low level of intelligence'. After spending over ten years in prison, she was discharged 'on arrangements being made for her emigration'.[18]

GAINING FROM MURDER

The three women who were executed in the second half of the nineteenth century were all involved in family disputes over land. These cases will be discussed more fully in the next chapter, so they are just summarized here. In 1853, Honora Stackpoole and her sister, Bridget, were hanged, together with Bridget's husband Richard, for the murder of Richard's cousin James Stackpoole, following a dispute over an inheritance. In 1870, Margaret Shiel and her brother, Lawrence, were hanged for shooting Patrick Dunne, a neighbour, with whom they were in dispute over a right of way to a bog.[19] In both of these cases, justice was swift and decisive. Where disputes arose over land, the judicial position was clear – it had to be publicly punished.

The Stackpoole murder was obviously premeditated and the women were held equally responsible for the planning and carrying out of the murder – James was beaten to death and his body left in a field near a local river. The story began when Honora and Bridget married into the Stackpoole family – Honora to Thomas and Bridget to his illegitimate nephew Richard. They lived on Thomas's small farm in County Clare with James (Thomas's legitimate nephew) and John Halpin (Honora's nephew). According to witness statements during the court case:

> Thomas Stackpoole had been at one time in respectable and comfortable circumstances, but being a drunken and dissipated person, he had squandered all his property.[20]

In fact he was in debt and 'all his furniture and crops were seized on the day he was taken prisoner' for the murder of James. The motive for the crime was well known. James was due to inherit 'landed property (about £70 per annum)' from his dead father who had emigrated to England. If he died before 'coming of age', the inheritance would go to Thomas. James did not live to see his birthday – he was beaten to death by his uncle, his cousin and their wives – a beating that was witnessed by Honora's 9-year-old daughter, Annie. Though Thomas played a part in the murder, he was not executed. The others were – Honora, Bridget and Richard were hanged in Ennis Prison on 29 April 1853.[21]

The murder of Patrick Dunne, a poor farmer from King's County, was regarded in a similar light to that of James Stackpoole, although there was more general sympathy for the brother and sister who carried out the murder. His death was the final act in a family feud between the Dunnes and the Shiels. Lawrence Shiel had got into a fight with Patrick Dunne a year prior to the crime. He was convicted of assault and spent six months in prison, during which time his sister Margaret (known as Peggy) swore that she would get even. On the evening of 26 February 1870, Patrick took a short-cut through the Shiel's farm to the bog over which there was disputed access. According to his statement as he lay dying, he was shot twice by Peggy, as Lawrence looked on. This is a very interesting piece of information, as it was most unusual, even in cases where guns were involved, for the woman to be the one who fired the shot. For this crime, Peggy and her brother were executed in Tullamore Prison on 27 May 1870 – just three months after their crime, in spite of memorials asking for clemency.[22] One wonders how the dispute about the 'right of way' was resolved.

Another woman who was judged to have murdered for gain was Catherine Dooley, a single woman who lived with her cousin John, on a farm in Queen's County. She was found guilty of his murder in 1884.

John was described as being a 'man of some means' who had 'a good deal of money in his possession at the time of the murder'. John Dooley had gone missing after a fair in Mountmellick on 20 July 1883. His disappearance was not reported to the police until 10 August and his body was found seven days later in his own garden 'about twenty yards from the house in which he resided'. He had died from a blow to the head from a blunt instrument. The money was missing. The jury found Catherine guilty of the murder and the motive seemed to be robbery although this was not proved as the money was never found. They recommended her to mercy, a recommendation that later helped in the decision to reduce the sentence to penal servitude for life. Catherine spent fourteen years in Mountjoy Prison and was discharged directly to hospital in Dublin in 1898.[23]

The final murder conviction in our discussion of women who killed men is a puzzle. We are not sure what the motive was, nor is it clear why the court handed down such a harsh sentence. Mary Brophy, a 23-year-old single Catholic housekeeper from Cork City, was sentenced to death in 1886 for the murder of her 18-year-old labourer brother, Timothy, with whom she was 'constantly in the habit of quarrelling'. He 'died from the effects of injuries to the neck and face inflicted apparently with a knife'. Mary was due to be hanged on 23 August 1886, but her sentence was commuted to penal servitude for life. During her time in prison, she communicated frequently by letter with her remaining two brothers, Philip and Daniel who, though they did not visit her, wrote to her. She was described as 'stout and strong' at the time of her entry to Grangegorman Prison but her health deteriorated and by 1892 'she was falling into consumption'.

After spending nine years in prison, Mary was discharged on the grounds of ill-health and admitted directly to Mercer Street Hospital in Dublin for the treatment of her consumption.[24] We do not know if she died in hospital or if she was well enough to be discharged home. As with other cases, for which the records are difficult to track, it is almost impossible to work out why Mary received the death penalty. Her weapon was a knife, a choice that did not usually reflect premeditation, nor was there an obvious motive for her crime. We can only conjecture that the attack was unprovoked and that the injuries she inflicted were unusually severe.

DOMESTIC VIOLENCE

In addition to the women convicted of murder and sentenced to death, there were other women convicted of the lesser crime of manslaughter or, in some cases, of assault, leading to sentences which varied in length from a few months to a life-time in prison (see Table 6.2). Of the sixteen cases selected for this discussion, six involved husbands and most of the others close relatives, reflecting the patterns of female crime noted elsewhere.[25]

Some of the cases in which the husband was the victim were clearly situations of domestic violence. The Lavelle family murder was an example of teenage children rallying around an abused mother. Mary was a 44-year-old Catholic housekeeper from County Mayo, who, together with her son, Thomas (aged around sixteen) and her daughter, Catherine (aged fifteen), was found guilty of the manslaughter of her husband in 1881. According to the *RIC Return of Outrages*:

> Upon the police hearing that he died under suspicious circumstances, the body was exhumed on 8th April. An inquest was held and it was found that the deceased had received a wound across his left arm, below the elbow, about four inches long, severing an artery … There were two other wounds on the same arm, a lacerated wound on the left hip and another on the left leg, about four inches long. There was also a puncture wound on the left shoulder and several slight wounds and bruises over the body.[26]

The police were well aware of the violence of this man towards his wife, as she had made a formal complaint against him two days before his death.

> It is supposed the injuries were inflicted by a spade and stable fork. Lavelle and his wife had been on very bad terms. On 31st March previously, she complained to the police that her husband had been continually beating her, and that she was in dread of her life. She was then advised to swear an information against him, which she said she would do.[27]

We can only conjecture that Edward again attempted to abuse his wife and that his son, Thomas, and daughter, Catherine, intervened to protect their mother. They made the mistake of hiding their crime by arranging a funeral as for a natural death. After being buried for four days, the body was exhumed on 8 April. Rumours had reached the police that there were suspicious circumstances surrounding the death. Mary, Thomas and Catherine were arrested and all three were found guilty of manslaughter at the Connaught Winter Assizes, held in Carrick on Shannon on 12 December 1881. Mary, though sentenced to penal servitude for life, was freed after eleven years in prison.

Thomas and Catherine each completed seven years of their ten year sentences, by which time they were in their twenties. Prison records for Mary show that they all maintained contact with each other and with two other sons, John and Edward, by letter and through prison visits.[28]

All three emigrated from Ireland to the US immediately on their release. Mary's ticket was paid for by her son. Her discharge plan was typical of many other convicts. She was discharged on 14 November 1892 to Liverpool docks. She sailed two days later to the US, having got an advance of her gratuity (earned in prison) of £2.5.7 to buy clothing (equivalent to approximately £170 at 2006 prices).[29] As this was not a great deal of money, we can only assume that she received the balance on her arrival at the other end of the journey. She was in her mid-fifties by then, a very advanced age to be starting a new life in a strange land. However, this was probably her only hope of a life free of the stigma of abuse and crime.

Some cases of murder arising from domestic violence did not lead to any conviction, due to insufficient evidence (see Table 6.3). Peter Mullin, from County Mayo, was shot dead by two men just before midnight on 20 December 1880. The post-mortem showed that he had four bullet wounds in his head and that three of them had been fired at him after he had fallen on the ground. It was well known in the area that he was a man 'of most violent temper' and that he was frequently violent towards his wife, Judy. On the day of the crime, he had gone with his wife and their 16-year-old son to the market at Ballinrobe. According to the police report:

> He drank freely during the day and left Ballinrobe much worse of drink, in company with his wife, son and eleven other persons. A dispute arose on the way, and deceased, finding that his wife did not arrive with him at home, went to the house of a neighbour, named Michael Cureen, to look for her.[30]

What happened next was the kind of assault that showed not only his violent nature, but his contempt for his wife and her friends, who were present during this abusive outburst.

> He found her at the fire in the kitchen, when he at once caught her by the hair, threw her down, and danced on her. Cureen and his family, with difficulty, tore him from his wife.[31]

While he was battering his wife, two of her nephews, Patrick Feerick and Anthony Sheridan, left the house and went outside. Nobody knows what happened next, but the police report builds a picture of a very quick killing.

> [Mullin] and his son then left [the Cureen house] and when they had walked about 250 yards from the house, passed two men sitting in the ditch of the boreen by which they went, the father being in front. The moment he passed the men, they rose and shot him in the back of the head. He fell and never spoke. They were so near him that the collar of his coat, through which the ball passed, was singed.[32]

Mullin's son of sixteen was present at the crime but he offered no information on the identity of the men who shot his father. The police conjectured that his wife's family was involved in the crime. They arrested Judy and her two nephews, Patrick Feerick and Anthony Sheridan, and held them for ten days when they came before a magistrate at the Hollymount Petty Sessions on 30 December. The magistrate discharged all three because there was no evidence against them. This was rough justice for Peter Mullin and a new lease of life for his wife.

There is no doubt that the local police knew the perpetrators of this crime. Ballinrobe is just a small town and the area has never been heavily populated. However, they must have failed to gather sufficient evidence to bring the case to the stage of a conviction. In other cases, information available informally to the police seemed to play a part in the outcome. An example of this was the death of John Bingham, a 45-year-old bill-poster from County Mayo. He died in September 1889, from the effects of injuries received from his wife and his mother-in-law. Because he had been 'in a bad state of health' before his death, the family was able to bury him without anyone alerting the coroner or the police. However, when rumours began to circulate about a possible assault, his body was exhumed very soon after burial, and he was found to have 'two deep cuts' in his head. According to the police report:

> *He was a man of intemperate habits and lived unhappily with his wife.* It is believed the wounds were inflicted by his mother-in-law, Mary Walsh and that his wife, Mary Bingham, also took part in the assault. A lodger in the house, named Catherine Gilfoyle, was alleged to have been an accessory after the fact.[33]

Though he was of intemperate habits, which we assume means that he drank to excess, there was no evidence of domestic violence. Because the injuries accelerated rather than caused John Bingham's death, and because his wife and mother-in-law pleaded guilty to aggravated assault, they were treated leniently by the court. They were each sentenced to four months imprisonment with hard labour. The lodger, Catherine Gilfoyle, was discharged because there was no evidence against her.

Not all cases of domestic violence involved husbands. Some tell the story of men who continued to be violent to the women in their households into their old age – lashing out at a daughter or a daughter-in-law. The women listed in Table 6.3, who were all arrested for a murder but who were not convicted, include two who killed a father-in-law and one a father. Here, we will discuss just one of these cases to illustrate the hatred that sometimes existed in homes where the young woman had to cope with an aggressive older male relative. This was the case of Michael Murray, a 77-year-old farmer from Curranarona, County Galway, who, according to police reports, was murdered in his own house on 27 September 1886.[34] The coroner recorded his death as a suicide in the first instance. Dr M.A. Lyden conducted an external examination of the body after it was found on the seashore near Murray's home, where he lived with his son, Martin, and daughter-in-law, Sabrina. The doctor was satisfied that the marks he found on the body were caused by crashing against sharp rocks and that 'death was caused by drowning'.[35]

Murray was buried, but about three weeks later, his stepson, Pat Flaherty, alerted the police to the fact that the death was suspicious. The body was exhumed, a new enquiry was opened, and Sabrina Murray and her husband, Martin, were arrested. They had just married, in February 1886, and Martin had been given some land and stock by his father. The father, however, had retained ownership of the house in which they all lived unhappily together.[36] The evidence presented to the court, the Galway Assizes of March 1887, was pretty damning. A post-mortem on the exhumed body, carried out by Dr Richard Kinkead, a Galway surgeon, overturned the findings of the previous medical report. He found marks on the head which were caused by a blow or heavy fall before Murray died and he concluded that 'the appearance of the heart and lungs would point to death caused by shock or concussion – [in] my opinion, death did not occur from drowning'.[37]

This finding was corroborated by Patrick Delap, a 13-year-old boy, who worked for Martin Murray. In a statement made to police on 30 October (a month after the death), he described a scene of violence initiated by Michael Murray but continued by Sabrina and her husband, Martin.

> Sabrina called me in and told me to bring in a bucket of water to wash the potatoes. I went for the water and brought it in and left it on the floor and then the old man threw it out. The old man said to me then – 'did I ask you to bring in the water?' Sabrina then went out and brought in another bucket and [she] spilt the water into the tub and put the potatoes into it. The old man stood up and spilt the potatoes and the water on the floor. Sabrina said – 'are you not a little afraid that I would choke you alive?'[38]

This was only the lead-up to the fight that ensued. Michael then mimicked Sabrina, in her hearing, and mocked her method of cooking potatoes. His method was to place them directly on the fire to roast, while hers was to boil them. At this point in the altercation, Martin came back into the house.

> The old man then struck Sabrina a blow of the tongs on her mouth. Sabrina then gave a shove to the old man and his left hand came against the wall, blood [was] coming out of Sabrina's mouth when the old man struck her ... He fell on the back of his head. The old man's hand was cut ... [He] got up again and struck Sabrina with his fist. Martin was there and he threw the old man out on the street and gave him a kick or two.[39]

At this point, accounts of what happened diverge. Sabrina and Martin maintained that Michael did not come back into the house and they did not know where he was until the body was found the next day. Patrick Delap told a different story. He told the police that he went back to the house later in the day, having tended to the cattle, as requested by Martin. He found the doors locked. He knocked but got no answer, although he was sure that there was someone inside the house. A few minutes later, Sabrina called him in. What he saw and heard next shocked him so much that he told police he was 'shivering with fear'.

> I noticed spots of blood on her [Sabrina's] hands ... I saw the old man in the pig's bed and he groaning [*sic*]. Sabrina said 'that is the death that God promised him, and that is the death that God promised me'.[40]

Sabrina asked Patrick to help her put Michael into his own bed, but the boy refused and left. In his statement, he said that Sabrina was not happy with him and was afraid that he might tell the police, who happened to be in the locality that day.

> When I was going out of the house, Sabrina said to me 'little would
> make me do the same thing to yourself'.[41]

Nobody else witnessed any of these events and the court decided that
the evidence was not sufficiently robust for a conviction. It was also
influenced by the fact that Sabrina was, by then (March 1887) 'far
advanced in pregnancy'. Martin was discharged before the case
reached the Galway Assizes, and Sabrina was acquitted.

The situation in which Sabrina found herself was not unusual then,
nor is it now, in societies where there is a tradition of newly-weds
moving into a house owned by the parents of one spouse. Michael and
his daughter-in-law deeply resented the fact that they had to live
together. This was an aggressive male who dominated his household
with verbal and physical abuse. What he did not expect was a violent
response. Unluckily for him, his decision to allow his son to bring his
new wife home resulted in his death just eight months after she
moved in.

In situations like this, it is hard to know who is to blame for the
tragedy that affected all of their lives. Perhaps the most culpable one
was Martin Murray, the man who put his wife and father into this
position? He was found to be innocent of any crime, but it is likely
that people in the locality knew that his wife could not have acted
alone in moving his father's body from the house to the shore, if that
is indeed what happened.

Not all manslaughter convictions involved domestic violence. Some
were cases in which greed was the motive, but where there were other
considerations, such as family pressure. One such case was the killing
of James Brosnan, a 52-year-old farmer from County Kerry. His wife
Margaret (aged 26) was arrested for his murder in 1879. His body had
been found in a meadow with 'three large cuts in the crown of his
head and his hat was cut through in three places'. Margaret had
obviously married James for his money. As part of the marriage
settlement, he had paid off the debt of £140 outstanding on the farm
occupied by Patrick Collins, his father-in-law, giving him the
controlling interest in it. Margaret and James had only been married
six months but there were rumours that 'an improper intercourse
existed between Mrs Brosnan and a neighbouring young man' and
also that 'her family treated Brosnan with the greatest contempt'. The
bad feeling between them was exacerbated by the fact that her family
thought James might sell his interest in the farm. Margaret, her father,
her brother and her nephew were all arrested for the crime. However,
they were acquitted because of lack of evidence and Margaret was

found guilty of manslaughter for which she was sentenced to twenty years penal servitude.[42] The judge in the case, Justice Douse, was sympathetic towards Margaret, whom he was saw as a victim of an arranged marriage motivated by greed.

> You have been made a victim by that selfish old father of yours by coercing you to marry a man against whom you had such dreadful animosity.[43]

Margaret was pregnant at the time of the trial, a fact taken into consideration by the court. They did not find her guilty of murder, which would have carried the mandatory death sentence. She had a baby girl in prison in February 1880. The baby was sent to an orphange in Cavan (probably St Joseph's) with no contact recorded in her file after that point. Margaret was released in 1890, by which time she had completed almost eleven years in prison. She was discharged to Liverpool docks and emigrated immediately from there – probably to her brother in Chicago. He had been in correpondence with her during her time in prison. We do not know what happened to the child as there is no evidence on the prison file that she was ever in contact with her mother.

We have now finished the discussion on the various verdicts handed down to women who killed men. The circumstances surrounding these killings were all different. In some cases, there had been an obvious dispute leading to a fight and in some there was known domestic violence. In some of these situations, the plea of temporary insanity or 'transitory frenzy', leading to violence, could have been used. However, if used, it was not successful. In some ways, this is a very good finding. Women are often viewed as 'mad' rather than 'bad' when they become involved in anti-social behaviour, because it is easier to see them as irrational and weak, rather than rational and strong, individuals. However, what we see here is an Irish criminal justice system that viewed women as completely capable of violent behaviour, leading sometimes to murder. This is an image of a strong woman, battling to preserve her place in a cruel world.

MARY RIELLY

The only exception to this pattern appears to be the case of Mary Rielly, a 30-year-old widowed nurse from County Galway, who was arrested in 1887 for the murder of a sick man in her care.[44] Though witness statements indicated that Rielly may have thought she was casting out a devil, the legal defence used the arguments discussed earlier on the link between alcohol consumption and temporary insanity. Mary was accused of throwing her victim on the fire as he lay ill. There were different versions of this story – the police version, the victim's version (given by the family), the media version and the perpetrator version.

Temporary insanity: The police story
According to the RIC *Return of Outrages*, events took place as follows:

> County of Galway, 23rd April 1887: Michael Dillon, farmer's son, aged thirty five years, was burned to death in his house at about three o'clock am. He had been suffering from fever for some time previously, and a woman named Mary Rielly was employed to nurse him. On the morning in question, the other inmates of the house were awakened by an unusual noise, and on going down into the kitchen, they found Dillon lying dead on a fire which had been lit in the centre of the floor, and Mary Rielly, in a state of wild excitement, throwing burning coals upon him. As the deceased was unable to leave his bed, the woman must have carried him to the kitchen, and placed him on the fire. *It is believed that she became temporarily insane from excessive drinking.*[45]

This version of events was consistent with most of the witness statements given during the court case. It also represented the official view of the crime. As Angela Bourke argues, in her discussion of the murder of Bridget Cleary, the RIC 'were the eyes, ears, and often the arms, of the British administration', in nineteenth-century Ireland.[46] Not only did they specialize in gathering information on all aspects of local life, but also in reporting it in a standardized form so beloved of Dublin Castle bureaucracy. In a county that was steeped in Irish language and folklore, the neutral tones of the English language gave the impression of order and control. Even the report of the arresting officer, Head Constable, Manus Colleary, upheld the notion of a perfectly rational and calm situation during the arrest:

> I arrested Mary Rielly in a house in Keans's Entry in the Town of Galway on the 23rd of April 1887. She appeared to me to be perfectly collected in her mind when I arrested her.[47]

The constable made no reference to the fact that Mary was a 30-year-old widow with four young children, some or all of whom may have been present at the time of her arrest. Neither did it convey any of the craziness associated with the crime in newspaper coverage. It is likely that this was indeed a low-key event as far as Constable Colleary was concerned. Crimes of a domestic nature were much less difficult for the police to deal with than either political or agrarian crimes because of the absence of any danger to the police themselves during the process of arrest. He had no reason to fear Mary or her family, so he went alone to arrest her.

Alcohol and 'transitory frenzy': The victim's story

This is the story of the Dillon family. It was comprised of a mother, two adult sons and a daughter-in-law. One of the sons, Michael, had typhus fever and they employed Mary to nurse him. On the night of the crime, Thomas (Michael's brother) slept in the barn with an employee, Peter Flaherty, while the mother and her daughter-in-law slept together in a room off the kitchen. Michael was being cared for in the kitchen by the nurse, Mary Rielly. Mary and the family were in the kitchen sharing a drink of whiskey until 11.00 p.m., when the family left to go to bed, leaving Mary alone with the sick man. There was no indication at that stage that anything was wrong. Early the next morning, they were all awoken by her screams. When they rushed into the kitchen, they found a naked Michael lying dead on the floor, surrounded by remnants of the fire. Mary was screaming and 'dancing' around him.

The description of events is contained in the statements given by witnesses before and during the court case at Galway Summer Assizes in 1887. It is clear from these statements that the witnesses had been asked if Mary was drunk at the time of the crime. Two indicated that she showed all the signs of having taken alcohol, while others were not sure. Winifred Dillon (mother of the dead man) gave the following statement:

> I awoke and found the two doors of the house open, the nurse Mary Rielly endeavoured to prevent my leaving my own room and flinging fire at me. She also threw a bottle at me. I was in terror of the nurse to leave the room. I saw from the door at which I was standing my son the deceased lying on the kitchen floor surrounded by fire, the nurse hopping about the floor with the bottle in one hand and a tongs in the other.[48]

Mary Dillon (wife of Thomas) could not confirm whether or not Mary was drunk. Her description of the scene on the morning after the crime showed a fairly violent Mary Rielly.

Mary Rielly prevented me from going into the kitchen, she had a tongs in one hand and a broom in the other. She struck me on the head with the broom. I then fainted. I fell on the ground in the room. When I came to my senses I tried to pass out into the kitchen … Mary Rielly struck me into the jaw with her hand when I came into the kitchen … I saw Michael Dillon lying on his back on the floor … Mary Rielly was there, she was jumping on the floor. There was a pint bottle of whiskey brought into the house the night previous, out of which there were three glasses taken. Mary Rielly got a half glass, myself took a half glass, and Peter Flaherty and my husband took one glass each. The bottle with the rest of the whiskey was put into the dresser which was left unlocked. I found the bottle broken in the kitchen in the morning. Sometime after I came out of the room, Mary Rielly was calling me a 'devil'.[49]

When questioned three days later, Mary Dillon was still uncertain about Mary Rielly's state of intoxication.

I saw no one in the kitchen up to that time but Mary Rielly who I could not say whether she was drunk or mad, there was a bottle of whiskey in the house, I saw the bottle broke on the floor.[50]

Two of the male witnesses were more certain that Mary was drunk. Peter Flaherty, who worked for the family, said that she asked him for a drink and Martin Beattie, whose daughter was married to Thomas, said she appeared to be drunk or out of her mind.

The purpose of eliciting evidence about alcohol consumption was to bolster the defence case. As discussed in an earlier chapter, there was a strong argument in nineteenth-century medical literature concerning the link between homicide and 'temporary insanity' or 'transitory frenzy' arising from over-indulgence in alcohol.[51] In this literature, the impulse to kill or to commit a violent act was often linked to delusions caused by alcohol. However, there was disagreement as to whether or not it removed or reduced responsibility for the crime.[52] The delusions that had preceded the crime sometimes continued after the crime and sometimes did not. Doctors were not always sure what these delusions represented. They could be a manifestation of chronic mental disorder, or simply the by-product of an alcohol induced 'transitory frenzy'. They could also be a clever ploy to cloak a cruel deed in words that sounded insane.

In coming to a conclusion on the behaviour of Mary Rielly, it was clear to all concerned that before the crime she was a perfectly sane woman with no history of mental disorder. Neither was there any evidence of subterfuge or deceit in her behaviour following the crime.

The only factor that could be identified as having a bearing on events was the fact that on the night in question she had access to a half bottle of whiskey, which was empty in the morning. This led to the decision by the jury that the crime was indeed the result of a 'transitory frenzy', based on a delusional state, brought on by over-indulgence in alcohol. This was in spite of the fact that no evidence was presented to the court that might have indicated that she had a problem with alcohol before or after the date of the crime.

Roasting a man alive: The media story

As might be expected, the media of the time made the most of the sensational aspects of the story. The three newspapers reporting the events – the *Galway Express*, the *Galway Vindicator* and the *Tuam Herald* – gave it coverage as part of its normal reporting on court cases heard during the County Galway Summer Assizes in July 1887.[53] However, though twenty-nine criminal cases were listed for the two-day sitting of the Assizes, only two received any attention – the Rielly case and that of a man (John Moloney) killed during a fight related to a local boycott. In the Moloney case, the Lord Chief Baron Palles, who was presiding over the assizes, said: 'We are living in very disturbed and turbulent times'. This was a period of high tension between tenant farmers and landlords in the west of Ireland. Virginia Crossman writes of falling agricultural prices in 1885–86, leading to rent strikes and evictions when landlords refused tenant requests for 'rent abatements'.[54] Large-scale evictions, when they did happen, often involved police and army, and resulted in arrests and convictions. This might explain the high number of cases at the Galway Summer Assizes and the relatively short amount of time devoted to the Rielly case.

Under the headline – 'Roasting a man alive' – both Galway news-papers, the *Galway Express* and the *Galway Vindicator* printed almost identical stories:

> Mary Rielly, a fever nurse, was indicted that she did at Claregalway in this county, kill and murder one Michael Dillon … The prisoner at the bar was employed to nurse the deceased Michael Dillon who was ill with fever. The evidence for the prosecution was to the effect, as deposed to by several witnesses, that Michael Dillon was left upon the night on which the occurrence took place in charge of the prisoner; that some of the members of the family were sleeping in the barn on account of the fever being in the house; that all were aroused early in the morning by the screams of the prisoner; and that upon going in they found the deceased lying almost naked on the floor, surrounded by fires. He was quite dead. Prisoner was seen standing over the body.[55]

Both newspapers reported the outcome of the case in fairly measured tones without any interpretation of events. The same could not be said for the *Tuam Herald*, which used the less inflammatory headline of 'Important Case', but offered a much more sensational story.

> In the case where a woman who was tending a man named Dillon, sick with typhus fever, and who burned him in the insane delusion that thereby she expelled the devil and restored his life, the jury found a verdict of manslaughter.[56]

Here, another aspect of life in rural Ireland is introduced into the events leading up to the death of Michael Dillon – the influence of superstition on the action of the nurse. Did she believe that Dillon was possessed by the Devil and that by burning him, she would restore him to health? The evidence presented by some witnesses planted the seed for the newspaper story. According to Peter Flaherty (who worked for the family):

> When I came to the kitchen door, I saw the deceased Michael Dillon stretched on the kitchen floor. He was surrounded by fire and fire scattered over the floor. I saw Mary Riley [*sic*] the nurse there having a tongs in one hand and a broom in the other gesticulating violently – Michael Dillon was then dead – I cannot say whether Mary Riley [*sic*] was drunk or not. When I came to the door the nurse said: 'Pether asthore give me a drink and I will soon have Michael Dillon here instead of the Devil'.[57]

The reader might wonder why, if a fire had got out of control in the kitchen, how it did not spread to the rest of the house? The next witness account, given by Thomas Dillon (brother of the dead man), gave the impression that the fire had spread farther than the kitchen:

> The nurse Mary Rielly was then dancing about the kitchen floor. She was apparently mad. I cannot say if she was drunk. There was fire scattered about the house and about the deceased. The man was dead at the time I saw him. I asked her the nurse, why she burned the deceased. She said she was not sorry for having done it and that she would soon have Michael back.[58]

The focus continued to be on Rielly's behaviour rather than on the extent of the fire. Dillon's story was confirmed by Martin Beattie (whose daughter was married to Thomas).

> I saw Michael Dillon lying on the floor, his head was about three feet
> from the fireplace and his face towards the door. The body was black as
> if thrown in the ashes. I saw fire scattered around. I saw Mary Rielly
> sitting down near the fire place. I asked her 'what was the matter since
> I was here last night?' She said she 'burned him, I done it, and the devil
> I burned in the place of Michael'. She appeared to be drunk or out of
> her mind.[59]

The discourse of devils and fairies appeared in the literature in
relation to three other famous cases in the 1890s in Ireland – that of the
Doyle family, in which a 13-year-old boy was beaten to death by his
family, that of 35-year-old James Cunningham, who was also beaten to
death by his family, and that of 26-year-old Bridget Cleary, who died
as a result of being held over an open fire by her husband and other
family members. In the Cunningham case (like the Rielly case), the
killers gave the impression of believing the victim to be possessed by
the Devil, while in the other two cases, it was alleged that the victim
was a 'changeling'. The insanity defence was used successfully in the
Cunningham case and the Doyle case – resulting in most members of
both families being sent to either a local asylum or the Central
Criminal Lunatic Asylum (Dundrum).[60] The same was not true for the
Cleary case in which the husband and other family members were
sent to prison.[61]

There are some similarities in the media coverage of the Rielly and
Cleary cases. The phrase 'roasted alive' was used in both accounts and
there was an acceptance of the possibility of superstition playing a real
part in the factors leading to the killing. In Bourke's seminal work on
the Cleary case, she argues that fairy legends were part of the ordinary
discourse of rural life in Ireland at the time, used as part of a
mechanism to maintain social equilibrium.

> Fairy-legends have been denigrated as superstition, and trivialized in
> ethnic stereotypes; like any other art form, however, they carry the
> potential to express profound truths and intense emotions … they are
> particularly well suited to the expression of ambivalence and ambiguity.[62]

However, when they were aired in official circles, such as a courtroom, they clashed with the rational discourse of the ruling elite. In
fact they represented a completely different 'symbolic universe' to that
occupied by the police and members of the court system. What is
interesting for us at this point of the discussion is that the media
reflected both of these worlds – the cool rational world of officialdom
in the city newspapers, the *Galway Express* and the *Galway Vindicator*,

and the superstitious world of the ordinary man or woman in the street in the more rural newspaper, the *Tuam Herald*.

Accidental death: The perpetrator's story

Mary Rielly disagreed with all previous versions of events, though her voice was not heard until some time after her conviction. It is likely that she made a statement at the time of her arrest or trial, but it is not included in the court papers of the time.[63] The only record we have of her story is contained in medical reports from Dundrum – information given to medical staff by Mary during her confinement there. According to Dr Isaac Ashe, the medical superintendent, Mary said that she was exhausted at the time of the crime, after having cared for her patient, Michael Dillon, for over a week. During the night in question, he fell out of bed onto the fire while she was asleep. She insisted that she did not, at any time, think he was a changeling or the devil. This is the story reported by Dr Ashe in June 1890, in his response to the request from the office of the inspectors of lunacy as to her state of mind:

> We have carefully examined Mary Reilly as requested by you, and find that she is at present completely recovered in mental health, no longer presenting the symptoms of melancholia formerly attributed to her. I may add that she entirely denies having entertained the idea that Michael Dillon, for whose murder she was tried, was a changeling; and states, as she has always done, that he was a restless patient during his sickness and must have got out of bed and fallen on the fire of himself, while she, having been awake nurse-tending him for seven days and nights consecutively, was in a state of profound slumber by his bedside.[64]

The possibility of an accidental death is confirmed in the summary of the medical evidence contained in the memorial (requesting her release) sent in June 1890 to the office of the Lord Lieutenant by Redmond McDonagh, solicitor acting on Rielly's behalf.

> The medical evidence for the prosecution left the facts in grave uncertainty, as it was not clear whether the deceased Michael Dillon … was, or was not, dead at the time the injuries were inflicted upon him by fire, as it appeared from the evidence of the doctors that the mark of these injuries would be left had they been inflicted some minutes after death. The Lord Chief Baron left the matter to the Jury, strongly observing upon the uncertainty of this testimony.[65]

The original testimony of Dr P.R. D'Alton, who carried out the post-mortem examination, was certainly not conclusive.

> I found the head, face, chest and extremities extensively burned. I
> believe that shock, the result of the burns above referred to, was in my
> opinion the cause of death. Deceased was suffering from fever and was
> under my care for some time and very seriously ill. Some of the burns
> were inflicted before and some after death. The burn on the scalp was of
> itself sufficient to cause death in his then state of health.[66]

As Mary Rielly was the only one present in the room at the time that
Michael Dillon fell or was pushed into the fire, her testimony was
crucial. However, at the time of her trial, Mary was not a good
witness. As explained by her solicitor, McDonagh, in his memorial to
the Lord Lieutenant, she remembered very little of the events of the
night of the crime.

> The Convict was a nurse, and had been for weeks in charge of the
> deceased. Worn out with sleeplessness and fatigue she seems (according
> to her own statement) to have little trace on her memory of the
> occurrence.[67]

It is clear from the witness statements that nobody saw what had
happened in the kitchen that night. Michael was already dead by the
time the family came into the room. Whether Mary's distress leading
to delusions occurred before or after her patient's death will never be
known. However, what is interesting is that the verdict of 'accidental
death' was not seriously considered as a possible option in the courtroom at the Galway Summer Assizes.

As Bourke argued in her discussion of the Cleary case, the kitchen
in Claregalway, the scene of the death of Michael Dillon, represented
not only the individual life of this family, but the larger events in Irish
society in the last two decades of the nineteenth century. This was a
society fraught by political unrest and economic deprivation.[68] For
most of the people in the west of Ireland, where this crime took place,
life was full of hardship. This was evidenced in the circumstances
surrounding the death of Michael Dillon. He had contracted typhus
fever, some members of the family were sleeping in the barn, and the
house in which four adults lived appeared to comprise of a kitchen, a
bedroom and a barn.[69] However, this family was not the poorest.
Michael's relatives employed a nurse to look after him, which indicated that they had some income from the farm.

Into the middle of the personal struggle for a good enough life
came the long arm of government, exemplified in the criminal justice
system. Years of bureaucratic control from England via Dublin had
resulted in a high degree of standardization and uniformity throughout

the public services. Classification was used in all aspects of official life, as demonstrated in the courts, prisons and hospitals. The death of Michael Dillon was classified as murder and Mary Rielly proclaimed insane.

Mary Rielly stood out from the crowd of other female criminal lunatics in Dundrum because of her crime. As already discussed, the women in Dundrum who had committed homicides had mainly killed children. For many of them, the insanity defence had a particularly female dimension, as the killing of children was often linked to 'puerperal mania' or other irregularities in the female reproductive system. These 'female maladies' were proposed only in relation to the killing of children and were not offered as a justification for killing an adult – male or female. It was to be expected, therefore, that there was no effort to link Mary Rielly's violent behaviour to menstruation or pregnancy. Though no information is given in the official records as to the ages of her children, there is no indication that Mary was pregnant or that she had recently given birth. We know that she was a young widow (aged thirty) with four children, and that she worked as a nurse to maintain her family. According to the local physician, Dr D'Alton, she was a caring and trustworthy woman, capable of looking after sick people in the community.

> I found the nurse Mary Rielly, attentive in the discharge of her duties when visiting the deceased Michael Dillon and appropriately fitted for the office of nurse tender.[70]

In other words there was no suggestion of disturbances in her mental state due to a 'female' condition. The explanation – of temporary insanity due to over-indulgence in alcohol – was the defence usually used for men who killed women. It had been discussed in this very court in the previous year to explain the killing of Mrs Brodie by her husband. It was once again deployed successfully in Rielly's defence and she was found 'guilty of manslaughter at a time when insane' and 'sentenced to be confined in Dundrum'.[71]

Thus, Mary Rielly became a criminal lunatic. Her sentence began in 1887 and lasted for only four years. According to the scant records on her time in Dundrum, she recovered her sanity and was discharged to the Richmond Asylum and immediately transferred to Ballinasloe Asylum in 1891, on the understanding that she would emigrate to the US, where her children and other members of her family lived.[72] Though the legal outcome for Rielly was extremely stigmatizing and probably ruined her life and that of her family, she avoided the alternative conviction of execution or penal servitude for life. She also set an Irish precedent for the successful use of the insanity defence for women who killed men.

NOTES

1 For discussion on gender patterns of crime and punishment, see K. Daly, *Gender, Crime and Punishment* (New Haven, CT: Yale University Press, 1994); Clarice Feinman, *Women in the Criminal Justice System* (Westport, CT: Praeger, 1994); Frances Heidensohn, *Women and Crime*, 2nd Edition (Basingstoke: Macmillan Press, 1996); A. Morris, *Women, Crime and Criminal Justice* (Oxford: Basil Blackwell, 1987); C. Smart, *Women, Crime and Criminology: A Feminist Critique* (London: Routledge and Kegan Paul, 1977); Sandra Walklate, *Gender and Crime: An Introduction* (London: Prentice Hall, 1995).

2 For discussion, see Alido V. Merlo, and Jocelyn M. Pollock, *Women Law and Social Control* (Boston: Allyn and Bacon, 1995). Elicka Peterson, 'Murder as self-help: Woman and intimate partner homicide', *Homicide Studies*, 3,1 (1999), pp. 30–46.

3 For further discussion, see Ngaire Naffine, *Female Crime and Criminology: A Feminist Critique* (Sydney: Allen and Unwin, 1987).

4 Judith Knelman, *Twisting in the wind: The Murderess and the English Press* (Toronto: University of Toronto Press, 1998), p. 17.

5 Ibid; Correspondence between the Chairman of the Prisons Board and the Lord Lieutenant, Dublin Castle, in NAI, CRF, Misc. 1888/no. 1862.

6 Knelman, *Twisting in the Wind*, p. 87; See also Ruth Harris, *Murder and Madness: Medicine, law and society in the fin de siécle* (Oxford: Clarendon Press, 1989).

7 Inez Bailey, *Women and Crime in Nineteenth Century Ireland: Mayo and Galway Examined* (Unpublished MA thesis, NUI, Maynooth, 1992); Carolyn A. Conley, *Melancholy Accidents* (Lanham, MD: Lexington Books, 1999); Sinead Jackson, *Gender, Crime and Punishment in Late Nineteenth-century Ireland: Mayo and Galway Examined* (Unpublished MA thesis, NUI Galway, 1999); Rena Lohan, *The Treatment of Women Sentenced to Transportation and Penal Servitude 1790–1898* (Unpublished Mlitt thesis, Trinity College, Dublin, 1989).

8 Thanks to Dr Bill Vaughan for bringing this case to my attention.

9 Information on the case in NAI, CRF, 1841/McC. 17 (McConkey).

10 Witness statement of Mary Ann Johnson on 20 March 1841, in NAI, CRF, 1841/McC. 17 (McConkey).

11 Memorials and letters dated 25 March to 28 April, in NAI, CRF, 1841/McC. 17 (McConkey).

12 Information on Mary Daly in NAI, CRF 1902 (Daly) and Crown and Peace Office: Crown files at Assizes, Queens County 1898–1902 (NAI, IC-46–100); Information on Ann Walsh in Correspondence on Death Sentence, Department of an Taoiseach, 1922–44 (NAI S7788A).

13 *RIC Return of Outrages for the year 1884*, Homicides, p. 11. (NAI, CSO, ICR2). The name is sometimes spelt Delaney.

14 NAI, PEN, 1898/121 (Delaney). I did not find any other case in which entry to the US was refused.

15 *RIC Return of Outrages for 1881* (NAI, CSO, ICR2), Homicides, p. 4; see also NAI, 1881/B41 (Buchanan).

16 Ibid.

17 Death Book for Ireland 1852–1932, NAI, PB.CN.S, no. 3–754–4.

18 Extra information contained in documents summarizing cases in which women had been sentenced to death, in the file on Mary Daly, NAI, CRF, 1902/ D76 (Daly).

19 NAI, CSORP, 1853/ 2421 (Stackpoole); NAI, CRF, 1870/ S7 (Shiel). The name is sometimes spelt Sheil.
20 Court reports contained in NAI, CSORP, 1853/ 2421 (Stackpoole).
21 Ibid.
22 NAI, CRF, 1870/ S7 (Shiel); NAI, CSORP, 1870/11011 (Dunne).
23 Information in the report to the CSO on females sentenced to death since 1881, in NAI, CRF, 1902/ D76 (Daly). Discharge details (name of hospital not given) on Penal Servitude Register 6: Convicts discharged from penal servitude 1893–1903 (NAI, GPB, PS/6).
24 *RIC Return of Outrages for 1886* (NAI, CSO, ICR2), Homicides, p. 11; see also NAI, PEN, 1895/76 (Brophy).
25 Feinman, *Women in the Criminal Justice System*; Harris, *Murder and Madness*; Knelman, *Twisting in the Wind*.
26 *RIC Return of Outrages for 1881* (NAI, CSO, ICR2), Homicides, p. 10.
27 Ibid.
28 NAI, PEN 1892/ 118 (Mary Lavelle).
29 Calculated from data by Lawrence H. Officer, *Purchasing power of British Pounds from 1264 to 2006*, available on www.measuringworth.com.
30 *RIC Return of Outrages for 1880* (NAI, CSO, ICR2), Homicides, p. 8.
31 Ibid.
32 Ibid.
33 *RIC Return of Outrages for 1889* (NAI, CSO, ICR2), Homicides, p. 10 Italics in original text.
34 *RIC Return of Outrages for 1886* (NAI, CSO, ICR2), Homicides, p. 8.
35 Medical report 30 September 1886, in court papers for the Galway Assizes on 15 March 1887, in Court Report of Galway C. and P. Crown Assizes, 1887. (Hereafter, Galway Court Report) (NAI, File no. 1C-19–153).
36 *RIC Return of Outrages for 1886* (NAI, CSO, ICR2), Homicides, p. 8.
37 Report on 6 November 1886, in Galway Court Report, 1887 (NAI, File no. 1C-19–153).
38 Witness statement of Patrick Delap on 30 October 1886, Galway Court Report, 1887) (NAI, File no. 1C-19–153).
39 Ibid.
40 Ibid.
41 Ibid.
42 Irish Crime Records, *RIC Return of Outrages for the year 1879* (NAI, CSO, ICR2), Homicides, p. 9; see also NAI, PEN, 1890/28 (Brosnan).
43 Cited in Conley, *Melancholy Accidents*, p. 68.
44 NAI, CRF, 1891/R7 (Rielly). The name was sometimes spelled Reilly or Riley.
45 *RIC Return of Outrages for 1887* (NAI, CSO, ICR2), Homicides, p. 8. Italics in original text.
46 Angela Bourke, *The Burning of Bridget Cleary* (London: Pimlico Press; New York: Penguin, 1999), p. 7; Angela Bourke, 'Reading a woman's death: Colonial text and oral tradition in Nineteenth-century Ireland', *Feminist Studies*, 21,3 (1995), pp. 552–86.
47 Witness statement on 4 May 1887, Galway Court Report (NAI, File no. 1C-19–153).
48 Witness statement on 25 April 1887, Galway Court Report (NAI, File no. 1C-19–153).
49 Ibid.
50 Ibid.
51 Anon., 'Psychological Retrospect'; D. Yellowlees, 'Case of Murder during Temporary Insanity induced by Drinking or Epilepsy', *Journal of Mental Science*, xxix, 127 (October 1883), pp. 382–7.
52 Yellowlees, 'Case of Murder', p. 386.
53 *Galway Express*, 23 July 1887, p. 4; *Galway Vindicator*, 20 July 1887, p. 4; *Tuam Herald*, 23 July 1887, p. 3.

54 Virginia Crossman, *Politics, Law and Order in Nineteenth-century Ireland* (Dublin: Gill and Macmillan, 1996), pp. 164–8.
55 *Galway Express*, 23 July 1887, p. 4.
56 *Tuam Herald*, 23 July 1887, p. 3.
57 Witness statement on 25 April 1887, Galway Court Report (NAI, File no. 1C-19–153).
58 Ibid.
59 Ibid.
60 These will be discussed in the next chapter.
61 For discussion of these cases, see Bourke, *The Burning of Bridget Cleary*; Michael J. F. McCarthy, *Five Years in Ireland 1895–1900* (3rd edition), (London: Simpkin, Marshall, Hamilton, Kent and Co; Dublin: Hodges, Figgis and Co., 1901).
62 Bourke, *The Burning of Bridget Cleary*, p. 206.
63 Summer Assizes report of 19 July 1887, Galway Court Report (NAI, File no. 1C-19–153).
64 Letter of 13 June 1890, NAI, CRF, 1891/R7 (Rielly).
65 Letter of 4 June 1890, NAI, CRF, 1891/R7 (Rielly).
66 Witness statement on 25 April 1887, Galway Court Report (NAI, File no. 1C-19–153).
67 Letter of 4 June 1890, NAI, CRF, 1891/R7 (Rielly).
68 For discussion, see Bourke, *The Burning of Bridget Cleary*; Crossman, *Politics, Law and* Order; David Fitzpatrick, 'Class, family and rural unrest in nineteenth-century Ireland', in P. J. Drudy (ed.), *Irish Studies 2: Ireland: Land, Politics, People* (Cambridge: Cambridge University Press, 1982), pp. 37–75.
69 Witness statement in NAI, Galway Court Report (NAI, File no. 1C-19–153).
70 Witness statement on 25 April 1887, Galway Court Report (NAI, File no. 1C-19–153).
71 Summer Assizes report of 19 July 1887, Galway Court Report (NAI, File no. 1C-19–153); *Galway Express*, 23 July 1887, p. 4.
72 NAI, CRF 1891/R7 (Rielly).

CHAPTER SEVEN

Family murders

> On the 6th March 1896, James Cunningham, shoemaker, aged thirty five years, was killed at about 10 o'clock pm by members of his family … The entire family appears to have become suddenly insane and the attack on the deceased seems to have been due to an impression that he was possessed of an evil spirit.[1]

THESE WORDS, FROM THE 1896 *RIC Return of Outrages* for County Roscommon, painted a picture of family violence directed inwards. The crime was explained in terms of insanity and a belief in the world of spirits. James showed 'signs of mental derangement' for a few days before he finally 'seized his father by the throat' during the family rosary. The family responded to his attack on their father by engaging in a frenzied attack on James.

> His three brothers rushed on him and after a struggle, overpowered him and forced him into a bedroom. Their sister then brought them a pot stick and a shovel and with these weapons they smashed in his face, causing immediate death.[2]

Violence, sometimes leading to death, is not unusual in families. In fact, the family could be described as one of the most violent institutions in society. It shares many of the characteristics of a total institution and, as such, places extreme stress on individual members to conform to rules that transcend and sometimes clash with those of the wider society. The family may also engage in a negative group response to situations that threaten its harmony or its survival.[3]

Family murders in nineteenth-century Ireland fell into a number of patterns. The victims were people who threatened the family's economic or social stability either from within or from without. The motives for the killings fell into three categories – to solve a disagreement over land, to remove a known wife beater or to destroy an evil spirit/bad fairy. As far as the authorities were concerned, land crimes were viewed as the most serious and were the most likely to lead to the death penalty. Finally, while many murders were viewed as rational acts deserving of punishment, some were explained in terms of group insanity (known in the medical literature as *'folie à deux'*).

FOLIE À DEUX

Dr Oscar Woods, the resident medical superintendent of the Killarney District Asylum, was one of the most prolific writers on *folie à deux* in the Irish medical press during the nineteenth century. He gained his knowledge from his own experience in two district asylums – Cork and Killarney – and from international medical literature, particularly that written by French 'alienists' (psychiatrists). He would have read the ideas of the influential French expert on the subject, Dr E. Marendon de Montyel, which were highlighted in the *Journal of Mental Science* in 1884.[4] According to Marendon de Montyel, *folie à deux* included three different types of case: *'Folie imposé'*, in which 'a lunatic imposes his delusions on a person intellectually and morally weaker than himself'; 'simultaneous insanity', in which two people 'hereditarily predisposed, contract at the same time the same form of insanity'; and 'communicated insanity', in which 'a lunatic communicates his hallucinations and delusions to one hereditarily predisposed to insanity'. In the first category, the person on whom the influence is exerted may not be insane (just 'weak minded'), while in the other two categories all participants may be judged insane. For 'communicated insanity' to exist, three conditions were necessary, according to Dr Marendon de Montyel – a hereditary predisposition, an 'intimate association and companionship between the two future co-lunatics' and 'incessant action by the lunatic upon his sane companion, so as to induce him to share his hallucinations and delusions'.[5] Some families, then as now, met all of the conditions for 'communicated insanity'.

Dr Woods, in his description of Irish cases in the *Journal of Mental Science* in 1897, wrote of both 'communicated insanity' and of 'simultaneous insanity' that had occurred within families admitted to Cork District Asylum, where he worked at the time.[6] Some of these cases, though not all, involved violence. In 1890, a young child was almost burnt to death by its mother, who believed 'it was a spirit'. The child's parents (both aged fifty), brother (aged twenty-one) and sister (aged nineteen) were found by the police barricaded into their home and 'fighting savagely'. All were admitted to Cork District Asylum in a 'state of acute hysterical mania, the females being much the worst and quite incoherent'. The victim, Patrick, who was described as 'weak-minded and strumous [*sic*]', had 'got a weakness while in

Chapel'. He continued to be sick until the incident that brought the family to the attention of the police. People in their local district believed that they had become insane from eating 'putrid' meat. After admission, they 'could not be got to answer questions, and rambled in an incoherent manner of visions they saw'.[7] After about two weeks in the asylum, they all recovered sufficiently to be discharged home.

Woods described two other cases in which there was an alleged link between the eating of bad meat and the onset of group insanity. In 1896, an entire family of adults, consisting of two brothers and three sisters (aged between twenty-four and forty-five years), was admitted to Killarney District Asylum with 'simultaneous insanity'. All were in delicate health and were 'violent and unmanageable'. The attack of insanity was attributed by the local people to the eating of tinned American meat and, by the local clergyman, to the eating of fowl bitten by a mad dog.[8] It is not clear whether the attitude of the local people reflected a suspicion of meat that was 'foreign' or meat that was tinned. The cause of the sickness was never discovered and the two men died shortly after admission. The three women recovered their physical and mental health and were discharged home within a few months. The precipitating factor for the attack of insanity seemed to have been the 'delicate health' of the oldest brother, John (aged forty-five) and the exhaustion suffered by the others in their efforts to care for him.[9]

In 1897, there were two further cases of 'communicated insanity' in Cork District Asylum – one involving a mother and son and the other, two sisters. Dr Woods had, by then, developed a theory as to the cause of these outbreaks.

> While, in some of these cases there was a strong hereditary predisposition, in nearly all there was a scrofulous and neurotic tendency ... Shock, acting on constitutions already enfeebled, appears to have been the exciting cause. The patient primarily attacked in each case proved to be the least hopeful as regards ultimate recovery. I look on all the cases as of the same type, highly neurotic persons living in remote districts, having little to divert their thoughts from their own surroundings, and when anxiety arose they were unable to bear the strain.[10]

Of special interest in these cases is the fact that most of the people who suffered from group insanity recovered their mental health fairly quickly and did not become institutionalized at a time when this could very easily happen in Ireland. Their physical health seemed more problematic, with some recovering and others dying. In the 1897 article, Dr Woods did not describe the treatment given to these patients, but he had already done so in an article he had written for the *Journal of Mental Science* some eight years earlier in relation to the murder of 13-year-old Patsy Doyle from County Kerry by his mother and other members of his family. After successfully treating Patsy's sisters, Woods wrote:

> No special medical treatment was found necessary. Aperient and tonic medicine with chloral as a night draught during the first week; plenty of nourishing food and out-door exercise was alone required.[11]

This approach to treatment (fresh food and exercise) was also taken by Dr M.J. Nolan, Assistant Medical Officer at the Richmond Asylum, Dublin, who joined the debate on *folie à deux* in the pages of the *Journal of Mental Science* in April 1889.[12] He described the case of two brothers, John C. (aged forty-five) and Richard C. (aged forty), who lived with their elderly mother on a remote farm. The brothers came to the attention of the police because of their eccentric behaviour following the death of their mother. According to Dr Nolan, the father of the family 'had died insane' leaving his wife and six children 'in abject poverty'. John and Richard remained on the family farm after the others had found work elsewhere.

> Prior to their admission, they had lived with her [their mother] in a small cottage in a very remote and desolate mountain district – she insane; they weak-minded. Studiously avoiding any intercourse with their neighbours, quarrelling between themselves, year after year, in monotonous toil, they eked out the barest necessaries of life. Though disagreeing on minor points, they were at all times united in their devotion to their mother who, for upwards of seven years prior to her death ... was bed-ridden from infirmity.[13]

During her illness, the mother told the brothers that they were of noble descent, that their uncle had married the Queen of England and that the countryside surrounding their farm was rightfully theirs. After her death, they began a campaign of reclaiming this land 'erecting fences, cutting down hay and growing crops'. When the police tried to stop them, violence erupted and the brothers were admitted to the Richmond Asylum, Dublin, as dangerous lunatics. During their five months in the Richmond, they showed remarkable similarity not only in the content of their delusions but also in the actual words used to describe them. Though they were kept apart in the asylum, they 'continued to reflect the mental condition one of the other' and they also had a dream of a visit from their dead mother on the same night. Some of the delusions began to disappear after a few months of treatment and the men recovered sufficiently to be discharged home.

We can surmise from the writings of Dr Woods and Dr Nolan that, for people who had not committed a serious crime during the 'outbreak' of 'simultaneous insanity', the consequences of coming to the attention of the authorities were positive. However, for those who killed someone during one of these outbreaks, the consequences could be life-changing – an indefinite confinement as a criminal lunatic in Dundrum Central Criminal Lunatic Asylum.

FAIRIES, CHANGELINGS AND EVIL SPIRITS

Folie à deux was often a feature of murders in which the victim was alleged to be a fairy 'changeling' or to be possessed by an evil spirit. In these cases, family members became involved in beating or burning the person until he or she died. The victims included Patsy Doyle, a 13-year-old 'epileptic, idiot' from County Kerry, Bridget Cleary, a 26-year-old seamstress from County Tipperary, and James Cunningham, a 35-year-old shoemaker from County Roscommon.[14]

These three murders occurred in the 1880s and 1890s, a time of rapid modernization and development in Ireland. On the wider stage, technological advances such as the X-ray, the cinema and the motor car were making an impact. At a local level, in the Irish countryside, literacy levels were improving, the Irish language was disappearing and bicycles were becoming a common mode of transport. However, in spite of these changes, traditional beliefs were still alive and well in rural areas. T.C. Croker commented in the second edition of *Fairy Legends and Traditions* (published in 1870) on superstitious stories surrounding the killing of a man and of a child during the 1820s.

> Deeply as I lament that such delusion should exist, these facts will sufficiently prove that I have not (as has been insinuated) conjured up forgotten tales, or attempted to perpetuate a creed that has disappeared. On the contrary, my aim has been to bring the twilight tales of the peasantry before the view of the philosopher; as if suffered to remain unnoticed, the latent belief in them may long have lingered among the inhabitants of the wild mountain and lonesome glen, to retard the progress of their civilization.[15]

The courtroom drama that unfolded in relation to the three murders discussed here provides evidence that Croker's words still held true at the end of the century. Writing at the time, the poet W.B. Yeats, introduced his *Irish Fairy and Folk Tales* with an anecdote that indicates how real these belief systems were for some people:

> Have you ever seen a fairy or such like? I asked an old man in County Sligo. Amn't I annoyed with them was the answer.[16]

While it would be untrue to say that these beliefs were widespread, they were part of the folklore that came into play at times of stress. For most of the time they were not tested by public scrutiny. However, problems did arise when these beliefs clashed with professional medical and legal opinion. This happened in court cases where this belief system was invoked to diminish responsibility for a serious crime, as happened in the murders of Patsy Doyle, Bridget Cleary and James Cunningham.

Patsy Doyle
In 1888, Johanna Doyle, a 40-year-old mother of eight children from County Kerry, was found 'guilty but insane' in relation to the murder of her 13-year-old 'epileptic, idiot' son, Patsy.[17] According to the police report, it was a very violent event.

> Patrick ... was found dead in his father's house at about four o'clock p.m. on 29th January. His skull, cheek bones, and jaws were fractured, apparently by blows from some heavy blunt instrument. Six members of the family, who were almost nude and appeared to be in a state of raging madness, were arrested by the police. *The deceased was an imbecile, and had not spoken or walked for some years previously. It is believed that his mother, in a fit of religious mania, killed him because she thought he had some connection with evil spirits.*[18]

When the RIC officers arrived at the family farm, they saw the 'dead body of a boy' and 'a number of the family grouped together'.[19] The mother, Johanna Doyle, a brother, Michael (aged twenty-two) and three sisters of the dead boy, Julia (aged twenty-four), Mary (aged eighteen) and Kate (aged fifteen) were admitted as dangerous lunatics to Killarney District Asylum. The two youngest children, Dan and Denis (who was also classified as 'an imbecile') were not involved. The father, Michael Doyle senior, 'a man of very feeble intellect', was brought before the two magistrates and sentenced to eighteen months of hard labour in prison, followed by two years of police supervision.

He was discharged three weeks later because of his poor health.[20] The other members of the family were sent to Killarney District Asylum. Michael senior refused to tell the police what he had seen. Instead, he said:

> My wife will tell you all. They are all more clever [*sic*] than I am, and say they have been to heaven, and I must believe them.[21]

Dr Oscar Woods was the resident medical superintendent at Killarney District Asylum when the five members of the Doyle family were admitted on the 30 January 1888, two days after Patsy's murder. He described their state of mind at the time:

> The three daughters were in a very violent state of acute hysterical mania, flinging themselves about; could not comprehend anything said to them; pupils largely dilated; pulse quick. Mother and son [were] very excited, but more collected and able to comprehend what was said to them. All patients were much bruised about the body, Julia's face and left eye being greatly torn.[22]

Dr Woods was so excited by the case that he presented a paper on it to the Irish branch of the Medico-Psychological Association in November 1888, a paper that was later published in the *Journal of Mental Science*. This was a classic case of *folie à deux*, or 'communicated insanity' in five members of one family. Julia had become insane first and had communicated her condition to the rest of the family. Dr Woods suggested that the outbreak of group insanity was caused by a combination of factors, a theory that he was able to substantiate in his later practice.

> No doubt the hereditary taint and the strong superstitious ideas instilled into their ignorant minds by the old country women, acting on people whose bodily health was somewhat undermined by bad food and loss of rest, had much to say to the cause of the attack.[23]

Though she was not the first to show signs of insanity, Johanna (the mother) took the lead role in the killing of Patsy. Her explanation was logical in its own terms.

> On Saturday night at cock-crow I took that fairy Patsy – he was not my son, he was a devil, a bad fairy, I could have no luck while he was in the house – carried him out of the house and threw him into the yard, and then got a hatchet and struck him three blows on the head. I then came back, and we all prayed and went to Heaven.[24]

Similar accounts of the crime were given by other members of the family. Mary told Dr Woods:

> [I] heard my mother in the yard when she took Patsy out, 'It is time for me to kill you, you young devil; I wonder if I have killed you enough now'. I was not shocked when I heard my mother kill him, as I heard people say he was a fairy and I believed them.[25]

This version of events reflected a particular belief system about the fairy kingdom and its forays into the human world. This view was romanticized by W.B. Yeats in *The Stolen Child*.[26] Yeats explained the phenomenon of the 'changeling' as follows:

> Sometimes the fairies fancy mortals and carry them away into their own country, leaving instead some sickly fairy child, or a log of wood, so bewitched that it seems to be a mortal pining away and dying and being buried. Most commonly they steal children ... Those who are carried away are happy, according to some accounts, having plenty of good living and music and mirth.[27]

After Patsy's death, his mother continued to believe that her son was a fairy 'changeling', but his brothers and sisters gradually came to realize that this was not so. When the excitement generated by his killing began to fade, they agreed that they believed that Patsy was a fairy because they had heard their mother and other people saying it. This was their excuse for doing nothing to intervene while their mother hit Patsy with a hatchet. It was also their excuse for taking part in kicking and beating their brother to death. Only the father, Michael Doyle, who had been described as a man of 'feeble intellect' had refused to take part in the violence. This is very interesting when one remembers the writings of Dr Marendon de Montyel on *'folie imposé'*. One might expect the 'feeble minded' father to be most susceptible to his wife's suggestions. However, this was not the case.

Johanna's belief (or, in medical terms, her main delusion) – that her son was a fairy 'changeling' – was steeped in traditional beliefs. Children who were born healthy and who later developed disabilities were most likely to be considered as 'changelings'. Patsy was probably born with an intellectual disability and with epilepsy. However, something different in his behaviour must have triggered the events leading to the beating that caused his death. The records we have of the case do not tell us if he became ill or unmanageable, but it is likely that the mother saw something different about him. This she interpreted as 'changeling' behaviour. Her intention was to drive out the evil fairy and bring back the human child. Unfortunately for her, what she had done was murder in the eyes of the law.

After spending a little over six months in the Killarney District Asylum, in the care of Dr Woods, Michael, Mary and Kate Doyle, were discharged as sane. Julia, the first to show signs of insanity, was still in the asylum a year later but she too recovered.[28] Only Johanna was returned for trial at the Summer Assizes of 1888 at Tralee. She was found guilty of murder but was judged to have been insane at the time of the crime. She was sent to Dundrum to be confined there indefinitely.[29] Dr Revington, the medical superintendent at Dundrum, described her on admission as 'a fierce wild Kerry peasant, scarcely able to speak English intelligibly'.[30] Poor Johanna was confined to an institution in Dublin, with people who could not even speak her language (Irish). There are records of other Irish-speaking patients in Dundrum, but none of an Irish-speaking staff member. Johanna's husband, Michael, began to petition for her discharge in 1893. He sent two memorials to the Lord Lieutenant in 1893 and 1895. These were signed by ten other people, including the Bishop of Kerry, John Coffey, and other Catholic clergy. In the second memorial, he spoke of home and the children.

> Since then (1882), I have only seen her four times and I should like to see her oftener, but as I am a poor man, I cannot afford to pay the heavy expenses which a journey from my home to Dundrum entails ... When I last saw her [she] expressed a wish to be brought home and she believed that she would improve in mind, if she were at home or near home, where she could see me and the children.[31]

Johanna was discharged to Killarney District Asylum in August 1895, on the recommendation of the medical staff at Dundrum (Dr Revington, medical superintendent, and Dr Nixon, visiting physician), who reported that she was still suffering from 'chronic mania and unfit to be discharged to the care of her friends'.[32] She may have ended her life in Killarney Asylum but at least, we assume, there were plenty of people there to converse in Irish with her.

Bridget Cleary

The story of the 'changeling' was to appear seven years later in relation to the murder of a County Tipperary woman by her husband and a group of relatives. In a case that became known as the 'witch-burning at Clonmel', Michael Cleary and eight others were tried for the murder of his 26-year-old wife Bridget in 1895.[33] The story of

Bridget's death, which aroused great interest at the time, has been the subject of many books and plays, including the seminal work by Angela Bourke.[34] The Tipperary police recorded the crime in graphic detail.

> Bridget Cleary, cooper's wife, aged twenty six years, disappeared on the night of the 15th March, and on 22nd March her body was found by the police buried in a shallow grave in a brake of furze, about three quarters of a mile from her house. *It appears that for some days previous to her disappearance, it was generally believed in the locality that she had been bewitched and her identity changed, and on the nights of 14th and 15th March, her husband, her father, and several others, in carrying out the prescription of a 'witch doctor' named Denis Gainey, subjected her to the most brutal ill-treatment.*[35]

This was not simply a case of a man killing his wife. It was a very different crime than those described in an earlier chapter. This husband did not kill his wife when he was alone with her. Nor did it happen accidentally during a fight. This was a deliberate act, carried out by Michael Cleary in a house full of people, most of whom were related to the victim.

> At midnight on 14th March, her husband Michael Cleary, her father Patrick Boland, her aunt Mary Kennedy, her cousins Patrick, William, James and Michael Kennedy and John Dunne, and two men named William Ahern and William Simpson, assembled in Cleary's house.[36]

There are different versions of the events leading up to Bridget's death, but the facts reported by the police in the *Annual Return of Outrages* echoed those told in court and reported in the newspapers. Bridget became ill and was confined to bed with 'a raging pain in her head'.[37] The doctor and the priest were both called to the house. According to Michael McCarthy's version of events, in his *Five Years in Ireland*, the doctor 'had no anxiety about the case' and the priest 'did not consider her dangerously ill'.[38] However, Bridget's health did not improve. After about ten days, her husband consulted a herb-doctor, Denis Gainey, seeking advice on what to do. This led to the train of events that culminated in her death.

> The deceased, who was clothed only in a chemise, was forcibly held by four men of the party, compelled to swallow a herb decoction and drenched with urine on the face, mouth and person. She was then placed on the kitchen fire and burned to some extent, while questions

were put to her as to her identity. She was afterwards replaced on her bed. On the following night this barbarous treatment was resumed by her husband, in the presence of her father and the Kennedys, *the motive being to drive out the witch which was supposed to possess her*. Paraffin oil was poured over her to increase the flames, and the lower part of the trunk, abdomen, hips and thighs burned until the bones and internal organs protruded.[39]

As in the Doyle case, the killing of Bridget Cleary was explained in terms of destroying the fairy that had taken her place. Johannah Burke, a neighbour, who was the star witness for the prosecution, said she heard voices from inside the house saying 'Take it, you witch', as they fed Bridget herbs and milk.[40] She and other witnesses also described an interrogation of Bridget by her husband, as he handed her the herbal drink and later some bread and jam: 'Are you Bridget Cleary, the wife of Michael Cleary, in the name of God?'[41] Bridget's failure to answer correctly on that fatal night led to him forcing her to the ground, pouring oil on her and pushing her onto the fire. When Johannah Burke tried to intervene, Michael Cleary said: 'Hold your tongue, Hannah, it is not Bridget I am burning'.[42]

A similar explanation had also appeared in the witness statements during the court case of Mary Rielly, the nurse from County Galway, in whose care Michael Dillon had died from the effects of falling or being pushed on a fire in 1887.[43] As Bourke notes, 'Iron and fire are both well known weapons against the fairies'.[44] Though the intention was never to murder a person, but rather to destroy a fairy or evil spirit, the outcome in both cases was death.

Michael Cleary, after killing his wife on the basis of what might seem an insane delusion, went on to act in a way that implied rationality and malicious intent. Unlike the Doyle family, or the Cunningham family (whose story is told next), Cleary and his companions tried to conceal the death by hiding the body and spreading the rumour that Bridget had mysteriously disappeared. However, there were witnesses who saw what had happened.

> At about 3.00 am her body was carried out in a sheet by Michael Cleary and Patrick Kennedy and buried in the place where the police found it.[45]

As far as the court was concerned, this act showed that Michael Cleary knew that what he had done was wrong. If, as in the Doyle case, Cleary had maintained his delusion that he had not killed his wife, but a fairy 'changeling', he might have persuaded people that he was insane. In Michael McCarthy's account, we hear that Michael Cleary 'said that he would go down towards Cloneen and pretend he was half mad'.[46] However, his efforts were not successful, as at no stage was a doctor called to examine him or any of the people involved in killing Bridget Cleary.

The lack of evidence of a continuing delusion meant that there was no insanity defence in the Cleary case. Michael Cleary (husband) was sentenced to twenty years of penal servitude for manslaughter. Patrick Kennedy was sentenced to five years of penal servitude and three others received lesser sentences for taking part in the crime. Mary Kennedy (Bridget's aunt) was discharged without punishment because of her advanced age. Michael Cleary spent fifteen years in prison and was released on licence to Liverpool in April 1910. He emigrated to Canada two months later.[47]

Of particular interest to the discussion here is the fact that this case had many of the elements of a crime committed during an outbreak of *'folie à deux'*. While Michael Cleary appeared to be the strongest proponent of the delusion that his wife was a fairy 'changeling', he was not alone in his beliefs. The herb-doctor, Denis Gainey, and Bridget's own father took part in the rituals leading up to her death – rituals designed to get rid of the evil spirit that inhabited her body. In other words, it is not clear who was the originator of the story that, in medical terms, would be regarded as a delusion. In the discourse associated with *'folie à deux'*, the events that took place in County Tipperary could be described as 'simultaneous insanity' or 'communicated insanity'. However, what was different about this case was the fact that the delusion did not seem to exert an undue influence over the participants after the event. Unlike the Doyles or the Cunninghams, members of the Cleary family behaved normally after the crime. They concealed the death by burying the body and made no attempt to confess to either the priest or the police. Their behaviour was 'bad' rather than 'mad'.

James Cunningham

Just one year later, in March 1896, superstition was again used to explain a family murder in County Roscommon. This time the crime was linked to insanity. According to the police report, the violence started during the family rosary in the Cunningham household in the town-land of Lisphelim.

It appears that for some days previously, the deceased [James] had shown signs of mental derangement, and that on the night of the 6th

March, while the family were at prayer, he suddenly seized his father by the throat. His three brothers rushed on him and after a struggle overpowered him and forced him into a bedroom. Their sister then brought them a pot stick and a shovel and with these weapons they smashed in his face, causing immediate death. *The entire family appears to have become suddenly insane, and the attack on the deceased seems to have been due to an impression that he was possessed of an evil spirit. Subsequent to their arrest the accused were seized at intervals with attacks of violent madness, lasting for hours.*[48]

According to Michael J. McCarthy, the controversial (and not unbiased) writer-barrister, in his *Five Years in Ireland*, the family lived in a 'comfortable dwelling-house' in a village where most of the people were inter-related and 'extremely superstitious'.[49] McCarthy quoted the newspaper, the *Freeman's Journal*, which reported that on the night of 6 March: 'Many of them [local people] including James Cunningham were under the impression that evil spirits were hovering round their dwellings.' The parish priest, Father Gately, who knew the family for fourteen years, objected strenuously to this view. He told the court and the newspaper that he had visited James Cunningham and found him 'religiously insane', that he was being tempted by the Devil 'to do away with' himself, but that at no time did he or his family refer to witches or fairies.[50] In his statement to the police, Father Gately described his visit to James a week before his death.

When we reached the door, James shook hands with me and said that he had good news for me that day that himself and his sister were saved. He remarked that he should go into a monastery and she into a convent. I said that the age was against them and that he should let that notion out of his mind. I had no doubt from his demeanour and conversation that he was deranged – suffering from religious mania. He mentioned that for twelve days the Devil had been tempting him to do away with himself and that God gave him grace to resist. I advised the family how to care for him and they all paid anxious attention to me and I again mentioned about not letting any dangerous weapons lie in his way. They said they had already taken precautions in that respect.[51]

McCarthy dismissed the priest's version of events as merely a reflection of his lack of knowledge of the local people. However, it is more likely that the priest was deliberately rejecting local super-stitions. Witness statements from the police, from neighbours and from members of the Cunningham family included many allusions to fairies and devils. For example, RIC Constable Christopher O'Brien, recounted what was said by Patrick Cunningham senior after his arrest.

> Shortly after leaving their house, Patrick Cunningham senior made a statement as follows – voluntarily: 'The Devil was in him. He was bringing more of them about the house to kill us all. We thought to keep them away with Holy Water, shaking it on the floor. I thought they would break in the door and pull down the house on us. They were on the loft and every place. I heard something say behind my back when James caught me by the throat "Now mind yourself". They should get him or kill us all. It should be done, O God help me it was a terrible night out and out'.[52]

The Cunninghams were more like the Cleary family than the Doyle family in a number of ways. They seemed to be fairly well off – living in a comfortable house with an income from a farm and from a shoemaking business run by James. They were also very well integrated into their immediate community. They sought help from the doctor and the priest when James became ill and often asked neighbours to help them with his care. They were aware of the fact that he might have to go into an asylum, but he refused to see a doctor.

On the night of the crime, the visiting neighbours had all gone home by ten o'clock. The Cunninghams knelt down to say the Rosary as usual, but during it, James jumped up and attacked his father. They immediately restrained him and beat him to death. The story, as told by Patrick junior to RIC Constable John Bowler, described the events just before the crime.

> After the Rosary, we said the Litany. We were saying it very loud when James got up and caught my father by the throat. At the same time, a big gush of smoke got in through the door and windows. We all got up and kept James from killing my father. He gave us a great tossing about. John got weak and Michael and myself shoved James into the room and Michael killed him there. James was astray in his mind since Saturday fortnight when he was in town.[53]

Statements by other members of the family confirmed the fear of evil spirits that had become associated with James's illness. Patrick junior told the police that they had given James £12 to go to America but that he refused to go because of what he referred to as *The Thing*.

> He [James] said that there were two men on the side of the road and they would not let him go. *The Thing* should get him for he was coming

for him every night. *The Thing* shouted down out of the loft when James
had hold of my father 'Mind yourself'.[54]

We cannot know in retrospect what the Cunninghams meant by the
phrase *The Thing*. Angela Bourke conjectures that they were at a loss
for words, being caught between the discourse of fairies and fairy
belief and that of the Catholic Church.[55] Accounts of the night's
activities also referred to a smell for which there was no logical
explanation. According to Patrick junior, in his statement to Head
Constable John Clerkin:

> When we were praying, a blast of wind having a terrible smell came
> through the window. James then jumped up in a fright, saying 'Now is
> your time' and got my father by the throat with his hands. He then
> caught John and my father again. Michael and I and the whole of us got
> up in a fright. We were scuffling, knocking round until at last we
> chanced to knock over as far as the room door ... I got James down on
> the table and held him with the right and striking him with the left ...
> During this time John was beating him with a tin saucepan. I could not
> tell what Michael was beating him with ... John after beating him with
> the saucepan got a shovel and struck him with it. My father was hitting
> him also.[56]

The Cunninghams did not try to conceal the death of James. They all
went immediately to the house of their nearest neighbour, William
Cunningham, who refused to let them in 'because of the lateness of
the hour'. However, they broke the kitchen window and let themselves
into the house. They stayed there until morning, when they went first
to the priest and then to the police station to give themselves up. After
going with them to the house and finding the body of James, the
police arrested all of the family – Patrick Cunningham senior (father),
John, Michael and Patrick junior (brothers) and Bridget (sister) – and
held them at Athlone RIC Barracks. There, they were very disturbed
and upset, especially at night, praying constantly and fending off the
police when they tried to restrain them. According to Constable J.P.
Dalton:

> After all the prisoners had been brought into the Barracks, they were
> shouting and wanting to get out and complaining about a fog rising in
> the lockup and saying they would not remain there unless they got a
> candle. They were given a candle and then appeared contented. At
> about two o'clock am, the prisoners commenced attacking the door and
> kicking in a furious manner. We had to handcuff them. About this time

they were constantly shouting 'daylight, daylight' and praying. They were very violent. They were spitting, stating they were driving away the evil spirits and saying that when the cock would crow they would go away (meaning the evil spirits).[57]

Within a few days of their arrest, all were seen by doctors, who were called to judge their mental state. Bridget was sent to Ballinasloe Asylum, where she was held for five months – until the Roscommon Summer Assizes. She was then discharged without trial. The four men were sent to Tullamore Prison, where they were examined by two doctors – Medical Officer, Dr John M.P. Kennedy and Dr G. Moorhead. They agreed that 'the defendants were suffering either from acute delirious mania or acute meningitis'. They were 'violent, wild and delirious', had 'hallucinations and were in a feverish state'.[58] In other words, they were not sure if the cause of the delusions and strange behaviour was physical or mental. As discussed earlier, there was a school of thought that promoted the use of health food and outdoor exercise in the treatment of *folie à deux*.

Michael did not improve and was admitted to Maryboro District Asylum. He stayed there until late July when he was certified as sane by the two inspectors of lunacy, Dr O'Farrell and Dr Courtenay. He was then transferred to Galway Prison, where he remained until his trial at the Galway Winter Assizes held in December 1896.[59] There, he was found guilty of murder 'at a time when insane' and sent to Dundrum. He was considered sane on admission and was discharged in less than a year. By then he was suffering from 'consumption' and died three months later. Patrick senior, Patrick junior and John were tried at the Roscommon Summer Assizes in 1896. Patrick senior was acquitted, while Patrick junior and John were found 'guilty but insane' and sent to Dundrum. Patrick junior completed two years and John five years of confinement before being freed.[60] Neither of them showed any signs of insanity during their time in Dundrum.

All of the Cunninghams regained their mental health fairly quickly after killing James, but did their lives ever return to normal? The story of James's possession by 'the Devil' may have been regarded by the courts as an insane delusion, but it provoked enough fear in the local people to keep them away from his funeral. As had happened at the funeral of Bridget Cleary, members of the RIC had to bury the body of James Cunningham at a ceremony that was boycotted by all his neighbours. McCarthy, in his *Five Years in Ireland*, gave a graphic report of the burial, featuring quotations from the *Freeman's Journal* on 11 March 1896.

'Lisphelan [*sic*] village is almost exclusively inhabited by relatives and namesakes of the deceased, *not one of them could be induced to lend assistance in the burial of the body*. Father Mulleady personally requested most of the neighbours *to assist the police*, but in vain! An instance is quoted of how one man, on being asked, made answer that 'he was only a first cousin by marriage'. Eventually the police, under the direction of the doctors, 'had to place the remains in a coffin', which 'at the last moment was found to be too small for the body', and had to be broken! 'The murdered man was not divested of his clothes; the coffin was placed in a cart and brought to the graveyard by the police. None of the relatives or friends took part'. Why, and a thousand times why, was this so?[61]

One can only conjecture that fear overcame compassion in the hearts of neighbours and friends. The very people who had helped to care for James before his death were not prepared to be seen at his funeral. Were they afraid of evil spirits or of insanity, or of both?

LAND DISPUTES

Anyone familiar with Irish history will be aware of the high levels of violence associated with land and tenancy rights in the late nineteenth century.[62] Though some decades (such as the 1880s) were more violent than others, there was a general perception by the authorities that violence could erupt at any time when there was a dispute over land.[63] This often led to harsher treatment of those found guilty of crimes that could be classified as 'agrarian', than those found guilty of crimes of a domestic or personal nature. Here, we focus on a small selection of cases in which family members were involved in a murder precipitated by a dispute over land. These cases are selected because they show the strength of family bonds when the family farm is under threat. The two most famous cases in the second half of the nineteenth century were those that led to the execution of more than one member of the same family. These were the cases of the Stackpoole family from County Clare and the Shiel family from King's County (Offaly). These cases have already appeared in our discussion on women who killed men, but they are explored in more detail here in the context of the impact of family relationships on motivation and action, and of the pivotal place given to evidence by children.

James Stackpoole
The Stackpoole murder happened in 1853, when 20-year-old James was killed by his uncle Thomas, his cousin Richard and their wives,

Honora and Bridget. They were helped by John Halpin, Honora's nephew, who lived with them. The motive was to prevent James from inheriting the house and land occupied by the whole family. They were afraid of being thrown off the farm by James when he became the owner of the property on his twenty-first birthday. Amazingly, the main informants about the murder were the Stackpoole children. Inspector D.B. Franks spoke of these unusual witnesses in his report:

> I attach copies of three of the leading informations on the case. Anne Stackpoole, who although only nine years and seven months old is one of the most intelligent children I ever met ... Her account of the actual murder is fully corroborated by her second sister, only seven years old, but also a very intelligent child and by her third sister five years old, whose evidence will be scarcely admissible, although she was the first person, who unsolicited, informed Mr Bardett Murray (?) J. P. when he went to the house the morning after the murder, that it was not she who did it, but her Daddy, Dick and Shawn Halpin, her mother and Biddy.[64]

The children may have been the first to tell the police what happened, but it was not long before Richard gave a full account of the crime. He told police that:

> On Saturday night, Thomas Stackpoole went to his house, pretended to be drunk, dragged him out on the road and gave him a slap of a stick and said, 'Jamesy is asleep upstairs, now or never, let us kill him and we will have the property'.[65]

Richard went with Thomas (Tom) at first, but slipped back to his own house without seeing James. Later that night, Honora (Tom's wife) came to Richard's house to ask him again to take part in the planned assault. Richard told the police:

> [She] put her arms around me and I went with her to Tom's house. John Halpin and I went upstairs, took Jamesy out of his bed, had a struggle in the room where Jamesy lost some blood from scratches received in the struggle. We forced him downstairs with difficulty, when we got him to the kitchen, I struck him two or three blows on the back with the tongs ... Honora Stackpoole held deceased around the body. John Halpin struck him with a brass candlestick. It broke on him. Thomas Stackpoole did not like how we were beating him. [He] took the tongs from me and said, 'damn your soul, this is the way to do it' and struck Jamesy on the head, knocked him down and gave him seven or eight blows. He was then dead.[66]

This scene of violence was witnessed not only by Honora and the children, but also by Richard's wife Bridget, who helped move the body out of the house. According to Richard's statement to Constable May:

> My wife [Bridget] was there. She told me in the morning that she carried the corpse in a sheet on her back to where it was found and that John Halpin accompanied her.[67]

Honora's nine-year-old daughter, Anne, gave testimony that implicated the two women in the planning and carrying out of the murder. She told the police of the conversation that had taken place between Bridget and Honora that night.

> I heard Bridget Stackpoole say to my mother that as Jamesy had promised to stop that night, that it would be a good time to kill him if they intended to do it at all. My mother said it would be a good time. Biddy said when he would be in bed would be the best time to do it.[68]

She added later that they also took part in the beating that led to his death – saying 'My mother and Biddy held him down until Dick got the tongs and struck him'. Anne's testimony condemned her mother (Honora) and Bridget to their deaths, but it exhonerated her father, Thomas. She said of the conversation between the two women:

> I don't think my father knew what they were saying as he was drunk and they were speaking in a low voice.[69]

Anne also described how her father tried unsuccessfully to cross a stile outside the house and fell over some straw in the yard when he came back from Richard's house.

> A few minutes after I heard my father in the yard trying to get in over the straw which was in the yard, I heard him falling at the door and afterwards saw his eyebrow cut. My mother went out and helped him in.[70]

Though Thomas Stackpoole took part in the murder by issuing instructions, the evidence presented by his daughter indicated that he was too drunk to strike any of the fatal blows. The judgement of the Ennis Assizes on 26 February 1853 was that Richard, Honora and Bridget were guilty of murder. They were sentenced to death. All three were hanged at Ennis Jail three months later on 29 April.[71] The execution was especially controversial because it involved two women –

a rare occurrence in Ireland. Neither the judiciary nor the government wanted to hang women, and the public was divided on the issue. However, the women, who were birth sisters as well as being 'in-laws', were viewed by many as greedy women who were totally responsible for their actions and deserving of their fate. We do not know what happened to the two children who gave evidence in the case. Records indicate that they were legally in the care of the State for many years after the crime, but as a major file on their case could not be located, it is not clear whether or not they went to an institution.[72]

Patrick Dunne

The second famous family murder, involving land, was the killing in 1870 of Patrick Dunne by his neighbours Margaret Shiel and her brother Lawrence, at Philipstown, King's County. The dispute between the Dunne family and the Shiel family was about the 'right of way' to a bog. The Shiels lived with their father and another brother on a farm beside a bog. Patrick Dunne and his mother, who were described as poor, lived in 'a cabin' nearby.[73] There was an ongoing dispute between the families over access to the bog. In 1869, Patrick Dunne and Lawrence Shiel had a fight after which Dunne brought a case against Shiel for assault – accusing Shiel of hitting him with a shovel. Shiel was in prison for six months for this assault and during that time, Margaret was heard to say that she would get even with Dunne even if she had to kill him herself. On 26 February, Lawrence took a short cut to the bog through the Shiel farm. Margaret and Lawrence were waiting for him and shot him twice. Before he died, he told police that Margaret had carried out the shooting while her brother looked on.

The brother and sister were found guilty of murder and sentenced to death. There was a general sympathy for their plight and there were a number of appeals on their behalf. One memorial, signed by over two hundred 'inhabitants of King's County', who were mostly shop-keepers and farmers, was sent to the Earl Spencer, the Lord Lieutenant of Ireland at the time, asking for mercy. Earl Spencer was asked to consider the case as a family dispute and 'in no way connected with agrarian disturbances'. However, the appeals fell on deaf ears. Ironically, on the day before the execution, a prison official from Tullamore had to send a telegram to the Lord Lieutenant to ask for more time to find a new executioner. The designated executioner had run away after being 'remarked' by some local people as he accom-panied the official to the prison to carry out his duties. The official wrote that it would be very difficult to find another executioner and that he might have to resort to asking one of the other prisoners to do it. The answer to his request was a telegram telling him that no delay would be allowed. At 8.00 a.m. on 27 May 1870, just three months after the murder of Patrick Dunne, Lawrence and Margarel Shiel were hanged at Tullamore Prison.[74]

These two cases were fairly straightforward in some ways, as there was evidence of motive and of pre-meditation. In others, the motivation was clear but the evidence of pre-meditation not so. RIC records for the second half of the nineteenth century show that there were at least seven other murders resulting from inter or intra familial disputes over land.[75] Sadly, sometimes the victim was not the intended target, but someone trying to break up a fight. In 1877, a dispute between the Corcoran family and the Guinan family in King's County, led to the death of Mary Guinan.

> [She] was kicked in the abdomen by Kieran Corcoran junior, as she was passing behind him. She immediately fell to the ground when Kieran Corcoran senior threw himself upon her and when he was pulled away, she was found unconscious and died in the course of a few minutes.[76]

This was another dispute about a 'right of way'. The Corcoran family, in an effort to protect what they viewed as their property, became involved in a fight that was never intended to include women. In the clipped words of the RIC report:

> A dispute having arisen between the Corcorans and others respecting the right of passage through certain lands, deceased endeavoured to separate them, whereupon she received the treatment stated.[77]

Three Corcoran men – Kieran junior, Kieran senior and Bernard – were tried at the Summer Assizes and all were acquitted. It was obvious to all that this death was accidental.

In a very similar killing in 1884, another woman was the victim. Again there were two families – the Kirke family and the Corrigan family – in a dispute over a drain that divided their farms. Unfortunately for her, Susan Kirke intervened in an attempt to stop a fight between her husband and son and the Corrigan brothers. According to the police report:

> Susan Kirke, farmer's wife, aged forty years, died from the effects of a blow of a stone, thrown, it is alleged by Martin Corrigan, who with his brother Patrick, was quarrelling with deceased's husband and son, regarding a drain which divided the Corrigan's farm from the Kirke's.

It would appear that Mrs Kirke was endeavouring to bring her husband and son away, when Corrigan threw the stone, which struck her between the shoulders, and the violence and fright induced a miscarriage which caused her death, hemorrhage [*sic*] having supervened.[78]

The Corrigan brothers were arrested and sent for trial at the Monaghan Summer Assizes in 1884. The jury disagreed on the verdict and the case was heard again at the Spring Assizes of 1885. Luckily for them, they were both acquitted. There was no evidence of an intention to kill Mrs Kirke – yet again, this death was judged to be an unfortunate accident. However, severe punishments were handed down where there was evidence of pre-meditation, such as there was in the killing of James Brosnan from County Kerry in 1879, of Bernard Morris from County Tyrone in 1880, and of Peter O'Neill from County Galway in 1885.

The killing of James Brosnan has already been discussed briefly in the previous chapter because his wife Margaret was the instigator of the crime. When James (aged fifty-two) married Margaret (aged twenty-six) in February 1879, he paid off the outstanding mortgage on the farm occupied by her family. James then became the registered tenant on the farm. The marriage was not a happy one, according to the police report.

They lived very unhappily together, it being rumoured that an improper intercourse existed between Mrs Brosnan and a neighbouring young man, and her family treated Brosnan with the greatest contempt, and threatened that they would be very soon revenged on him, as were apprehensive that he was about to sell his interest in the farm.[79]

The possibility of the farm moving out of their control was sufficient motive for murder. However, it is not clear from the accounts that remain of this crime, whether or not the final assault on Brosnan was planned. His wife and her family were not the only suspects in the crime. Just before his death, the victim had 'a dispute' with his own nephew, also called James Brosnan, about money given for safe-keeping to his wife. She, it appears, was not willing to return the money, when he asked for it. His death, as reported in the RIC *Return of Outrages* could have been caused by anyone.

James Brosnan, farmer, was found dead in a meadow convenient to his house on 21st August. Upon examination, it was ascertained that he had been murdered. There were three large cuts on the crown of his head, and his hat was cut through in three places.[80]

The post-mortem revealed that he had been killed three days earlier, on 18 August, and his body left where he had died. The police arrested his wife, Margaret, and her brother, Denis Collins, and her father, Patrick Collins. They also arrested James Brosnan junior, the nephew of the dead man. This murder was regarded by the police as a particularly vicious crime and efforts were made to ensure that all the guilty parties would be held responsible. However, as in many other cases of local crime, the prosecution found it very difficult to locate any witnesses who would link their neighbours to the murder. In the end, James Brosnan was discharged before the case went to court as there was no evidence against him. Margaret Brosnan, Patrick and Denis Collins were all tried at the 1879 Winter Assizes held at Limerick. Margaret was found guilty of manslaughter and sentenced to twenty years of penal servitude and the Crown 'abandoned the prosecution' against Patrick and Denis Collins. Margaret joined her brother, who had already emigrated to Chicago, after eleven years in prison.[81] They had to leave behind the land that had caused the violence and its consequences.

In the following year, 1880, in County Tyrone, another family became involved in a dispute over land that led to the death of one of them. This was not a premeditated murder and the family made no effort to conceal the death. Unfortunately for the victim, Bernard Morris, he was caught in a fight from which he had little to gain, apart from the approval of his wife's family. All of the people involved in the dispute were related to each other. Bernard earned his living not from the land, but from his work as a tailor and a water bailiff. The actual events were recorded by the RIC as follows:

> Bernard Morris, tailor and water bailiff, was fired at by Patrick Morris senior, at about three o'clock p.m. and wounded in the right thigh. He died from the effects of the injuries. *Patrick Morris senior held a field which Bernard Morris claimed to be the property of his mother-in-law. On the day in question, the latter, accompanied by her son-in-law, went to drive cattle off the field.* Patrick Morris, who owned the cattle, fired a shot from a fowling piece, which he carried, the ball passing through Bernard Morris right thigh and smashing the bone. Pat Morris junior and Anne Morris also kicked him in the chest.[82]

It is clear from the police report of this crime that this was a fight that went too far. Patrick senior, Patrick junior and Anne Morris were all arrested and brought before the court at the 1880 Winter Assizes. Patrick senior pleaded guilty to manslaughter and was sentenced to seven years penal servitude. Anne Morris pleaded guilty to assault and was sentenced to one year imprisonment. Patrick junior was discharged, as there was no evidence against him. What is not clear from this case (and others like it) is whether or not the dispute was over tenancy or ownership of land. Very high levels of illiteracy and of poverty in the Irish countryside meant that both tenancy and owner-ship rights were often not transmitted legally, leaving the way open for disputes.

Peter O'Neill

Sometimes a clear legal position did not prevent relatives who shared rights to land from fighting over it. In County Galway in 1885, a brother and sister conspired to get rid of the illegitimate son of their deceased brother, because of a farm they had all inherited. According to the police report:

> Peter O'Neill, farmer, was murdered by William and Margaret O'Neill, who inflicted severe cuts on the head with a stone from the effects of which he died almost immediately. *The deceased and accused were cousins and had constant quarrels in relation to a farm which they held conjointly, and which was left to them on their uncle's death about three years ago.*[83]

William and Margaret were arrested, tried at the 1885 Winter Assizes in Galway, and sentenced to fourteen years penal servitude each. Their prison records tell us how important the land was to both of them, but especially to William. At the time of the crime, he was just twenty-four and Margaret thirty years of age. The man they killed was forty and had probably occupied the farm since they were children.

Prison records also tell us that they were both literate and intelligent and determined to make a good life after discharge. They wrote constantly to each other and to their sister, Nellie, who lived in Connecticut, US. William also wrote a number of times to a Colonel O'Hara, who appeared to be overseeing the management of the farm. That this was not an easy task was obvious from some of the correspondence in William's prison file. In March 1887, Pat Fahey, who seemed to be occupying the O'Neill house or working the land, wrote to William about some of the difficulties he was having with Mr Walsh, the solicitor dealing with the O'Neill business.

> Dear William, I am writing those few lines hoping to find [you] in good health as the departure of this leaves us all at present. Thank God for his mercy to us all. Dear William if you don't settle things better before 1st May you will be out of the land. Walsh is wanting to put you out of

the land. Dear William the land is surveid [*sic*] from North Poles to South but no meran [*sic*] made yet. Dear William Tom Walsh would not give us as much Land as we would sow the Dung in ... Dear William it is well how we have no occasion to come into this house but keeping it for you and Walsh said he would put us out in the street.[84]

We don't know what William thought of this letter, but it was not important enough for him to keep it – it was the only personal letter in his prison file. He did not answer the letter but wrote several times to Colonel O'Hara around this time. Mr Walsh was mentioned eight years later in a letter from Margaret to William. This letter is still in Margaret's prison file, so it may never have been sent. By then, they had spent nine years in prison and while Margaret was planning to join her sister in America on discharge, William was determined to return home to the eleven-acre farm that had caused so much trouble. On 13 December 1894, Margaret wrote:

I am very happy to know you heard from Mr Walsh of late and that he had your house and land waiting for you. Did he make any mention of the expense of fencing in your half of the land since the first time? I remember one time you wrote to me saying that Mr Walsh stated that it would cost £20 to make the fences and that you told him to make the fences and that you would give him the £20 when you would get out, or your land, it would not be an easy matter for us to make up £20 after coming out of Prison and it would grieve me very much to see you hand your land over to any man on that condition.[85]

Margaret went on to suggest that they might be able to raise the capital together by emigrating. It is obvious from her letter that she would like to go to America after leaving prison, but she was looking for William's approval.

I expect to be discharged in April, if you sent on a petition, they might have mercy on you and have you discharged with me, it would be a very hard trial on me to go either home or abroad without you, may God direct us to the best.[86]

It seems that William did not reply to this letter. Margaret was released in April 1895 and went to live with Nellie in Connecticut. A year later, they tried again to persuade William to join them. By then, he was in Maryboro Prison, having spent nine years in Mountjoy Prison and one in Cork Prison. Nellie (Ellen) wrote to Mr Conlon of the General Prison Board in February 1896.

I wish to let you know that we are very uneasy about my brother William O'Neill we wrote him a letter in November last asking him to make up his mind to come to this country when his time was expired I hope he got it. Now we are wondering why he doesn't write to us I hope he is not sick. Margaret O'Neill is living in Bridgeport and she gets along nicely. We would rather a thousand times he would come to this country than go home to live in that place again for we had too much trouble on account of that place. It has been a dreadful trouble to us …

I would be so glad if my brother would only make up his mind and come here. It is very sad to think of him. He is the only one of the family in Ireland now. Mr Conlon I hope you will be so kind as to write to me when you get this and let me know as far as you can judge how his health is and if he write to Mr Walsh about the place lately or what you think he intends to do for we are very anxious to know. I hope he will do what is best then poor fellow.Please answer this.

Yours respectfully, Ellen O'Neill. Direct to Mrs William Young[87]

In spite of his sister's wishes, William did not emigrate. He had worked hard during his eleven years in prison, learning carpentry and tailoring, and earning a gratuity of £9.13.2 (equivalent to approximately £768 in 2006).[88] He told the prison authorities that he would spend his gratuity on 'working clothes and stock' as he was returning to his farm in Streamford, County Galway. Here was a man whose farm meant everything to him. He had already sacrificed his freedom for it and now he was prepared to turn his back on the closest members of his family in order to work on it.

What we learn from this and other cases in which families became involved in land disputes that led to a murder, is the importance of land to people who relied on it totally for basic subsistence. While punishment was often harsh for behaviour labelled as 'agrarian crime', disputes over land continued to be part of life in Ireland well into the twentieth century. We end this chapter on family murders by referring to two cases already discussed in detail in the last chapter. These are stories of domestic violence, where the family united to protect an abused woman. In the Lavelle family, the father, Edward, was an abusive husband.[89] He met his death during an altercation in which his teenage daughter and son came to their mother's rescue. They, like their mother, served their sentences in prison before leaving Ireland to start a new life in the US. The other story had a happier outcome for the perpetrators of the crime. Peter Mullin's abuse of his wife after a drinking session in Ballinrobe was his last act of violence. He was shot by two men, in the presence of his teenage son, as he walked home that evening.[90] There was not enough evidence to convict the chief suspects – his wife's two nephews.

These, and other cases discussed in this chapter, are probably only a tiny proportion of murders involving family members. Some seemed irrational and insane, while others appeared completely rational. All showed that there is no place more dangerous than the home.

NOTES

1   *RIC Return of Outrages for 1896* (NAI, Police Reports 1882–1921, Box 4), Homicides, p. 8.
2   Ibid.
3   For discussion, see Frans Koenraadt, 'Domestic homicide – filicide and infanticide in Holland', Paper presented to the Annual Congress of the IALMH, Paris, 1996.
4   Anonymous, 'Contribution to the Study of *Folie à Deux*, by Dr E. Marendon de Montyel', *Journal of Mental Science*, xxix, 128 (January 1884), pp. 598.
5   Ibid.
6   Oscar Woods, 'Notes of some cases of *Folie à Deux* in several members of the same family', *Journal of Mental Science*, xliii, 183 (October 1897), pp. 822–5.
7   Ibid., p. 823 (referring to the D. family).
8   For discussion on 'calamity meat' (feoil thubaiste), see Angela Bourke, *The Burning of Bridget Cleary* (London: Pimlico Press, New York: Penguin, 1999), p. 30.
9   Woods, 'Notes of some cases', p. 823 (referring to the C. family).
10 Ibid., p. 825.
11 Oscar Woods, 'Notes of a Case of *Folie à Deux* in Five Members of one Family', *Journal of Mental Science*, xxxiv, 148 (January 1889), pp. 535–9, p. 538.
12 M.J. Nolan, 'Case of *Folie à Deux*', *Journal of Mental Science*, xxxv, 149 (April 1889), pp. 55–61.
13 Ibid., p. 55.
14 See Bourke, *The Burning of Bridget Cleary*; Angela Bourke, 'Reading a woman's death: Colonial text and oral tradition in nineteenth-century Ireland', *Feminist Studies*, 21, 3 (1995), pp. 552–86.
15 T.C. Croker, *Fairy Legends and Traditions* (London: W. Tegg, 1870, 2nd edition. First published 1825), p. xxix.
16 W.B. Yeats, *Irish Fairy and Folk Tales* (London: W. Scott Ltd., c. 1893), p. ix.
17 *RIC Return of Outrages for 1888* (NAI, CSO, ICR2), Homicides, p. 11.
    Dundrum, Female Casebook 1893–1920s, p. 29, Case F772; Woods, 'Notes of a case' (1889).
18 *RIC Return of Outrages for 1888*, Homicides (NAI, CSO, ICR2), p. 11. The italics are in the original text.
19 Woods 'Notes of a case' (1889), p. 535.
20 NAI, CRF 1895/D. 34 (Doyle).
21 Woods, 'Notes of a case' (1889), p. 536.
22 Ibid.
23 Ibid., p. 539.
24 Ibid., p. 536.
25 Ibid., p. 538.
26 Yeats, *Irish Fairy and Folk Tales*, p. 56.
27 Ibid., p. 45. See also, O'Connor, *Child Murderess and Dead Child Traditions*.
28 Woods, 'Notes of a case' (1889), p. 538.
29 *RIC Return of Outrages for 1888* (NAI, CSO, ICR2), Homicides, p. 11.
30 Dundrum Female Casebook, 1888, Case F772, p. 29.

31 Memorial 1895, in NAI, CRF 1895/D. 34 (Doyle).
32 Report from Dundrum dated June 1895 in NAI, CRF 1895/D. 34 (Doyle).
33 Anonymous, 'The witch burning at Clonmel', *Folklore: Transactions of the Folklore Society*, vi, 4 (December 1895), pp. 373–84.
34 Bourke, *The Burning of Bridget Cleary*; Bourke, 'Reading a woman's death'.
35 *RIC Return of Outrages for 1895* (NAI, Police Reports 1882–1921, Box 4), Homicides, p. 12. Italics in original text.
36 Ibid.
37 Bourke, *The Burning of Bridget Cleary*, p. ix.
38 Michael J.F. McCarthy, *Five years in Ireland 1895–1900*, 3rd Edition (London: Simpkin, Marshall, Hamilton, Kent and Co and Dublin: Hodges, Figgis and Co., 1901), pp. 145–6.
39 *RIC Return of Outrages for 1895* (NAI, Police Reports 1882–1921, Box 4), Homicides, p. 12. Italics in original text.
40 Anonymous, 'The witch burning at Clonmel', p. 375.
41 Ibid., p. 374; McCarthy, *Five Years in Ireland*, p. 156.
42 McCarthy, *Five Years in Ireland*, p. 158.
43 *RIC Return of Outrages for 1887* (NAI, CSO, ICR2), Homicides, p. 8.
44 Bourke, *The Burning of Bridget Cleary*, p. 80.
45 *RIC Return of Outrages for the year 1895* (NAI, Police Reports 1882–1921, Box 4), Homicides, p. 12.
46 McCarthy, *Five Years in Ireland*, p. 161.
47 Bourke, *The Burning of Bridget Cleary*, p. 202.
48 *RIC Return of Outrages for 1896* (NAI, Police Reports 1882–1921, Box 4), Homicides, p. 8.
49 McCarthy, *Five Years in Ireland*, p. 175.
50 Ibid., p. 177.
51 Court Report of Roscommon C. and P. Crown Assizes, Summer 1896, (hereafter Roscommon Court Report 1896); Witness statement of Fr Gately on 6 March 1896 (NAI, File 1C-64–72).
52 Roscommon Court Report 1896. Witness statement of Constable Christopher O'Brien on 14 April 1896. (NAI, File 1C-64–72).
53 Ibid. Witness statement of Constable John Bowler on 14 April 1896..
54 Ibid. Witness statement of Constable J. P. Dalton on 14 April 1896. (Emphasis added).
55 Personal communication, November 2005.
56 Roscommon Court Report 1896. Witness statement of Head Constable John Clerkin on 14 April 1896. (NAI, File 1C-64–72).
57 Ibid. Witness statement of Constable J. P. Dalton on 14 April 1896.
58 Ibid. Witness statement of Dr J.M.P. Kennedy on 14 April 1896. Medical report for Petty Sessions at Lecarrow, 10 March 1896 (NAI, CRF 1918/ c. 43 [Cunningham]).
59 Report from Office of Inspectors of Lunatics, 21 July 1896 (NAI, CRF 1918/ c. 43 [Cunningham]).
60 Memorial from Charles O'Donoghue and others, 18 May 1917; Note on file. John died in 1917 (NAI, CRF 1918/ c. 43 [Cunningham]).
61 McCarthy, *Five Years in Ireland*, pp. 185–6. (Emphasis as per original text.)
62 See Virginia Crossman, *Politics, Law and Order in Nineteenth-century Ireland* (Dublin: Gill and Macmillan, 1996), pp.153–92.
63 See Mark Finnane, 'A decline in violence in Ireland? Crime, policing and social relations, 1860–1914', *Crime, History and Societies*, 1, 1 (1997), pp. 51–70.
64 Witness statement of RIC Inspector Franks on 11 October 1852. (NAI, CSORP, 1853/ 2421 [Stackpoole]).
65 Ibid.
66 Witness statement of RIC Constable Thomas May (no date). (NAI, CSORP 1853/ 2451 [Stackpoole]).
67 Ibid.

68 Witness statement of Anne Stackpoole, 4 October 1853. (NAI, CSORP 1853/ 2421 [Stackpoole]).
69 Ibid.
70 Ibid.
71 NAI, CRF 1853/ S. 6 (Stackpoole).
72 A file on the Stackpoole children is listed in the papers of the CSO, but the final file referred to was missing. The first file reference is NAI, CSORP 1854/ file no. 20397.
73 NAI, CRF, 1870/ S.7 (Shiel); NAI, CSORP, 1870/11011 (Dunne); NAI, CSORP 1870/ 6528 (Shiel).
74 NAI, CSORP, 1870/11011 (Dunne); NAI, CSORP 1870/ 6528 (Shiel).
75 *RIC Return of Outrages 1838–1921* (NAI, CSO ICR1; NAI, CSO ICR2; NAI, Police Reports 1882–1921, Box 4).
76 *RIC Return of Outrages for 1877* (NAI, CSO, ICR1), Homicides, p. 7.
77 Ibid.
78 *RIC Return of Outrages for 1884* (NAI, CSO, ICR2), Homicides, p. 4.
79 *RIC Return of Outrages for 1879* (NAI, CSO, ICR2), Homicides, p. 9.
80 Ibid.
81 NAI, PEN 1890/ 28 (Brosnan).
82 *RIC Return of Outrages for 1880* (NAI, CSO, ICR2), Homicides, p. 5. Italics in original text.
83 *RIC Return of Outrages for 1885* (NAI, CSO, ICR2), Homicides, p. 7. See also PEN file.
84 Letter from Pat Fahey, dated 20 March 1887. [NAI PEN 1896/ 72 (William Neill)]. The police mistakenly thought they were cousins. The name is sometimes 'Neill' and sometimes 'O'Neill'.
85 Letter from Margaret to William, dated 13 December 1894. (NAI PEN 1895/ 39 [Margaret Neill]).
86 Ibid.
87 Letter from Ellen O'Neill to Mr Conlon, dated 3 February 1896. (NAI PEN 1896/ 72 [William Neill]).
88 Calculated from data by Lawrence H. Officer, *Purchasing power of British Pounds from 1264 to 2006,* available on www.measuringworth.com.
89 *RIC Return of Outrages for 1881* (NAI, CSO, ICR2), Homicides, p. 10.
90 *RIC Return of Outrages for 1880* (NAI, CSO, ICR2), Homicides, p. 8.

CHAPTER EIGHT

Leaving behind crime and madness

WE BEGIN THIS CHAPTER with two quotations from the reports of the inspectors of lunacy in Ireland, as they discuss the prospect of discharging some patients from Dundrum. It is clear from these reports and from other correspondence between the lunacy inspectorate and the office of the Chief Secretary to the Lord Lieutenant, that they saw emigration as a positive outcome for people who had been involved in some of the most notorious crimes in Ireland.

> We shall have occasion, however, in the course of the present year, to lay before his Excellency the Lord Lieutenant, for his consideration, seven or eight cases as fit subjects for freedom. Of these cases three were acquitted of homicide; but being now for over four years under our immediate supervision and certified by the attendant physicians to be free of every symptom of mental derangement, at the same time that they have been uniformly quiet, industrious, and well conducted, we feel justified in the course we propose – the more so as they undertake to emigrate; two having already received money for the passage out to join their families.[1]

And

> Of the male cases discharged, two who had been charged with murder, were, on their recovery set free, their friends providing for their being sent to America.[2]

The people referred to in these reports were not named, but we know of a number of people, already discussed in previous chapters, who were discharged on condition that they took the boat out of Ireland. In the case of Dr Terence Brodie, we know that the petition for his release was helped by the fact that he said he was 'willing to leave the country permanently'.[3] In Mary Rielly's case, her convict record file tells us that 'her passage (was) paid to America, although she did not go directly from Dundrum, but was discharged to her home in

Galway.[4] The approach to discharge, used for Rielly and Brodie, was not a normal part of the general practice within the asylum system – lunatics were not channelled towards emigration by the authorities. However, it was part of the criminal justice system – convicts and ex-convicts were encouraged to leave the country.

Some questions come to mind when we read the accounts of people who took part in this form of what could be called 'assisted' emigration. Was it official government policy to encourage and assist people who had committed serious crimes to leave Ireland after discharge from prison or Dundrum? Did the receiving country (the US, Canada, South Africa or Australia) willingly embrace people who had a history of violence and insanity as immigrants? What does the willingness to emigrate tell us about the people involved – was it a sign of individual empowerment or of passivity? How can we conceptualize these people – as exiles or as emigrants?

There has been substantial scholarship on emigration from Ireland and on the criminal justice system within Ireland, some of which is of relevance here.[5] According to David Fitzpatrick, at least eight million men, women and children emigrated from Ireland between 1801 and 1921.[6] This large scale movement of people from Ireland in the nineteenth century was characterized, for the most part, by voluntary emigration by people who funded their own passage. However, as shown by Gerard Moran and Bob Reece, it also included schemes of assisted emigration, funded variously by landlords, the Poor Law (workhouse schemes) and by philanthropists.[7] In addition, it included people from the criminal justice system, through transportation schemes, which began in the eighteenth century, as shown in the work of Brian Henry, Maria Luddy and Rena Lohan.[8] What is less well known is the fact that after the abolition of transportation in 1853, convicts continued to be released on 'licence' on condition that they emigrate. These people are the focus of the final chapter of this book. Some had been convicted of murder, a crime that carried the death sentence, and some spent time in the Central Criminal Asylum, Dundrum.

In order to understand why these people agreed to go, and what emigration from Ireland meant to them, we look to research on current migrations into the US and Europe. The concept of 'emigration' usually refers to people going voluntarily from one country to another in search of a new and better life. It includes the notion of 'choice', though it is accepted that for many emigrants, such as Irish people who went to North America during the nineteenth century, there may be few incentives to stay at home. However, current scholarship on voluntary and forced movements of people demonstrates that the distinction between the categories of 'voluntary emigrant' and 'forced exile' were, and still are, often blurred. As Orm Overland observes, in his study of current refugee communities in the US:

> The words *emigrant* and *exile* may speak of different kinds of departure, the one voluntary (although there may be pressing reasons behind the decision), the other forced and enforced by the threat of violence and loss of life or freedom. In extreme cases, such as leaving for adventure or for banishment, the difference between emigrant and exile are clear. There may, however, be such pressing political or economic reasons behind a decision to emigrate that it is not always useful to distinguish too clearly between the *emigrant* and the *exile*.[9]

Overland's concerns are echoed in the work of migration scholars Lucassen and Lucassen, who question the adequacy of conceptual models of migration based on what Proudfoot and Hall refer to as the 'straightforward binarism between free and unfree emigration'.[10] The people we are talking about here are individuals who seemed to have had less choice than most, as they had already made themselves unwelcome in their local community by virtue of a conviction for a crime which, in some cases, was linked to insanity. These were people who were discharged from the criminal justice system within Ireland on condition that they would leave Ireland never to return.

EMIGRATION

The movement of people from Ireland took place within the context of the colonization policies of the British government. Some of the views underlying these policies were expressed in the report of the Select Committee on Colonization from Ireland in 1847. The Committee stated their commitment to two major principles – that all colonization should be for improvement and in keeping with the primary duties of the State; and that it must be voluntary.

> The maintenance of law and order, the protection of life and property, the fulfilment of duties as landlords, the performance of obligations and the prosecution of industry by tenants and the labouring classes, together with the diffusion of moral principles and of knowledge amongst all, must ever be the main, as they are the natural causes of progressive improvement, and of the wealth as well as the happiness of nations ... Colonization can never be considered as superseding the performance of such duties.

and

> Another misapprehension against which the Committee feel it their
> duty to guard is the supposition that they have lent their countenance
> to any scheme of emigration which is not perfectly voluntary on the
> part of the emigrant. A compulsory emigration would not be more
> repulsive to the spirit of our free constitution than it would be fatal to
> the success of the emigration itself.[11]

The Select Committee went on to affirm the sentiments of the 1830
Report on the Irish Poor, that 'emigration as a remedial measure is more
applicable to Ireland than to any other part of the Empire'.[12] This was
because it provided an alternative for labourers drawn to England
because of higher wages, preventing an 'influx of labourers' into areas
that could not sustain them. But, lest there be any allegation of com-
pulsion, the witnesses appearing before the 1847 Select Committee
were often asked about the attitude of the Irish people to emigration.
All reported positive attitudes, with some speaking of 'the deep and
pervading anxiety for emigration, as exhibited by the people themselves'
and others of 'the general success of the Irish emigrant to the colonies'
as demonstrated by the amount of money and the number of pre-paid
sailing tickets sent back home, resulting in 'chain emigration'. In the
words of the report, due to the success of other emigrants, people are
encouraged to follow in their footsteps – 'emigration begets emigration'.[13]
The truth of this sentiment is echoed in current studies on migration,
which confirm the importance of pre-migration socialization that
strengthens the myth of a 'good life' in the new country.[14]

Though predominantly drawn from unskilled or semi-skilled backgrounds, each decade of emigration from Ireland was characterized by
differences not only in numbers of people but also in their socio-
economic backgrounds. Before the 1820s, many people emigrated
from Ireland as labourers and domestic servants. In the 1830s,
according to Graham Davis, those who emigrated from Ireland to the
US had some money which made them more independent when they
arrived.[15] In the 1840s (around the time of the Famine), there was mass
migration of people from all walks of life, but the majority were
labourers or domestic servants. At this time, it is estimated that Irish
people constituted around half of all immigrants to the US. 1852 was
the peak in terms of numbers, with approximately 250,000 people
travelling from Ireland to the US – most of them self financing.[16] The
large influx of Irish immigrants in the mid-century led to an increase
in the blatant prejudice again Irish people, prejudice often overtly

shown in cartoons in newspapers and in *Punch* magazine. By the late nineteenth century, many of the men who went to the US became involved in canal building, lumbering and civil construction in the north-eastern part of the US and formed small but tight communities in Boston, Providence and New York. This led to chain migration from Ireland to large cities where Irish neighbourhoods were established. It was to these communities that relatives in difficulties in Ireland were invited.[17]

This pattern was acknowledged and welcomed by both the British and American governments as it meant that the newly arrived immigrants would not be a burden on the State. In the official correspondence on emigration in 1847 we read:

> In the emigration which takes places annually from this country to North America, including the US ... It would appear that a large proportion of the people consists of persons proceeding to join their friends, who in many cases have remitted the means of transit to those by whom they are followed. In these instances, it may be expected that no difficulty will arise. The newly arrived emigrants will disperse themselves throughout the various localities where their friends are already established, and where from the manner in which they are sent for, it may be presumed that they will find the means of subsistence.[18]

However, not everyone could afford to join their friends in the New World and not everyone had friends there.

ASSISTED SCHEMES

The policy of providing 'assisted' emigration schemes had originated in the early nineteenth century, and was based on the twofold assumption that it would get rid of 'redundant' populations at home and help develop colonial settlements in the New World.[19] It was also assumed that assisting emigration of redundant pauper labourers from Ireland would prevent them from coming to England and Scotland. In the words of the *Report of the Select Committee on Colonization from Ireland 1847* (quoting from an 1830 Report on the Irish Poor):

> Emigration as a remedial measure is more applicable to Ireland than to any other part of the Empire. The main cause which produces the influx of Irish labourers into Britain is undoubtedly the higher rate of wages which prevails in one island than in the other.[20]

Assisted emigration schemes decreased in the late 1840s, as it became clear that people wanted to go to the US rather than to Canada or Australia. As the numbers going voluntarily to the US increased, the demand for participation in assisted emigration schemes diminished. In the light of this decrease in interest in emigrating to the colonies, group schemes to Canada and Australia were explored by the Select Committee on Colonization from Ireland, 1847.[21] This suggestion was based on the realization that communities made up of families rather than of individuals had a better chance of success. For example, emigration officials suggested schemes to help whole villages with clergymen to set up villages in Canada.[22] Efforts to encourage these group schemes continued until late in the nineteenth century, as evidenced in the work of the Select Committee on Colonization in 1889.

Witnesses told the Committee of the difficulties encountered by different assisted emigration schemes, with suggestions for solutions. For example, the Right Honourable the Earl of Meath, chairman of an association created for the purpose of creating and fostering public opinion in favour of State colonization and emigration, suggested that, in order to be a successful member of a crofter scheme in Canada the emigrant should be of 'good character'. However, when questioned as to the manner in which this character reference could be ascertained, his reply showed his trust in the system, a view that was not echoed by his questioner:

> *Question*: When you speak of certificates of good character, I suppose you are aware of the general worthlessness of testimonials with regard to the character of emigrants, as proved by experience?
> *The Earl of Meath*: I think not necessarily so, in the case of a man coming from the country his clergyman and his squire generally know something about him.
> *Question*: We have had evidence before this committee that people who give these certificates constantly give certificates which are illusory and deceptive?
> *The Earl of Meath*: No doubt this is so.[23]

The fact that only those of 'good character' were acceptable to the receiving countries and that certain categories of people were not welcome, was clearly demonstrated in the words of Charles P. Lucas, Secretary to the Emigrant's Information Office (part of the Colonial Office in London), another witness called by the 1889 Select Committee.

> *Question*: You find the colonies will only take that class of people whom it is desirable that any country should keep, whereas we cannot get rid

of the class of people whom it would be well for us to have sent out of the country?

Charles Lucas: I think that is so, generally speaking.[24]

Question: Is it your opinion that there are a great many of the inferior class, who although they cannot find sufficient work in this country, might find work in the colonies?

Charles Lucas: Yes, I think that certainly.

Question: Are those the persons whom you would recommend to be emigrated?

Charles Lucas: I would recommend them for their own sakes. Whether the colonies would like to have them is another question.[25]

It is worth remembering that the discussion here was not about criminals, just about people of the 'inferior classes'. Another witness, Mr James H. Tuke, Almoner of an emigration fund provided by the Society of Friends, suggested that there were other reasons for the failure of State-funded assistance schemes – the lack of sufficient money by the new immigrant to enable him and his family to become a landowner, and the negative reactions of the authorities to anyone associated with Poor Law assistance from Ireland. He proposed solutions to both problems.

> I would advise no colonist to be sent out who did not possess 100 shillings of their own ...

And

> I believe that it is immensely important ... that the emigrants should have no apparent or real connection whatever with the Board of Guardians ...

And

> We are all aware of the difficulties which the American government have thrown in the way of assisted emigrants in the last three or four years and their memorials on the subject.[26]

The sentiments on negative attitudes to assisted emigration expressed by Tuke were echoed in the words of Charles P. Lucas.

> *Question*: When you said that you thought the colonies would regard with suspicion any scheme of state colonization or emigration, had you any recent colonization scheme in your mind?
>
> *Charles Lucas*: No, I spoke generally. I think that any state-aided emigration from this country would be regarded with suspicion.[27]

Official documents on voluntary and assisted emigration form the background to the practice of assisting convicts to emigrate from Ireland on their discharge from prison. It is clear that the official view of emigration is that it was best if it was voluntary, and if it connected those leaving Ireland to family members already in the destination country. It is also clear that the receiving countries did not want people who might be a burden on the State. It was essential for new immigrants to have money on arrival for the purchase of land or to procure a living. Any evidence of government sponsorship was best avoided if possible, as it gave the impression that the immigrants had been paupers at home. Finally, the receiving countries did not want people of bad character – if they were unwanted at home, they were likely to be unwelcome elsewhere.

These sentiments are fully borne out in the convict records examined for this book. Convicts were asked if they had any relatives they could go to and had to provide evidence of this through letters from the person with whom they would live on arrival. The relatives were also expected to provide a sailing ticket, if possible, thus avoiding any government involvement in its purchase. It was not necessary to have a financial assistance scheme as those discharged in this way had earned money while in prison, money handed to them on arrival in their adopted country. On the question of being of good character, there is little evidence in the convict files that this was of concern to the prison officials. After all, these people were not ordinary emigrants – they had committed a crime.

TRANSPORTATION REPLACED BY PENAL SERVITUDE

As already discussed in an earlier chapter, the assumptions underlying convict transportation schemes were similar to those in 'assisted' emigration schemes, but with the additional intention of getting rid of trouble-makers, among whom were convicts. As an alternative to capital punishment, it provided a second chance for people who would otherwise have been executed or condemned to years in prison. Thousands of people were transported either directly from Ireland or through English ports. The numbers of convicts transported to the US are estimated, by Henry, as amounting to 14,400 people.[28] In addition, Reece estimates that over 40,000 convicts were transported to Australia directly from Ireland, with 8,000 of Irish birth transported from Britain.[29] Even after it was clear that convicts were not welcome in the US or Canada, the government in Ireland continued to use this method of getting rid of convicts.[30] For the names of some of the women transported from Ireland under these schemes, see Table 1.2 in Chapter One.

Without transportation, the Irish prison system had to cope with much larger numbers of long term prisoners, some of whom had committed very serious offences. As discussed earlier, this meant the building of more prisons, including one for women. It also led to the overhaul of the prison regime and the introduction of training in trades and other employable skills.[31] The legislation that underpinned this new approach – the Irish Convict System Act in 1854 – introduced a number of new regulations, which included a system whereby a 'licence' (also known as 'ticket of leave') could be issued to well-behaved convicts.[32] This allowed for their early discharge, with the proviso that they would be supervised by local police and brought back to prison if they engaged in any unruly or criminal activities.[33]

The law enabling a 'ticket of leave system' came into force in Ireland in 1856.[34] A copy of the conditions under which the license was granted was given to the person as he or she left the prison, so there was no doubt that any infringement of the law would lead to re-arrest.[35]

Many of the convicts released early did not live up to the expectations of the authorities, and when they did not comply with the conditions of the licence, they found themselves back in prison again.[36] There were complaints from the English public about 'ticket of leave men', but in Ireland, the level of complaint was relatively low. This may have been because the surveillance in Ireland was more stringent or it may have been because many of those released in Ireland, under this system, left the country.

When transportation was first abolished in the early 1850s, crime in Ireland was at its height and the prisons were full. In early 1855, for example, the number of convicts in the prison system was estimated as 3,427.[37] This meant that there was great pressure on prison governors to discharge as many as possible. The situation changed after the Famine, as the level of crime and the number of convicts decreased. By 1884, the number had dropped to 837.[38] However, even though the numbers had decreased, there were still men and women in the prison system, most of whom had been sentenced to death and had their sentence commuted to penal servitude for life, who could be detained for many more years.

During the 1880s, there was a concerted effort to discharge women who had been sentenced to death, especially those who had killed a child. Table 8.1 gives the names of some who were discharged on licence in 1886 and 1887, on condition that they emigrated directly to the US. In each case, the family had agreed that emigration was the best option, a relative in the US had agreed to take responsibility for the newly arrived immigrant, and the prisoner was of good conduct.

Table 8.1 *Women convicted of murdering a child and discharged on condition of emigration*

Name	Age	Year of discharge	County	Destination (Port)	Prison
Mary Ellen Pritchard	26	1886	Antrim	Montreal (Dublin)	6 years
Eliza Smith (Leigh)	24	1887	Monaghan	Boston (Liverpool)	5 years
Mary Darby	45	1886	Tyrone	US (Liverpool)	20 years
Margaret Slavin	45	1886	Fermanagh	Boston (Dublin)	5 years
Anne Aylward	43	1886	Kilkenny	New York (Liverpool)	15 years
Mary Brennan	47	1886	Leitrim	Philadelphia (Liverpool	7 years
Margarel Halloran	41	1887	Kerry	Boston (Liverpool)	5 years

Note: All were delivered directly to the docks with a ticket and gratuity money.

Sources: Convict records, including a file on convicts discharged from penal servitude 1886–92 (NAI GPB PS 5).

Some of these women were young, such as Mary Ellen Pritchard and Eliza Smith, each of whom had killed a new-born illegitimate baby and had been found guilty of murder. Mary Ellen had completed six years and Eliza five years in prison. They were lucky to be in the prison system at a time when the Lord Lieutenant was doing his utmost to release women sentenced to death for infanticide.[39] For older women, emigration must have been much more complicated. It would be very difficult for someone like Mary Brennan (aged forty-seven) or Margaret Slavin (aged forty-five) to adjust to a new life and to gain employment. The fact that they had not spent too many years in prison may have made it easier for them to cope. In contrast, Anne Aylward (aged forty-three) was not only fairly old to be a new immigrant in a country full of promise for the young, she had also spent fifteen years of her life in prison. However, she and the others had the support of their families and the well established Irish communities of Boston, New York, Philadelphia and Montreal.

The policy of encouraging convicts to emigrate continued in the 1890s, applying not only to women who had committed infanticide, but also to others who had committed serious crimes. For the purposes of illustration, we are focusing on women here, but that is not to say that men did not follow the same path. Hundreds of men and women left the prison system in this way. In Table 8.2, we see the names of some of the women found guilty of murder or manslaughter in relation to the killing of a husband or a male relative. These women all served substantial periods of time in prison. The youngest, Catherine Lavelle, was only fifteen when she became involved in the family fight that led to the death of her father. She and her brother Thomas both served seven years in prison, before being discharged with a view to emigration. Her mother, Mary, served a longer stretch (eleven years), which meant she was quite old (fifty-five) when she was discharged. She, like Margaret Brosnan, had children to receive her when she arrived in the new country. It seems that families of convicted individuals were more likely to emigrate after the scandal caused by a crime. Even Catherine Delany, who had poisoned her husband, had someone to receive her. Her children had corresponded with her and the Chief Secretary's office quite frequently in order to secure her release. Unfortunately for Catherine and her family, she was refused entry when she reached the US.

Table 8.2 *Women convicted of the murder or manslaughter of a man and discharged on condition of emigration*

Name	Age	Year	County	Victim	Destination (port)	Prison
Catherine Lavelle	22	1888	Mayo	Father	Jersey (Liverpool)	7 years
Mary Lavelle	55	1892	Mayo	Husband	Jersey (Liverpool)	11 years
Margaret Brosnan	37	1890	Kerry	Husband	Chicago (Liverpool)	11 years
Margaret O'Neill	40	1895	Galway	Cousin	Connecticut (Dublin)	10 years
Catherine Delany	59	1898	Tipperary	Husband	Boston (Cork) (refused entry)	14 years

Note: Some delivered directly to the docks with a ticket and gratuity money.

Sources: Convict records, including files on convicts discharged from penal servitude 1886–1892 and 1893–1903 (NAI GPB PS 5 and PS 6).

GRATUITIES

In addition to the licence issued to the discharged prisoner, each was given the gratuity earned while in prison. For example, Mary Lavelle, asked for and was given an advance on her gratuity of £2.5.7 to buy clothes (equivalent to approximately £170 at 2006 prices).[40] The money was released by the Prisons Board to a 'Mr Doody, that he may forward it to the agent in Liverpool to be handed to prisoner on her arrival in America'.[41] Gratuities came into existence as part of the new penal system introduced in the 1850s. This was a highly organized method of rewarding and punishing those in prison, with the ultimate goal of re-integration into society as a disciplined and skilled worker. For those who might previously have been executed or transported, penal servitude provided a chance to pay a debt to society, with the prospect of returning to normal life. The sentence of penal servitude was divided into three stages. The first, the penal stage, was a period of strict separate confinement in Mountjoy Gaol (men and women). The second, the reformatory stage, was spent working with other convicts and learning a trade if appropriate. This took place in other prisons, depending on the convict's ability and health. For the men, there were prisons for outdoor labour, for trades, and for those who could not work (classified as invalids). The women stayed in Mountjoy Gaol but worked in association with others.

The third stage, the intermediate stage, was aimed at preparing the convict for re-entering society. With the exception of convicts who had been found guilty of murder or manslaughter, individuals were transferred from Mountjoy, and other secure prisons, to more open institutions. Men were sent to agricultural prisons, such as Lusk and Smithfield in Dublin, which were much more open, and women were sent to 'refuges', such as Goldenbridge and Harcourt Road in Dublin and Blackrock Road in Cork, which were run mainly by religious orders helped by 'benevolent ladies'.[42] It was at this third stage, that convicts could be released on licence/ticket of leave.

As part of this regime, prisoners were encouraged to be 'good' and to make progress through the stages of reform. Good behaviour was rewarded by a system of 'marks' and 'gratuities'. Marks were awarded once a month, under the headings of discipline, school and industry, with a maximum of three marks for each heading. Prisoners were classified into six classes: penal, probationary, 3rd, 2nd, 1st, and exemplary. Each class had to be earned with a designated number of marks. For example, with eighteen marks, a prisoner could move from 3rd class to 2nd class. The mark system meant that good and bad behaviour determined the speed at which the prisoner moved through the system. As with good behaviour, bad behaviour was also recorded and prisoners could be demoted and thus lengthen their time in prison.[43]

In addition to a speedy journey to freedom, the classification and mark system was also rewarded in monetary terms. Gratuities were awarded for 'good conduct and industry'.[44] None could be earned in the penal and probationary classes, but a prisoner in the 3rd class earned 1d per week, while one in the 2nd class earned a basic 2d per week. In addition, for very good behaviour, there was a possibility of earning an extra 2d per week for those in 1st, 2nd, or 3rd class.[45] Prisoners who were sick could receive an exemption from working and could still earn the gratuity relevant to the class.

The gratuity was paid to the convict either in a lump sum at discharge or in instalments while on licence. As seen in the case of Mary Lavelle, some of this money was given to an agent to be passed on to the newly arrived immigrant on arrival. It is difficult to estimate how much money a convict actually earned, as the final sum is rarely given in convict files. However, it is likely that it was less than one pound for every year in prison, as evidenced in the case of William O'Neill (who, with his sister, Margaret, killed their cousin). William was a hard worker, and was promoted very quickly through the class system. The gratuity due to him after eleven years in prison was estimated as £9.13.2. This would amount to a purchasing power of approximately £754 at 2006 prices.[46] It is unlikely that the women discussed earlier would have earned as much as this, but it gives some indication of the rewards available to those who worked well within the prison system.

One of the interesting facts about the gratuities payments is that they did not appear in any official document as a subsidy to emigration. Even then, it was not connected in any way to emigration of any kind. Information on the amount spent on gratuities did appear in the annual reports of prisons, but in such a way as to make it impossible to calculate what each prisoner received. It was given as an overall expense within the prison system, without any details on the recipients.

TRANSPORTATION UNDER ANOTHER NAME

Notwithstanding all the efforts to reform convicts while in prison, there were lots of complaints about the 'ticket' system in England, with local people objecting to the discharge of convicts on licence into their midst.[47] The positive outcomes of transportation policies were not easily forgotten and the idea of sending some convicts to complete their sentences in Western Australia was discussed by the Commission on Transportation and Penal Servitude in 1863.[48] The ploy of hiding the fact that the people being sent to the new world were convicts had already been tried. During the eighteenth century, many of the convicts transported from England and Ireland were 'sent in the guise of indentured servants'.[49] Blank indenture forms signed by a Lord Mayor or a Chief Magistrate meant that a ship's captain could sell his cargo as indentured servants.[50] Convicts could buy the indenture papers on board the ship and be free on arrival if they had the money to do so.

Another way of achieving the aim of exiling convicts without 'technically' transporting them, was to allow 'certain classes of convicts to go into voluntary exile overseas', by allowing them or their relatives in Australia to deposit money with the authorities as a guarantee that they would not return.[51] On a more informal basis, the idea of 'voluntary exile' continued to be a feature of the Irish criminal justice system in Ireland throughout the nineteenth century. It is clear, from convict records, that the encouragement to emigrate was extended not only those who were on licence, but also to those who were discharged unconditionally from prison. In discussing the problems of discharging convicts in 1884, the Royal Commission on Prisons in Ireland, recommended that local 'societies' were needed to help them get employment, but noted with praise that:

> There is, however, in Dublin an agent of the Prisons Board whose duty it is to look after discharged male convicts, and to assist them to obtain employment or to emigrate.[52]

Many of the men and women, discussed in earlier chapters, left Ireland as part of this system. Mary and Catherine Lavelle, Margaret O'Neill, Margaret Slavin, Margaret Brosnan, Mary Ellen Pritchard, and many others were released on licence/ticket of leave. They had originally been convicted of murder, had their death sentences reduced to penal servitude for life, and served a number of years in prisons under conditions of penal servitude. These women were subject to the regulation governing marks and gratuities and, if hard-working, were rewarded with money and a sailing ticket, paid for either by relatives or from their own gratuities.

Others, who benefited indirectly from this 'assisted' emigration policy, had been found guilty of murder but insane at the time of the crime and sent to Dundrum as criminal lunatics. Their sentences were not time-limited but rather were at the discretion of the Lord Lieutenant. Because there was no system of marks or gratuities in the asylums, Mary Rielly, Terence Brodie and others like them, relied on the State and on their relatives for the purchase of a sailing ticket.[53] Those from the prison system were escorted to the docks – sometimes in England (Liverpool) and sometimes in Ireland (usually Dublin) – and handed into the care of a shipping agent. Unless refused entry on embarkation, they were completely free on arrival in the US. The licence/ticket of leave system did not have any legal jurisdiction outside of the UK and the strict controls introduced by the US government to keep undesirables, such as convicts or insane people out, were capable of being breached. Anyone who has visited Ellis Island, New York, the embarkation point for immigrants, will share my amazement at the fact that the Irish ex-convicts got through the system without being stopped. No doubt, they threw away any official papers they were carrying (such as the 'ticket of leave' document) and did not mention the fact that they had been found guilty of murder, or even worse, been found 'guilty but insane'. On either count, they would not have been welcome.

According to the US census carried out in the year 2000, roughly thirty-four million Americans reported Irish ancestry. Most of these people, when searching for their ancestral roots, expect to find poverty. Few expect to find crime and insanity among the reasons for the original decision by their ancestor to leave Ireland. However, as shown here, it is highly likely that this is the ancestral heritage of many Irish Americans today. Thinking back to the questions that were asked at the beginning of this chapter, we can now come up with some answers. Transportation may have finished in the 1850s, but Ireland continued to send convicted people to the US and elsewhere through the use of the 'ticket of leave' system. This was not an official policy outlined in any legislation or even as a recommendation from a Select Committee. It was an unofficial policy that required no special funding and was hidden in the files of individual convicts.

To the historian, the size of the scheme (number of participants) appears to be completely hidden. Apart from an overall figure for the cost of gratuities to the prison service for any given year, there was no financial heading for it in published reports on prisons. Neither is there detailed information on individual discharges. Convicts, according to law, were released to the place of their original conviction, unless they had requested a different location. A simple list, showing the point of discharge would have highlighted the fact that many were discharged to Liverpool and Dublin rather than to their home counties.

There is no doubt that Irish officials were aware of what they were doing. All of the countries that had been used during the transportation era to receive convicts – the US, Canada and Australia – made perfectly clear their opposition to the 'dumping' of unwanted people on their shores. These countries did not want people who had committed a serious crime (such as murder or manslaughter) or who had a history of insanity. Irish officials chose to ignore the opposition from the New World in the interests of the home countries.

On a more positive note, these stories of exile also show the strength of family bonds. Many families did not abandon their relatives convicted of serious crimes, even those who were labelled as 'criminal lunatics'. They maintained contact with them and with the Lord Lieutenant of Ireland, to whom they wrote memorials, pleading for clemency. Their devotion paid off eventually, sometimes after many years of correspondence. The fact that appeals for release were sometimes supported by a pre-paid sailing ticket and a welcoming address in the US or Canada, showed the strength of family ties. It also demonstrated a belief in the possibility of a new life, far away from the scandal and shame that was almost inevitable at home.

NOTES

1 *Asylums Report*, HC 1854–55 (1981) xvi. 137, p. 153.
2 *Asylums Report*, HC 1883 (c. 3675) xxx. 433, p. 19.
3 Extract from the memorial from Dr Terence Brodie to the Lord Lieutenant of Ireland. NAI, CRF, Misc. 1420/1897 (Correspondence in relation to the discharge of Brodie).
4 Note written by the inspector of lunacy on Mary Rielly, in file on Transfers from Dundrum, NAI, CRF Misc. 392/1891.
5 Patrick Carroll-Burke, *Colonial Discipline: The Making of Irish Convict System* (Dublin: Four Courts Press, 2000); D. Fitzpatrick, *Irish Emigration 1801–1921: Studies in Irish Economic and Social History 1* (Dundalk: Economic and Social History Society of Ireland, 1990); Brian Henry, *Dublin Hanged* (Dublin: Irish Academic Press, 1994); Rena Lohan, *The Treatment of Women Sentenced to Transportation and Penal Servitude 1790–1898* (Unpublished Mlitt thesis, Trinity College, Dublin, 1989); Gerard Moran, *Sending out Ireland's Poor* (Dublin: Four Courts Press, 2004); Bob Reece, *The Origins of Irish convict Transportation to New South Wales* (Basingstoke: Palgrave, 2001);
6 Fitzpatrick, *Irish Emigration 1801–1921.*
7 Moran, *Sending out Ireland's Poor;* Reece, *The Origins of Irish Convict Transportation.*
8 Henry, *Dublin Hanged* Ireland-Australia transportation database (available on www.nationalarchives.ie) Lohan, 'The Treatment of Women'.
9 Orm Overland, 'Visions of Home: Exiles and emigrants', in Peter I. Rose (ed.), *The Dispossessed: An Anatomy of Exile* (Massachusetts: University of Massachusetts Press, 2005), pp. 7–26, p. 7.
10 Jan Lucassen and Leo Lucassen (eds), *Migration, Migration History and History: Old Paradigms and New Perspectives* (Bern: Peter Lang, 1997); Lindsay Proudfoot and Dianne Hall, 'Points of Departure: Remittance emigration from South-West Ulster to New South Wales in the later nineteenth century', *International Review of Social History*, 50 (2005), pp. 241–77, p. 242
11 Colonization from Ireland: Report of the Select Committee House of Lords, HC 1847 (737) (737–11) vi. 1 and 563, p. 4. (Hereafter, Colonization from Ireland 1847).
12 Ibid., p. 7.
13 Ibid., p. 14.
14 Proudfoot and Hall, 'Points of Departure', p. 242, Note 4.

15 Graham Davis, 'Shovelling out paupers?: Emigration from Ireland and the south
    west of England, 1815–1850'. Paper given at the Westward Ho: Movement and
    Migration Conference, University of Exeter, April 2003.
16 Ibid.
17 See file on Catherine Delany (letters from relatives in Providence, NJ, and Rhode
    Island, NY; NAI, PEN, 1898/121 (Delaney).
18 *Papers related to emigration to the British provinces in North America with Appendix*, HC
    1847 (777) xxxix. 19, p. 21.
19 *3rd Report of the Select Committee on emigration from UK, 1827*, quoted in Davis,
    'Shovelling out paupers?'
20 Colonization from Ireland 1847, p. 7.
21 Colonization from Ireland 1847.
22 *Papers related to emigration to the British provinces in North America with Appendix*, HC
    1847 (777) xxxix. 19, p. 22.
23 *Report from the Select Committee on Colonization 1890*, Minutes of evidence. p. 190,
    HC 1890 (354) xii. 1; See also *Report from the Select Committee on Colonization, with
    proceedings of the committee, Minutes of evidence, Appendix and Index*, HC 1889 (274)
    x. 1. (Hereafter, *Select Committee on Colonization 1889*).
24 *Select Committee on Colonization 1889*, p. 91, HC 1889 (274) x, 1.
25 Ibid., p. 98.
26 Report from the Select Committee on Colonization 1890, Minutes of evidence, HC
    1890 (354) xii. 1. pp. 201, 205, 211. (Hereafter, Select Committee on Colonization 1890).
27 Select Committee on Colonization 1889, p. 93.
28 Henry, *Dublin Hanged*, p. 156.
29 Bob Reece (ed.) *Exiles from Erin: convict lives in Ireland and Australia*, (Dublin: Gill
    and Macmillan, 1991), p. 1.
30 Carroll-Burke, *Colonial Discipline*.
31 Copies of correspondence relative to the management and discipline of convict
    prisons, and the extension of prison accommodation, with reports of
    commissioners, HC 1854 (344) lviii. 6. For discussion, see Carroll-Burke, *Colonial
    Discipline*, pp. 95–9.
32 Irish Convict System Act 1854, 17 & 18 Vic c.76.
33 First report of the directors of convict prisons in Ireland for 1854, HC 1854–55
    (1958) xxvi. 609, p. 3.
34 Ibid.
35 Copy of licence in the convict file NAI PEN 1892/118 (Mary Lavelle). See Chapter
    1 for extract.
36 For discussion, see Carroll-Burke, *Colonial Discipline*, pp. 216–18.
37 Ibid., p. 104.
38 *Second Report of the Royal Commission on Prisons in Ireland 1884*, HC 1884 (c. 4145)
    xlii. 671, p. 698.
39 Correspondence between the Chairman of the Prisons Board and the Lord
    Lieutenant, Dublin Castle, in NAI, CRF, Misc. 1888/no. 1862.
40 Calculated from data by Lawrence H. Officer, *Purchasing power of British Pounds
    from 1264 to 2006*, available on www.measuringworth.com.
41 Letter from the Superintendent of Grangegorman to the General Prisons Board on
    14 November 1892, in NAI PEN 1892/118 (Mary Lavelle).
42 Carroll-Burke, *Colonial Discipline*, pp.103–21.
43 For further discussion see ibid., p. 119.
44 Fourth Report of the directors of convict prisons in Ireland for 1857,, HC 1857–58
    (2376) xxx. 95, p. 96, cited in Carroll-Burke, *Colonial Discipline*, p. 120.
45 Carroll-Burke, *Colonial Discipline*, p. 121.
46 Prison report of 9 May 1896, in file on William O'Neill, NAI PEN 1896/72 (Neill);
    Calculated at the rate of £1 in 1895 = purchasing power of £79.37 in 2006. See
    calculator for the British Pound on www.measuringworth.com.

47 Carroll-Burke, *Colonial Discipline*, p. 212.
48 Report of the commission on transportation and penal servitude 1863 Vols. 1 & 2, HC 1863 (3190 I) xxx. 1283, 36, cited in Carroll-Burke, *Colonial Discipline*, p. 212.
49 Reece, *The Origins of Irish Convict Transportation*, p. xv.
50 Ibid., pp. 13–16.
51 Ibid., p. 1.
52 *Second Report of the Royal Commission on Prisons in Ireland 1884*, HC 1884 (c. 4145) xlii. 671, p. 703.
53 The idea of gratuities was discussed in Dundrum in the 1890s.

Epilogue

THE AIM OF THIS book was to explore the cases of people sent to the Central Criminal Lunatic Asylum for Ireland at Dundrum, County Dublin, for serious crimes such as murder or manslaughter, within the broader context of crime and punishment in Ireland. Statistics gathered from the year of Dundrum's opening, in 1850, to the end of the nineteenth century, show that almost 60 per cent of the people confined there had been involved in the killing of a child or an adult (See Table 2.3). It was of great interest to me that the gender of the offender had a significant impact on the judgments of the court in relation to sentencing and on the judgments of the Lord Lieutenant in relation to discharge.

Though it was part of the criminal justice system, Dundrum was not like a prison. People sent there directly by the courts remained at the discretion of the Lord Lieutenant, a discretion that was exercised carefully, subject to the recommendations of the inspectorate of lunacy and of the medical superintendent at Dundrum. The decision to release a 'criminal lunatic' was also subject to the agreement of the families involved in the crime – that of the victim and that of the offender. Then, as now, it was also influenced by public opinion. Someone regarded as dangerous could not easily be released. However, offenders who had killed a family member were not viewed as dangerous in the same way as those who had killed a stranger.

Of course, not all of the patients in Dundrum had come directly from the courts. Indeed, a substantial number were transfers from the prison system – offenders who showed signs of a mental disorder after conviction. Their discharge was much more straightforward and did not require any recourse to the Lord Lieutenant. If they recovered their sanity, they were transferred back to prison if the sentence had not been completed, or released home if it had. If they did not recover their sanity, they were transferred to their local asylum on completion of their 'tariff' time.

In retrospect, it is easy to see patterns of crime and punishment that were not clear at the time. Killings that took place within the domestic sphere (as opposed to the political sphere) pre-dominated in the stories of the criminal lunatics confined to Dundrum. It was not unusual to find wifekillers among the men and childkillers among the women. What this meant was that the insanity defence was being used most successfully by men who killed a female relative (including a wife) and by women who killed one or more children. Crime statistics for nineteenth-century Ireland show that while the killing of a woman by a man was not a common crime, the killing of a child (usually a baby) by a woman was. However, domestic killings did not feature very prominently in overall crime statistics. Around the time of the Famine, when crime rates were at their highest, the most common form of crime was an offence 'against property', although a substantial number of crimes did involve injuring or killing a person. These crimes were very often connected to disputes over land and animals.[1] In the second half of the century, the overall crime rates declined as did the rate of homicides. While many killings continued to be related to land disputes, a steady decrease in the killing of babies was a major contributor to this downward trend in overall homicide rates.[2]

Though crime rates were falling in Ireland in the second half of the nineteenth century, the prison system was expanding. This was mainly due to the fact that it had to cope with the containment of offenders who, before 1853, had been transported to the US, Canada or Australia.[3] Alongside the expansion in the prison system, came a parallel growth in the asylum system, bringing with it a greater understanding of the impact of mental disorder on human behaviour.[4] Dundrum occupied a pivotal position between the two systems and it was often seen as the solution to the problems in both. Before it opened, asylum managers argued that they could not manage offenders within asylums, while prison managers insisted that prison discipline suffered as a result of the presence of lunatics in prisons. However, because Dundrum could only accommodate 120–140 people, there had to be some cross-over and co-operation between the two systems to facilitate new admissions. These admissions were tightly controlled by the inspectorate of lunacy, with offenders who had committed a serious crime given priority. However, because some offenders who had committed trivial offences were clearly mentally unstable and difficult to handle within the prison system, they also were accepted temporarily in Dundrum. It is clear from the reports of the medical staff there that these prison transfers were regarded as much more difficult to manage than patients coming directly from the courts. The latter had been found to be insane at the time they committed a murder, but often recovered their sanity fairly quickly and were compliant and easy to control. These were the patients whose cases were presented to the Lord Lieutenant as suitable for release.

The most prominent group in this category were women who had killed a baby at a time when there was a 'disturbance of the mind', due to 'puerperal' or some other type of mania. As already discussed, great compassion was shown to these women, particularly if they were single and young. While the theories of mental disorder that linked the female reproductive system to weakness and irrationality may be highly suspect in today's world, they did provide a narrative that excused some of these vulnerable women from responsibility for an act that could have been viewed as murder. Others were not so lucky. For them, the death sentence continued to be handed down until the Infanticide Act was passed in 1949. However, no woman was actually executed for killing a child in the second half of the nineteenth century and many, whose death sentence was commuted, spent years doing penal servitude in prison. The only escape was a sailing ticket to a new life in the US, which for many was a second chance for a life free from scandal and stigma, but for a few was an additional punishment in the form of exile.

The other prominent group in the category of patients found to be insane at the time of their crime, but who recovered their sanity fairly rapidly, were men who had killed a wife or a close female relative, during a 'frenzy' brought on by alcohol or extreme stress. As in other countries, Irish crime statistics show that the killing of women by men happens less frequently than the killing of men by men.[5] However, then, as now, a substantial number of men were extremely violent towards the women in their households, violence that sometimes led to death. One of the most common precipitating factors in a violent attack was the consumption of a large amount of alcohol in the hours or days leading up to the crime. While every case was discussed in its own right in the courts, there was a tendency to excuse these men of full responsibility for the crime, especially if there had been no previous report of domestic violence. Some of these men were acquitted completely of the crime, while others received various sentences, including penal servitude in prison and, for those found guilty of murder, the death penalty. The use of a weapon, such as a gun or a knife, was regarded very seriously by juries, and the use of poison was almost certain to lead to a conviction for murder (see Tables 4.2 and 4.3). The insanity defence was also a possibility, a defence that was used very successfully by men who killed during a 'transitory frenzy' brought on by alcohol consumption. This resulted in a committal to Dundrum for an indefinite period of time. Though this could have meant a lifetime of confinement, a quick return to sanity, accompanied by remorse, often led to an early discharge and a chance to begin a new life outside of Ireland. This was especially the case where there was family support in Ireland or the US.

Women who killed men had quite a different experience of the criminal justice system. While there is no evidence of this kind of killing being a common occurrence, the manner in which the crimes were committed and the subsequent handling of the cases reveals a great deal about the impact of gender on both crime and punishment in Ireland. The motivations for killing a husband, father-in-law, or neighbour included love, jealousy, greed and self-defence. The weapons used included poison, a knife, a pistol, a hatchet, and a spade. As with men who killed women, the use of poison indicated pre-meditation and almost always led to a murder conviction. Likewise, the range of sentences included the death sentence and imprisonment, with or without penal servitude, for varying lengths of time (see Tables 6.1 and 6.2). While the judicial and political authorities in Ireland were not very happy about the execution of a woman, the sentence was carried out in cases where there was evidence of premeditation and collusion between the perpetrators of the crime. An option that was virtually missing for these women was the use of the insanity plea. We only found one instance (during the second half of the nineteenth century) in which this defence was used successfully. In this case, the established arguments on the link between over-indulgence in alcohol and the onset of a violent 'frenzy' were used to explain the crime. Luckily for this woman, she recovered her sanity and was discharged after four years, on condition of emigration. The use of the US as a safety valve, for people who had been through the criminal justice system in Ireland, is an interesting one. In today's world, where inter-country migration is a controversial topic, we have not, as yet, heard of any country deliberately off-loading its ex-prisoners to Ireland. One wonders what the politicians or the public would think of such a policy, if it were uncovered.

Another group of people discussed earlier in this book, were those who became involved in family murders. As with other murders, the motivations included love, greed and self-defence. We know that families are dangerous environments. They provide the backdrop for accidents, child-abuse, violence and all kinds of emotional and financial treachery. It is not surprising that murders are planned and carried out by family members in order to protect or defend the safety and status of the family as a unit. Because the cases explored here happened in Ireland in the nineteenth century, it is also not surprising that some of the killings were motivated by disputes over land. Perhaps, what is surprising is that it did not happen more often. However, the most tragic stories of family murder are not those over land, but those in which families were pushed to the edge of sanity by the illness or disability of one of its members. In modern Ireland, it is hard to imagine that a child (or an adult) would have to be killed as the final act of coping with the strain of caring for a sick or disabled son or daughter. While the media and the public may have been excited by what seemed like 'group insanity', the fact remains that some families were so isolated and vulnerable that murder was their only way out of a crisis caused by being unable to manage a mental illness or intellectual disability.

As a final word, I want to say that I hope that the reader will not become locked in the past as a result of reading this book. Many of the cases have echoes in today's world. There is very little public under-standing of the impact of mental disorder on criminal behaviour. There is also very little sympathy for people who have been found 'not guilty' of serious crimes on the grounds of mental disorder. These attitudes reflect the fact that it is only now that the issue of human rights for mentally disordered offenders is being discussed at the European Court of Human Rights. Some people (offenders with a mental disorder) continue to be held indefinitely in, what is now, the Central Mental Hospital at Dundrum and in other high security hospitals throughout the world, because of the lack of legal protection and of low security options for their care and containment. In Ireland, as in other countries, many will never return home after discharge because of the stigma attached to crime and to mental disorder. We can only hope that some of this will change in the next one hundred years.

NOTES

1   Woodward, 'Transportation convictions'.
2   O'Donnell, 'Lethal violence in Ireland, 1841–2003'.
3   Carroll-Burke *Colonial Discipline*; Lohan, *The treatment of women*; Reece, *Exiles from Erin*.
4   Mark Finnane, *Insanity and the insane in Post-Famine Ireland* (London: Croom Helm, 1981); Malcolm, *Swift's Hospital*; Joseph Robins, *Fools and Mad: A History of the insane in Ireland* (Dublin: Institute of Public Administration, 1986).
5   Conley, *Melancholy Accidents*.

The legal basis for admissions to the Central Criminal Asylum for Ireland, Dundrum, 1850–1900

Lunacy (Ireland) Act 1821 (1 & 2 Geo. 4, c. 33): Applied to persons acquitted on the ground of insanity, of treason, murder, or other offences; to persons indicted and found insane at the time of their arraignment, or brought before any criminal court to be discharged for want of prosecution, appearing insane.

Criminal Lunatics (Ireland) Act 1838 (1 & 2 Vic. c. 27): Applied to persons apprehended under circumstances denoting a derangement of mind, and a purpose of committing an indictable crime (termed dangerous lunatics); to persons who have become insane under sentence of imprisonment or transportation, or under any warrant in default of surety to keep the peace.

Central Criminal Lunatic Asylum (Ireland) Act 1845 (8 & 9 Vic. c. 107): Defined 'criminal lunatics' as meaning any person acquitted on the ground of insanity, or found to have been insane under the provisions of the *1821 Act (1 & 2 Geo. 4, c. 33).*

and

It also gave a discretionary power to the Lord Lieutenant to 'direct the removal also to the Central Asylum, of persons under sentence of imprisonment or transportation in any gaol etc or district asylum, who may have become insane'.

Trial of Lunatics (Ireland) Act 1883 (46 & 47 Vic. c. 38): Referred to the trial of insane people charged with offences. From this point onwards, the verdict became 'guilty but insane', for a person found to be insane at the time of any crime, including murder.

APPENDIX 2

Rules made by the Chief Secretary to the Lord Lieutenant of Ireland,

pursuant to the provision of the Capital Punishment Amendment Act 1868 (31 & 32 Vic. C. 24) for regulating the execution of capital sentences in Ireland.[1]

1. For the sake of uniformity, it is recommended that Executions should take place in the week following the third Sunday after the day on which sentence is passed, on any week-day but Monday, and at 8.00 am.

2. The mode of Execution, and the ceremonial attending it, to be the same as heretofore in use.

3. A public notice, under the hands of the Sheriff and the Governor of the Prison, of the date and hour appointed for the Execution, to be posted on the Prison Gate not less than twelve hours before the execution, and to remain until the Inquest has been held.

4. The Bell of the Prison, or, if arrangements can be made for that purpose, the Bell of the Parish or other neighbouring Church, to be tolled for fifteen minutes after the Execution.

5. The person or persons engaged to carry out the Execution should be required to report themselves at the Prison not later than four o'clock on the afternoon preceding the Execution, and to remain in the Prison from the time of their arrival until they have completed the Execution, and until permission is given them to leave.

NOTES

1   A copy of the rules, ratified again by George Wyndham, on 23 August 1902, is contained in the *Death Book 1852–1930*, NAI, GPB CN 5.

List of selected statutes on mental disorder and crime

Transportation Act 1717	6 Geo. 1 c. 12
Criminal Lunatics Act 1800	39 & 40 Geo. 3 c. 94
Lunatic Asylums (Ireland) Act 1817	57 Geo. 3 c. 106
Lunacy (Ireland) Act 1821	1 & 2 Geo. 4 c. 33
Lunacy (Ireland) Act 1825	6 Geo. 4 c. 54
Lunacy (Ireland) Act 1826	7 Geo. 4 c. 14
Criminal Lunatics (Ireland) Act 1838	1 & 2 Vic. c. 27
Private Lunatic Asylums (Ireland) Act 1842	5 & 6 Vic. c. 123
Central Criminal Lunatic Asylum (Ireland) Act 1845	8 & 9 Vic. c. 107
Irish Convict System Act 1854	17 & 18 Vic. c. 76
Lunatic Asylums (Ireland) Act 1846	9 & 10 Vic. c. 115
Offences Against the Persons Act 1861	24 & 25 Vic. c. 100
Lunacy (Ireland) Act 1867	30 & 31 Vic. c. 118
Capital Punishment Amendment Act 1868	31 & 32 Vic. c. 24
Lunacy Regulations (Ireland) Act 1871	34 & 35 Vic. c. 22
Private Asylums (Ireland) Act 1874	37 & 38 Vic. c. 74
Lunatic Asylums (Ireland) Act 1875	38 & 39 Vic. c. 67
Trial of Lunatics Act (Ireland) 1883	46 & 47 Vic. c. 38
Lunacy (Ireland) Act 1901	1 Edw. 7 c. 17
Infanticide Act 1922 (England and Wales)	12 & 13 Geo, 5 c. 18
Infanticide Act 1938 (England and Wales)	1 & 2 Geo. 6 c. 36
Infanticide Act 1949	1949, No. 16
Mental Health Act 2001	2001, No. 25
Criminal Law (Insanity) Act 2006	2006, No. 11

APPENDIX 4

Inspectors of Lunacy and senior medical staff at Dundrum 1850–1900

INSPECTORS OF LUNACY[1]

Dr Francis White	1846–57 (died in 1859 as a result of injuries received in a railway accident. Inspector of Prisons from 1841)
Dr John Nugent	1847–89 (formerly, travelling physician to Daniel O'Connell)
Dr George William Hatchell	1857–89 (died 1890)
Dr G. Plunkett O'Farrell	From 1890 (formerly, Inspector of Reformatories and Industrial schools)
Dr E. Maziere Courtenay	From 1890

MEDICAL SUPERINTENDENTS AT DUNDRUM 1850–1900[2]

Dr G.M. Corbet [3]	From 1850
Dr Isaac Ashe	From 1872 (formerly RMS Londonderry Asylum)
Dr F. MacCabe	From 1872–73 [4]
Dr George Revington [5]	From 1892 (formerly RMS Manchester Asylum)

NOTES

1 Most of this information is from Anonymous, 'Changes in the Irish Lunacy Board', *Journal of Mental Science*, xxxvi, 153 (April 1890), pp. 309–10. Other sources are Finnane, *Insanity and the insane*, pp. 52, 55, 68, 69; Kirkpatrick, *History of the care of the insane*, pp. 36–7; Robins, *Fools and Mad*, p. 92. My apologies for any errors.
2 Some information from Anonymous, 'The Irish Question', *Journal of Mental Science*, xxxviii, 162 (July 1892), pp. 414–15.

3   Inspectors of lunacy report book 1852 (NAI, OLA 6/1, Item 472).
4   His name appears in the list of salaries in the Inspector's report, but does not appear elsewhere – *Asylums Report*, HC 1874 (c. 1004) xxvii, 363, Appendix F, Table 14, p. 257.
5   *Asylums Report*, HC 1893–94 (c. 7125) xlvi. 369, pp. 440–42.

Selected Bibliography

PRIMARY SOURCES: UNPUBLISHED PAPERS

Central Mental Hospital, Dundrum, County Dublin, Ireland.
- Registers of admissions, discharges and deaths 1850–1920s
- Male and Female Casebooks 1893–1920s
- Physician's Book 1872–1920
- Letter Book 1878–88
- Register of inmates/ patients 1850–1900

National Archives of Ireland
- General Prison Board Records
- Death Books (Male and Female) 1852–1930 (GPB CN5)
- Penal Servitude Registers 1877–1914 (GPB PS 2–7)
- Individual penal servitude files (PEN file, based on year of discharge and name of convict)
- Individual convict record files (CRF file, based on year of discharge and name of convict)
- General convict record files referring to more than one convict, or an issue raised in one case, usually have a 'miscellaneous' reference (CRF MISC. files)

Royal Irish Constabulary Records:
- Returns of outrages reported to the constabulary office (monthly and yearly) 1838–1921 (CSO ICR 1–3; Police Reports 1882–1921).

Court Reports
- Roscommon: Court Report of Roscommom C. and P. Crown Assizes 1896 (1C–64–72).
- Galway: Court Report of Galway C. and P. Crown Assizes 1887 (1C–19–153).

Miscellaneous
- Inspectors of Lunacy Report Book, 1852. (OLA 6/1: Item 472).
- Ireland-Australia tranportation database (Available on www.national archives.ie)

University theses

Bailey, Inez, Women and Crime in Nineteenth-century Ireland: Mayo and Galway Examined, (Unpublished MA thesis, NUI, Maynooth, 1992).

Lohan, Rena, The Treatment of Women Sentenced to Transportation and Penal Servitude 1790–1898 (Unpublished M.Litt. thesis, Trinity College, Dublin, 1989).

Jackson, Sinead, Gender, Crime and Punishment in late Nineteenth-century Ireland: Mayo and Galway Examined, (Unpublished MA thesis, NUI Galway, 1999).

PRIMARY SOURCES: PUBLISHED WORK

Parliamentary papers (in chronological order)

Annual reports on the district, criminal and private lunatic asylums in Ireland, with appendices. (Short title used in text: *Asylums Report*)

HC 1845 (645) xxvi. 269
HC 1846 (736) xxii. 409
HC 1847 (820) xvii. 355
HC 1849 (1054) xxiii. 53
HC 1851 (1387) xxiv. 231
HC 1852–53 (1653) xli. 353
HC 1854–55 (1981) xvi. 137
HC 1857 (2253 Session 2) xvii. 67
HC 1859 (2582 Session 2) x. 443
HC 1861 (2901) xxvii. 245
HC 1862 (2975) xxiii. 517
HC 1863 (3209) xx. 621
HC 1864 (3369) xxiii. 317
HC 1865 (3556) xxi. 103
HC 1866 (3721) xxxii. 125
HC 1867 (3894) xviii. 453
HC 1867–68 (4053) xxxi. 303
HC 1868–69 (4181) xxvii. 419
HC 1870 (c. 202) xxxiv. 287
HC 1871 (c. 440) xxvi. 427
HC 1872 (c. 647) xxvii. 323
HC 1873 (c. 852) xxx. 327
HC 1874 (c. 1004) xxvii. 363
HC 1875 (c. 1293) xxxiii. 319
HC 1876 (c. 1496) xxxiii. 363

HC 1877 (c. 1750) xli. 449
HC 1878 (c. 2037) xxix. 395
HC 1878–79 (c. 2346) xxxii. 455
HC 1880 (c. 2621) xxix. 459
HC 1881 (c. 2933) xlviii. 469
HC 1882 (c. 3356) xxxii. 479
HC 1883 (c. 3675) xxx. 427
HC 1884 (c. 4160) xl. 427
HC 1884–85 (c. 4539) xxxvi. 635
HC 1886 (c. 4811) xxxiii. 559
HC 1887 (c. 5121) xxxix. 591
HC 1888 (c. 5459) lii. 595
HC 1889 (c. 5796) xxxvii. 641
HC 1890 (c. 6148) xxxv. 609
HC 1890–91 (c. 6503) xxxvi. 521
HC 1892 (c. 6803) xl. 365
HC 1893–94 (c. 7125) xlvi. 369
HC 1894 (c. 7466) xliii. 401
HC 1895 (c. 7804) liv. 435
HC 1896 (c. 8251) xxxix. Part 2. 1
HC 1897 (c. 8639) xxxviii. 527
HC 1898 (c. 8969) xliii. 491
HC 1899 (c. 9479) xl. 501

Other reports (in chronological order)

Report of the Select Committee on the aged and infirm poor of Ireland 1804,
    HC 1803–04 (109) iv. 771.
Report of the Select Committee on the lunatic poor in Ireland 1817, HC 1817
    (430) vii.1.
*Report of the Inspectors General on the general state of prisons in Ireland
    1823,* HC 1824 (294) xxii. 269.
*Report of the Select Committee (House of Lords) on the state of the lunatic
    poor in Ireland 1843,* HC 1843 (625) x. 439.
*Report of the Inspectors General on the district, local and private lunatic
    asylums in Ireland 1843,* HC 1844 (567) xxx, 69.
*Report of the Inspectors General on the district, local and private lunatic
    asylums in Ireland 1844,* p. 324, HC 1845 (645) xxvi. 269.
*Papers related to emigration to the British provinces in North America with
    Appendix,* HC 1847 (777) xxxix. 19.
Colonization from Ireland: Report of the Select Committee House of Lords,
    HC 1847 (737) (737–11) vi. 1 and 563.

Criminal tables for Ireland 1852, HC 1852–53 [338] lxxxi. 347.

*Ireland: Tables showing the number of criminal offenders committed for trial
    or bailed for appearance at the assizes and sessions in each county, in the
    year 1851*, HC 1852–53, (1556) lxxxi. 71.

*Copies of correspondence relative to the management and discipline of convict
    prisons, and the extension of prison accommodation, with reports of
    commissioners*, HC 1854 (344) lviii. 6.

First report of the directors of convict prisons in Ireland for 1854, HC
    1854–55 (1958) xxvi. 609.

Report of the Commission of inquiry into lunatic asylums in Ireland 1858,
    HC 1857–58 (2436) xxvii.1.

Judicial statistics forIreland 1863, HC 1864 (3418) lvii. 653.

*Report of the Royal Commission on capital punishment 1866, together with
    the minutes of evidence and appendix*, HC 1866 (3590) xxi. 1.

Criminal and judicial statistics for Ireland 1868, HC 1868–69 (4203) lviii.
    737.

Report by the Commissioners in lunacy on Broadmoor Asylum 1868, HC
    1868–9 (244) li. 477.

Judicial and criminal statistics for Ireland 1871, HC 1872 (c. 851) lxx. 247.

*Report of the Commissioners appointed to inquire into the working of the
    penal servitude acts, Vol. iii, Minutes of evidence, continued with
    appendix and index 1878*, HC 1878–79 (c. 2368), xxxviii. i.

*Report of the Commission appointed by the Home Department to enquire into
    the subject of Criminal Lunacy* (England & Wales), HC 1882 (c. 3418)
    xxxii. 841.

*Preliminary report of the Royal Commission appointed to inquire into the
    administration, discipline, and condition of prisons in Ireland 1884*, HC
    1883 (3496), xxxii. 803; *First report with evidence and appendices 1884*,
    HC 1884–5 (4233), xxxviii. 1; *Second Report 1884*, HC 1884 (4145),
    xlii. 671.

Report from the Select Committee on colonization 1889, with proceedings
    of the Committee, Minutes of evidence, Appendix and Index, HC
    1889 (274) x. 1.

Report from the Select Committee on colonization 1890, with Minutes of
    evidence. HC 1890 (354) xii. 1.

Judicial and criminal statistics for Ireland 1892, HC 1893 (c. 7534) xcv. 105.

Contemporary literature

Abraham, G.W., *Law and Practice of Lunacy in Ireland* (Dublin:
    Ponsonby, 1886).

Anonymous. 'Contribution to the Study of *Folie à Deux*, by Dr E. Marendon de Montyel', *Journal of Mental Science*, xxix, 128 (January 1884), pp. 598.

Ashe, Isaac, 'Some observations on general paralysis', *Journal of Mental Science*, xxii, 97 (April 1876), pp. 82–3.

Churchill, Fleetwood, 'On the mental disorders of pregnancy and childbed', *Dublin Quarterly Journal of Medical Science*, xvii (February 1850), pp. 38–63.

Cox's Criminal Law Cases: Report of cases in all courts of England and Ireland (London: John Crockford, Law Times Offices), Vol. xiv: 1877–82.

Croker, T.C., *Fairy Legends and Traditions* (London: W. Tegg, 1870, 2nd Edition [1825]).

Head, F.B., *Fortnight in Ireland* (London, 1852).

Houstoun, Matilda Charlotte, *Twenty Years in the Wild West: or Life in Connaught* (London: 1879).

Lockhart Robertson, C., 'A case of homicidal mania, without disorder of the intellect', *Journal of Mental Science*, vi, 34 (July 1860), pp. 385–97.

McCarthy, Michael J.F., *Five Years in Ireland 1895–1900* (3rd Edition) (London: Simpkin, Marshall, Hamilton, Kent and Co and Dublin: Hodges, Figgis and Co., 1901).

Maudsley, Henry, 'Homicidal Insanity', *Journal of Mental Science*, ix, 47 (October 1863), pp. 327–43.

Nolan, M.J., 'Case of Folie à Deux', Journal of Mental Science, xxxv, 149 (April 1889), pp. 55–61.

North, S.W. 'Insanity and Crime', *Journal of Mental Science*, xxxii, 138 (July 1886), pp. 163–81.

Williams, J.W., 'Unsoundness of Mind, in its Medical and Legal Considerations', *Dublin Quarterly Journal of Medical Science*, xxxvi (November 1854), pp. 260–87.

Woods, Oscar, 'Notes of a Case of *Folie à Deux* in Five Members of one Family', *Journal of Mental Science*, xxxiv, 148 (January 1889), pp. 535–9.

Woods, Oscar, 'Criminal Responsibility of the Insane', *Journal of Mental Science*, xl, 171 (October 1894), pp. 609–21.

Woods, Oscar, 'Notes of some cases of *Folie à Deux* in several members of the same family', *Journal of Mental Science*, xliii, 183 (October 1897), pp. 822–5.

Yeats, W.B., *Irish Fairy and Folk Tales* (London: W. Scott Ltd., c. 1893).

Yellowlees, D., 'Case of Murder during Temporary Insanity induced by Drinking or Epilepsy', *Journal of Mental Science*, xxix, 127 (October 1883), pp. 382–7.

SECONDARY SOURCES

Allen, H., *Justice Unbalanced: Gender, Psychiatry and Judicial Decisions* (Milton Keynes: Open University Press, 1987).

Berrios, G.E. and H. Freeman (eds), *150 Years of British Psychiatry 1841–1991* (London: Gaskell, 1991).

Bluglass, R. and P. Bowden (eds), *Principles and Practice of Forensic Psychiatry* (Edinburgh: Churchill Livingstone, 1990).

Bourke, Angela, 'Reading a woman's death: Colonial text and oral tradition in nineteenth-century Ireland', *Feminist Studies*, 21,3 (1995), pp. 552–86.

Bourke, A., *The Burning of Bridget Cleary* (London: Pimlico Press New York: Penguin, 1999).

Brewer, John D., Bill Lockhart & Paula Rodgers, *Crime in Ireland 1945–95* (Oxford: Clarendon Press, 1997).

Bynum, W., *Science and the Practice of Medicine in the Nineteenth Century* (Cambridge: Cambridge University Press, 1994).

Carroll-Burke, Patrick, Colonial Discipline: *The Making of the Irish Convict System* (Dublin: Four Courts Press, 2000).

Clarkson, Leslie A. and E. Margaret Crawford, *Feast and Famine: A History of Food and Nutrition in Ireland 1500–1920* (Oxford: Oxford University Press, 2001).

Conley, C., 'Homicide in late-Victorian Ireland and Scotland', *New Hibernia Review,* 5, 3 (Autumn 2001), pp. 66–86.

Conley, Carolyn A., *Melancholy Accidents* (Lanham, MD: Lexington Books, 1999).

Connell, K.H., *Irish Peasant Society: Four Historical Essays* (Oxford: Clarendon Press, 1968).

Connolly, S.J., 'Illegitimacy and pre-nuptial pregnancy in Ireland before 1864: the evidence of some Catholic parish registers', *Irish Economic and Social History*, 6 (1979): 5–23.

Connolly, S.J. (ed.), *Kingdoms United? Great Britain and Ireland since 1500: Integration and Diversity* (Dublin: Four Courts Press, 1999).

Crossman, Virginia, *Politics, Law and Order in Nineteenth-century Ireland* (Dublin: Gill and Macmillan, 1996).

Daly, K., *Gender, Crime and Punishment* (New Haven, CT: Yale University Press, 1994).

Daly, Mary, *Social and Economic History of Ireland since 1800* (Dublin: The Educational Co., 1981).

D'Cruze, Shani (ed.), *Everyday Violence in Britain 1850–1950: Gender and Class* (Harlow: Longmans/Pearson, 2000).

Drudy, P.J. (ed.), *Irish Studies 2: Ireland Land, Politics, People* (Cambridge: Cambridge University Press, 1982).

Emsley, Clive, *Crime and Society in England 1750–1900*, 2nd Edition, (London and New York: Longman, 1996).

Feinman, Clarice, *Women in the Criminal Justice System* (Westport, CT: Praeger, 1994).

Finnane, Mark, *Insanity and the Insane in Post-Famine Ireland* (London: Croom Helm, 1981).

Finnane, Mark, 'Irish psychiatry, Part 1: The formation of a profession', in G. E. Berrios and H. Freeman (eds), *150 Years of British Psychiatry 1841–1991* (London: Gaskell, 1991), pp. 306–13.

Finnane, Mark, 'A decline in violence in Ireland? Crime, policing and social relations, 1860–1914', *Crime, History and Societies*, 1, 1 (1997), pp. 51–70.

Fitzpatrick, D., *Irish Emigration 1801–1921: Studies in Irish Economic and Social History 1* (Dundalk: Economic and Social History Society of Ireland, 1990).

Foster, Roy F., *Modern Ireland 1600–1972* (London: Penguin Books, 1988).

Gelsthorpe, Lorraine and Allison Morris (eds) *Feminist Perspectives in Criminology* (Milton Keynes: Open University Press, 1990).

Gibbons, P., N. Mulryan and A. O'Connor, 'Guilty but insane: the insanity defense in Ireland 1850–1995', *British Journal of Psychiatry*, 170 (1997), pp. 467–72.

Gibbons, P., N. Mulryan, A. McAleer and A. O'Connor, 'Criminal responsibility and mental illness in Ireland 1850–1995: Fitness to plead', *Irish Journal of Psychological Medicine*, 16, 2 (1999), pp. 51–6.

Greer, Desmond, 'Crime, justice and legal literature in nineteenth-century Ireland', *Irish Jurist (n. s.)*, 37 (2002), pp. 241–68.

Griffin, B., *The Bulkies* (Dublin: Irish Academic Press, 1998).

Griffin, Brian, *Sources for the Study of Crime in Ireland, 1801–1921*, (Dublin: Four Courts Press, 2005).

Guillais, J., *Crimes of Passion: Dramas of Private Life in Nineteenth-century France* (Oxford: Polity Press, 1986).

Harris, Ruth, *Murder and Madness: Medicine, Law and Society in the fin de siècle* (Oxford: Clarendon Press, 1989).

Healy, David, 'Irish psychiatry, part 2: Use of the Medico–Psychological Association by its Irish members – plus ca change!', in G.E. Berrios and H. Freeman(eds), *150 Years of British Psychiatry 1841–1991* (London: Gaskell, 1991), pp. 314–20.

Heidensohn, Frances, *Women and Crime*, 2nd Edition (Basingstoke: Macmillan Press, 1996).

Henry, Brian, *Dublin Hanged* (Dublin: Irish Academic Press, 1994).

Hoffer, Peter C. and N. E. Hull, *Murdering Mothers: Infanticide in England and New England 1558–1803* (New York: New York University Press, 1981).

Jackson, Mark, *New-born Child Murder: Women, Illegitimacy and the Courts in Eighteenth-century England* (New York and Oxford: Oxford University Press, 1993).

Jones, K., *Lunacy, Law and Conscience* (London: Routledge, 1951).

Jones, Kathleen, *A History of the Mental Health Services* (London: Routledge, 1972).

Kennedy, Liam, 'Bastardy and the Great Famine: Ireland 1845–1850', *Continuity and Change*, 14, 3 (1999), pp. 429–52.

Kirkpatrick, T.P.C., *History of the Care of the insane in Ireland to the end of the Nineteenth Century* (Dublin: University Press, 1931).

Knelman, Judith, *Twisting in the Wind: The Murderess and the English Press* (Toronto: University of Toronto Press, 1998).

Lambert, R.S., *When Justice Failed* (London: Methuen, 1935).

Lee, Joseph, *The Modernization of Irish Society 1848–1918* (Dublin: Gill and Macmillan, 1973).

Lucassen, Jan and Leo Lucassen (eds), *Migration, Migration History and History: Old Paradigms and New Perspectives* (Bern: Peter Lang, 1997).

McAuley, Finbar and J.P. McCutcheon, *Criminality: A Grammar* (Dublin: Round Hall Sweet and Maxwell, 2000).

McDonnell Bodkin, M., *Famous Irish Trials* (Dublin: Blackhall Publishing, 1997 [1918]).

McLoughlin, Dympna, 'Infanticide in Nineteenth-century Ireland', in Angela Bourke, S. Kilfeather, M. Luddy, M. McCurtain, G. Meaney, M. NiDonnchadha, M. O'Dowd and C. Wills (eds), *Field Day Anthology of Irish Writing, Vol. 4: Irish Women's Writing and Traditions* (Cork: Cork University Press, 2002), pp. 915–22.

Malcolm, Elizabeth, *Swift's Hospital* (Dublin: Gill and Macmillan, 1989).

Malcolm, Elizabeth, *The Irish Policeman, 1822–1922: A Life* (Dublin: Four Courts Press, 2005).

Menzies, Robert, 'Contesting criminal lunacy: Narratives of law and madness in west coast Canada 1874–1950, *History of Psychiatry*, xii (2001), pp. 123–56.

Merlo, Alido V. and Jocelyn M. Pollock, *Women Law and Social Control* (Boston, MA: Allyn and Bacon, 1995).

Moran, Gerard, *Sending out Ireland's Poor* (Dublin: Four Courts Press, 2004).

Moran, R., *Knowing Right from Wrong: The Insanity Defense of Daniel McNaughton* (New York: The Free Press, 1981).

Morris, A., *Women, Crime and Criminal Justice* (Oxford: Basil Blackwell, 1987).

Naffine, Ngaire, *Female Crime and Criminology: A Feminist Critique* (Sydney: Allen and Unwin, 1987).

North, S.W., 'Insanity and Crime', *Journal of Mental Science*, xxxii: 138 (July 1886), pp. 163–81.

O'Connor, A., *Child Murderess and Dead Child Traditions: A Comparative study* (Helsinki: Academia Scientiarum Fennica, FF. no. 249, 1991).

O'Donnell, Ian, 'Lethal Violence in Ireland, 1841–2003', *British Journal of Criminology*, 45 (2005), pp. 671–95.

O'Donnell, Ian and Finbarr McAuley (eds), *Criminal Justice History* (Dublin: Four Courts Press, 2003).

Oxley, D., *Convict Maids: The Forced Migration of Women to Australia* (Cambridge: Cambridge University Press, 1996).

Partridge, Ralph, *Broadmoor: A History of Criminal Lunacy and its Problems* (London: Chatto and Windus, 1953).

Peterson, Elicka, 'Murder as self-help: Woman and intimate partner homicide', *Homicide Studies*, 3,1 (1999), pp. 30–46.

Prior, Pauline M., *Gender and Mental Health* (London: Macmillan; New York: New York University Press, 1999).

Prior, Pauline M., 'Dangerous Lunacy: The Misuse of Mental Health Law in Nineteenth-century Ireland', *Journal of Forensic Psychiatry and Psychology*, 14,3 (2003), pp. 525–53.

Prior, Pauline M., 'Roasting a man alive: The case of Mary Rielly, criminal lunatic', *Eire-Ireland*, 41,1 & 2 (Spring/Summer 2006), pp. 169–91.

Prior, Pauline M., 'Mentally Disordered Offenders and the European Court of Human Rights', *International Journal of Law and Psychiatry*, 30, 6 (2007), pp. 546–57.

Prior, Pauline M. and D.V. Griffiths, 'The Chaplaincy Question: The Lord Lieutenant of Ireland versus the Belfast Lunatic Asylum', *Eire-Ireland*, 33, 2 & 3 (1997), pp. 137–53.

Proudfoot, Lindsay and Dianne Hall, 'Points of Departure: Remittance emigration from South-West Ulster to New South Wales in the later nineteenth century', *International Review of Social History*, 50 (2005), pp. 241–77.

Reece, Bob (ed.), *Exiles from Erin: Convict Lives in Ireland and Australia* (Dublin: Gill and Macmillan, 1991).

Reece, Bob, *The Origins of Irish Convict Transportation to New South Wales* (Basingstoke: Palgrave, 2001).

Robins, Joseph, *Fools and Mad: A History of the Insane in Ireland* (Dublin: Institute of Public Administration, 1986).

Rose, P.I. (ed.), *The Dispossessed: An Anatomy of Exile* (Massachusetts: University of Massachusetts Press, 2005).

Ross, Ellen, *Love and Toil: Motherhood in outcast London 1870–1918* (New York and Oxford: Oxford University Press, 1993).

Rublack, Ulinka, *The Crimes of Women in Early Modern Germany* (Oxford: Clarendon Press, 1999).

Scull, A., *Museums of Madness: The Social Organization of Insanity in Nineteenth-century England* (London: Allen Lane, 1979).

Scull, A. (ed.), *The Asylum as Utopia: W.A.F. Browne and the Mid-Nineteenth Century Consolidation of Psychiatry* (London: Tavistock/Routledge, 1991).

Shorter, E., 'Mania, Hysteria and Gender in Lower Austria 1891–1905', *History of Psychiatry*, 1 (1990), pp. 3–31.

Showalter, Elaine, *The Female Malady: Women, madness and English Culture, 1830–1980* (London: Virago Press, 1987).

Smart, C., *Women, Crime and Criminology: A Feminist Critique* (London: Routledge and Kegan Paul, 1977).

Smith, Roger, *Trial by Medicine: Insanity and Responsibility in Victorian Trials* (Edinburgh: Edinburgh University Press, 1981).

Vaughan, W.E. (ed.), *A New History of Ireland, V: Ireland under the Union, 1. 1801–1870* (Oxford: Clarendon Press, 1989).

Shortt, S.E.D., *Victorian Lunacy: Richard M. Bucke and the Practice of Nineteenth-century Psychiatry* (Cambridge and New York: Cambridge University Press, 1986).

Walker, N., *Crime and Insanity in England, Vols. 1 and 2* (Edinburgh: Edinburgh University Press, 1968 and 1973).

Walklate, Sandra, *Gender and Crime: An Introduction* (London: Prentice Hall, 1995).

Wilbanks, William, 'Homicide in Ireland', *International Journal of Comparative and Applied Criminal Justice*, 20,1 (Spring 1996), pp. 59–75.

Williamson, Arthur, 'The beginnings of state care for the mentally ill in Ireland', *Economic and Social Review*, 10,1 (January 1970), pp. 281–90.

Woodward, Nicholas, 'Transportation convictions during the Great Irish Famine', *Journal of Interdisciplinary History*, xxxvii, 1 (Summer 2006), pp. 59–87.

Index